# Hawthorne's Narrative Strategies

# Hawthorne's Narrative Strategies

*Michael Dunne*

UNIVERSITY PRESS OF MISSISSIPPI
*Jackson*

**Library of Congress Cataloging-in-Publication Data**
Dunne, Michael, 1941–
Hawthorne's narrative strategies / Michael Dunne.
p.   cm.
Includes bibliographical references and index.
ISBN 0-87805-761-7 (alk. paper)
1. Hawthorne, Nathaniel, 1804–1864—Technique.   2. Reader-response
criticism.   3. Narration (Rhetoric)   4. Fiction—Technique.
I. Title.
PS1891.D86   1995
813'.3—dc20      94-43866
CIP

British Library Cataloging-in-Publication data available

# Contents

Acknowledgments     vii

1. Introduction     3

2. Varieties of Narrative Authority in Hawthorne's *Twice-told Tales* (1837)     22

3. Narrative Voice in the Sketches     47

4. Narrative Levels and Narrative Authority     70

5. Narrativity and Historicity     101

6. Narrative Transformations of Romanticism     129

7. Narrative Transformations of Domesticity     155

8. Conclusion     186

Works Cited     193

Index     201

# Acknowledgments

In the course of a critical project extending over many years, an author acquires many obligations. I am most fundamentally indebted to all the scholars involved in producing *The Centenary Edition of the Works of Nathaniel Hawthorne*, which I have used as my primary source throughout this book. My approach to Hawthorne has also been influenced by all the critics mentioned in my list of works cited, as well as by many whose work has been slightly superseded by those listed. My earliest personal obligation is to Otis B. Wheeler, under whose direction I first began to study Hawthorne's works. Since Professor Wheeler taught by example as well as by precept, I continue to profit from his instruction today. Later on, many scholars have directly aided me as readers, editors, and program chairs. I am grateful in particular to Nicholas Canaday, C. E. Frazer Clark, J. Lasley Dameron, Allison Ensor, Joseph Flibbert, Rita Gollin, James Meriwether, Siegfried Mews, Michael R. Richards, Thomas Woodson, and Sally B. Young. I am especially grateful to the editors who have granted me permission to revise and reprint material that earlier appeared in *The Nathaniel Hawthorne Journal, 1978, South Atlantic Review* 54 (1989), and *Tennessee Philological Bulletin* 26 (1989) and 29 (1992).

Allen Hibbard, Thomas Harris, David Lavery, John McDaniel, John Paul Montgomery, and Michael Neth, my colleagues at Middle Tennessee State University, have provided assistance and encouragement at various stages of this project. I am thankful for their support. Ellen Donovan read an early draft of this entire book. I am deeply grateful for her generous and insightful criticism. Several talented graduate students assisted me along the way. Jane Powell Campbell updated Lea Newman's bibliography for me. Rebecca King assisted in the early stages of manuscript preparation. William Prather checked the accuracy of my quotations. I hope that the final version of this book will not disappoint these young scholars. Betty McFall of the MTSU Todd Library cheerfully provided valuable assistance throughout this project as she has often done before. As before, I am extremely grateful to her. The Research Committee of Middle Tennessee State University assisted me several times with released-time grants and has helped fund publication of this book. I hereby gratefully acknowledge this assistance.

Despite his disagreement with parts of my argument, Frederick Newberry provided detailed and consistently helpful advice. My debt to him is great, as is my gratitude. I am also indebted to my editor Seetha A-Srinivasan for seeing another project through the presses.

My wife Sara, who has patiently listened to me talk about Hawthorne for many years, heard parts of this book delivered as conference papers, and she also helped me prepare the index. My sons Paul and Matthew provided continuing emotional support and tracked down sources for me. I love all three and thank them here.

Hawthorne's Narrative Strategies

ONE

# Introduction

As Richard Brodhead has shown in *The School of Hawthorne* (1986), Nathaniel Hawthorne's fiction has attracted critical scrutiny for as long as there has been a generally recognized entity called "American literature." Brodhead writes that Hawthorne "is the only American author always to have been part of our significant past" (8). Brodhead and other critics operating on principles derived from the new literary history have argued further that the "Hawthorne" who has been a central figure in the American literary canon for a century and a half is not a constant figure, either as a creative artist or as a thematic composite constituted by a group of published texts. Supporting evidence abounds. In his book *The Marble Faun: Hawthorne's Transformations* (1992), Evan Carton claims, about reviews of Hawthorne's work written by Henry Wadsworth Longfellow and Herman Melville, "To a large extent, each of these literary contemporaries depicted Hawthorne as the kind of writer that he imagined or desired himself to be" (4). Brodhead sees American authors in the late nineteenth century engaging in the same sort of historically inflected appropriation: "What they are really doing is making new Hawthornes for their purposes: inventing, from within their own writing projects, new versions of what his meaning as a model might consist of" (66). I would add that as critics we also appropriate Hawthorne, consciously or unconsciously, according to our own personalities and convictions.

Jane Tompkins agrees in her *Sensational Designs* (1985), maintaining that the "very essence [of literary works] is always changing in accordance with the systems of description and evaluation that are in force." As a result,

"Even when the 'same' text keeps turning up in collection after collection, it is not really the same text at all" (196). Brodhead and Tompkins argue that readers of various historical periods have found in Hawthorne's works those values, attitudes, and insights into human nature that correspond to the qualities valorized in their very diverse cultures. Just as America has been a significantly different nation in 1860, 1900, 1930, 1960, and 1990—with different dispositions toward economic possibility, the place of hieratic art in the culture, the opportunities available to women, and the appropriateness of various forms of sexual behavior—so the deep truths that readers have consistently found within the pages of Hawthorne's works have varied.

This historical perception seems to me indisputably true, and not only because Brodhead and Tompkins supply such convincing evidence in support of the argument. Contemporary critics proceeding from very different assumptions have arrived at similar conclusions. Paul Ricoeur, for example, writes: "With written discourse, the author's intention and the meaning of the text cease to coincide. . . . Not that we can conceive of a text without an author; the tie between the speaker and the discourse is not abolished, but distended and complicated" (95). That is to say, even without believing in the "death of the author," we should question whether criticism can actually uncover the "real" biographical or ideological Hawthorne behind the fiction. Past experience suggests that however persuasively we might present the discovery of this Hawthorne, in two, or ten, or twenty years there will be another, equally credible Hawthorne coming along to take his place.

One explanation for this hermeneutic procession is offered by Wolfgang Iser in *The Implied Reader*:

> With all literary texts, . . . we may say that the reading process is selective, and the potential text is infinitely richer than any of its individual realizations. This is borne out by the fact that a second reading of a piece of literature often produces a different impression from the first. The reasons for this may lie in the reader's own change of circumstances, still, the text must be such as to allow this variation. On a second reading familiar occurrences now tend to appear in a new light and seem to be at times corrected, at times enriched. . . . This is not to say that the second reading is "truer" than the first—they are, quite simply, different. . . . (280–81)

Iser's remarks seem apt in connection with what Brodhead and Ricoeur have written and also in terms of my own experience. My second, third, and tenth readings of Hawthorne's works over the last quarter century have demonstrated that the fiction does, in Iser's words, "allow this variation." Continued familiarity also suggests that still another reading might over-turn—without necessarily invalidating—all my earlier interpretations.

These widely variant readings are attributable to what we may think of as Hawthorne's characteristic narrative posture, illustrated clearly in this passage from "Young Goodman Brown":

> Aloft in the air, as if from the depths of the cloud, came a confused and doubtful sound of voices. Once, the listener fancied that he could distin-guish the accents of town's-people of his own, men and women, both pi-ous and ungodly, many of whom he had met at the communion-table, and had seen others rioting, at the tavern. The next moment, so indistinct were the sounds, he doubted whether he had heard aught but the murmur of the old forest, whispering without a wind. Then came a stronger swell of those familiar tones, heard daily in the sunshine, at Salem village, but never, until now, from a cloud of night. (11:82)

Depending on one's critical disposition at the time of reading the passage, it can be understood to establish the sounds as real, or it can be interpreted as attributing the sounds to Goodman Brown's delusion, or to his guilty conscience, or to the manipulations of Satan. It might be proposed from still another critical angle that the author is using Brown's uncertainty to undermine the reader's epistemological certainties.

Or perhaps some other reading will best account for the significance of this passage and of similar passages in the tale, such as the following:

> Some affirm, that the lady of the governor was there. At least, there were high dames well known to her, and wives of honored husbands, and wid-ows, a great multitude, and ancient maidens, all of excellent repute, and fair young girls, who trembled, lest their mothers should espy them. Either the sudden gleams of light, flashing over the obscure field, bedazzled Goodman Brown, or he recognized a score of church-members of Salem village, famous for their especial sanctity. Good old Deacon Gookin had arrived, and waited at the skirts of that venerable saint, his revered pas-tor. (11:85)

Again, our commitment to a particular reading can help us negotiate among the uncertainties provoked by the passage. Because of the authority proposed and retracted in the surrounding sentences, we might decide that the definite statement "Good old Deacon Gookin had arrived" means that the deacon is present in the forest, or that Goodman Brown only imagines him to be there, or that Satan has conjured up the deacon's image to delude Brown. As George Haggerty has written, "Hawthorne employs a grammatically complex and rhetorically subtle mode of literary discourse that substitutes a nearly fully effective Gothic textual procedure for the isolated and ineffective Gothic 'content' of earlier works" (108). I would agree with Haggerty that variant readings are unavoidable because of the way Hawthorne constructs his narrative discourse, but I would not limit the effects to Hawthorne's Gothic tales.

A passage from *The Blithedale Romance* will serve equally well to show why Hawthorne invites constant reinterpretation. In this episode, Miles Coverdale, Hollingsworth, and Silas Foster have fished the body of the principal female character, Zenobia, from the pond in which she drowned, probably in an act of suicide. The illustrative passage does not focus on the Gothic properties of Zenobia's rigid corpse, however, but rather on Coverdale's reaction to the body:

> One hope I had; and that, too, was mingled half with fear. She knelt, as if in prayer. With the last, choking consciousness, her soul, bubbling out through her lips, it may be, had given itself up to the Father, reconciled and penitent. But her arms! They were bent before her, as if she struggled against Providence in never-ending hostility. Her hands! They were clenched in immitigable defiance. Away with the hideous thought! The flitting moment, after Zenobia sank into the dark pool—when her breath was gone, and her soul at her lips—was as long, in its capacity of God's infinite forgiveness, as the lifetime of the world. (3:235)

These words authorize various conclusions: Zenobia may or may not have committed suicide; she may or may not have regretted her action; she may or may not have prayed at the last moment for salvation; salvation may or may not have been her reward. Depending on our overall interpretive strategy for the book—or for Hawthorne's life and/or career—some combination of these alternatives will seem most appropriate to us. Because, as Iser explains, "the potential text is infinitely richer than any of its individual realizations," we should remember that whatever view we adopt will require

us to ignore considerable evidence to the contrary in this passage and elsewhere in the book. This is what makes Hawthorne's writing both fascinating and inexhaustibly complex. This is also what has convinced me not to
propose my own "selective" reading but to focus instead on what I am calling Hawthorne's narrative strategies, the methods by which he keeps us
reading long enough to arrive at our interpretations.

Charting these strategies is not the critical method I would have adopted
ten or twenty years ago. When I began reading and writing about Hawthorne in the mid-1960s at Louisiana State University, his status as a major
American writer was unquestioned, even in that setting so much unlike the
ones in which Hawthorne wrote. In retrospect it is clear that this eminence
was attributable in part to Hawthorne's compatibility with the New-Critical
standards then unquestionably ascendant, especially as these values were
promulgated in Cleanth Brooks and Robert Penn Warren's influential textbook *Understanding Fiction* (1943, 1959), the first edition of which contained an interpretation of Hawthorne's "The Birthmark." Highly ingenious
practical applications of New-Critical principles could be found in the secondary works to which graduate students were directed in those days,
books such as Richard Harter Fogle's *Hawthorne's Fiction: The Light and the
Dark* (1952, 1964), Charles Feidelson's *Symbolism and American Literature*
(1953), and Roy R. Male's *Hawthorne's Tragic Vision* (1957). Developments
in literary criticism during the past thirty years might lead most of us today
to withhold total agreement with the stylistic/thematic presuppositions of
modernist organicism central to these books. On the other hand, I doubt
that most of us would dismiss these critics' interpretations as just plain mistaken.

The problem may be illustrated by a representative assertion from Fogle
about a descriptive passage in "Rappaccini's Daughter":

> The fountain and shrub are both emblems for Beatrice Rappaccini. The
> shrub is the false Beatrice, the noxious prodigy of Rappaccini's invention;
> the fountain is the true Beatrice, her perishable body and her immortal
> soul. The shrub must die, for its complexities could never be explicated.
> Thus Hawthorne, while refusing to provide a natural or human solution,
> balances his tragic earth with a clear vision of heaven. (234)

In a sense, what Fogle says is "true." At least, it may help us to keep track
of some striking images in the tale. On the other hand, most of us probably

feel somewhat uncomfortable with Fogle's objectification of Beatrice and with the assumptions about gender that this implies. To continue reading Hawthorne today, we require a critical method other than Fogle's. A passage chosen almost at random from *Hawthorne's Tragic Vision* leads to the same conclusion. Male writes, "In *The Marble Faun*, the parallel between sculpture and life is introduced in the title, established in the first paragraph, and maintained throughout the book. The process of transfiguration is as central in art as it is in life" (163). Reading this, we probably feel some obligation to assent, and not simply because of Male's assertive syntax. By checking *A Concordance to the Five Novels of Nathaniel Hawthorne* (671–72), we can count the references to sculptors and sculpture in *The Marble Faun*. Choosing a few representative cases, we can analyze the thematic parallels that Male suggests. On the other hand, we must also feel that there are issues in the book more pressing than the preoccupation with artists so characteristic of modernist criticism. We feel that we must look elsewhere for other questions and other answers.

I would propose the same to be true of the critical approach that supplanted New Criticism for many readers of Hawthorne. Growing out of the highly influential *The Sins of the Fathers: Hawthorne's Psychological Themes* (1966) by Frederick C. Crews, psychological readings of Hawthorne and his work have continued to appear, including *Family Themes and Hawthorne's Fiction: The Tenacious Web* (1984) by Gloria C. Erlich and *Salem Is My Dwelling Place: A Life of Nathaniel Hawthorne* (1991) by Edwin Haviland Miller. As in the case of New-Critical/modernist readings, psychological interpretations of Hawthorne seem to me simultaneously valuable and limited.

In this arbitrarily chosen passage, Crews writes about Miles Coverdale:

> A man of mature years who dwells with awe and titillation on the possibility that a mature woman may not be virginal, who must suppose that her experience has been at the hand of a fiendish seducer, who hopes for the love of a sexless girl but can do nothing to win her, and who turns his sexual rival into an imaginary paternal tyrant—such a man may justly be called a casualty of Oedipal strife. (204)

The insight is provocative. Coverdale's sexuality is surely twisted in some ways. Reading Coverdale's speculations and fantasies about Zenobia and

Priscilla is so unpleasant that we probably feel slightly uncomfortable. Even recognizing Coverdale's disabilities, however, we probably suspect that we have not totally explained the hold that Hawthorne's book has on us. Miller is also provocative in this randomly chosen remark about another character, Clifford Pyncheon: "Psychologically . . . Clifford's soap bubble turns out by accident (he is much too cowardly to take the offensive) to be his means of attacking his betrayer and emasculator, the man who has denied him maturity through false imprisonment" (331). Miller's point immediately seems well taken. As we follow this bubble incident, it seems at first intended primarily as an opportunity for sketch-like speculations about beauty and impermanence. Then as Judge Pyncheon becomes the victim of a light-hearted assault, we probably move from delighted surprise to a sense that justice is somehow served in the passage. We are happy that Clifford is getting even with his evil cousin, even to such a limited degree. We are happy to see Jaffrey inconvenienced, even so slightly. If we do not precisely adopt the term *emasculation*, we surely agree with Miller that Jaffrey has greatly deprived Clifford and that this deprivation has made Clifford somehow less than a fully functioning adult.

Do such psychological insights explain why so many readers have drawn so many rich interpretations from *The Blithedale Romance* and *The House of the Seven Gables*, however? Although highly perceptive remarks are scattered throughout the many psychological readings of Hawthorne's life and works, we must recognize that psychology textbooks can provide us with portraits of far more deranged characters, as well as far more ingenious strategies of revenge and far more pathetic cases of arrested psychic development. In fact, we probably know real people with debilitating psychological difficulties equal to anything in Hawthorne. We do not read and reread psychology textbooks decade after decade, however. Nor do we find the real-life cases as fascinating as we find Coverdale, Clifford, and Hawthorne. Despite the brilliance of Crews, Miller, and other psychological critics, Hawthorne's fiction is not primarily the place to look for an anatomy of mental illness or a guide to mental health. Oedipal problems do not justify our interest either in Coverdale or in his creator. Hawthorne's continuing appeal must be explained otherwise.

A variety of explanations has been offered by the school of critics concerned with Hawthorne and history. Of course, Hawthorne's historical engagement has long been recognized. Even during the ascendancy of the ahistorical New Critics, some scholars, such as G. Harrison Orians, adopted a historical approach to Hawthorne, primarily by focusing on the putative sources of Hawthorne's work in the history of New England. In our time, however, Hawthorne's relations with history have been substantially redefined in Michael Colacurcio's exhaustive study, *The Province of Piety: Moral History in Hawthorne's Early Tales* (1984). Since nearly all critical studies published since Colacurcio's have acknowledged the centrality of his work to the shaping of contemporary Hawthorne scholarship, we may take his contribution as established. Like F. O. Matthiessen in another age, Michael Colacurcio occupies a place in all critical discourse about Hawthorne— including mine.

Incisive treatments of Hawthorne's historical materials have also appeared in the work of Frederick Newberry (1987), Susan Mizruchi (1988), and Emily Miller Budick (1989), among others. As my Chapter 5 will show, I am indebted to all these historical interpreters of Hawthorne. As that chapter will also show, however, I choose to place my primary emphasis elsewhere. After explaining that Hawthorne's contemporaries thought of John Endicott as "the typal forebear of leaders in the Revolutionary War," for example, Newberry goes on to claim, "Such a view of Endicott depends, of course, upon an understanding of national typology, a political adaptation of Biblical hermeneutics current in Hawthorne's time and considerably adumbrated in recent years" (18). As in the case of psychological interpretations, the alleged cause seems unequal to the effect. Generations of readers have been drawn to Hawthorne's work. As George Dekker observes, "Hawthorne always gets his chapters in books, his week in courses about the American novel" (72). Can it be that these readers are turning and returning to Hawthorne for history lessons, however sophisticated the vocabulary? Do even half of them, or one-third, do so? It seems equally unlikely that our continuing fascination with Hawthorne can be explained by Budick's claim: "At the center of Hawthornean romance . . . is the basic problem of the skeptical dilemma, of determining whether or not the elements of the dualism, the self and the world, exist at all" (84). All thinking persons must confront these issues, but this philosophical quest probably does not provoke our reading and rereading of fiction. Since so many stimulating interpretations have blithely ignored this skeptical dilemma, moreover, we must doubt that the question is central to Hawthorne's work.

Variants of the historical approach inspired two excellent books published in 1991. *The Anatomy of National Fantasy: Hawthorne, Utopia, and Everyday Life*, by Lauren Berlant, and *The Office of The Scarlet Letter* by Sacvan Bercovitch, both use *The Scarlet Letter* as their primary document to investigate the meaning of democratic citizenship in Puritan, mid-nineteenth-century, and contemporary America. Focusing on Hawthorne's characteristic opposition between the ideal and the actual, Berlant reinflects the political conflict between the self and society in terms of gender. Hawthorne's social status as a privileged white male largely determines the shape and outcome of this conflict, according to Berlant:

> Delegitimating Hester's utopian theory by addressing, interpreting, and disparaging her body, [Hawthorne] turns the possibility of postpatriarchal social thought into an advertisement for abstract citizenship in the liberal political sphere. This is why, to counter her thoughts, he deconstructs her gender. (140)

Hawthorne's narrator certainly seems uncomfortable with Hester's nonconformity, as Berlant demonstrates, and the overall plot of the book seems designed to frustrate Hester's desires. Thus, we must assent logically to Berlant's analysis, even as we question whether Hawthorne's contemporaries found this message in *The Scarlet Letter*, whether the late-nineteenth-century authors mentioned by Brodhead did, whether readers twenty years from now will see the book in these terms. In his essay "The Limits of Edgar Allan Poe," Tzvetan Todorov writes that "Poe has benefited—and continues to benefit—from the attention of critics who have seen in his work the most perfect illustration of a certain ideal—which turns out however to be a different ideal in each case" (93). Surely, we may say the same of Hawthorne.

Ironically, Bercovitch's language echoes Berlant's while advancing an opposed thesis. According to Bercovitch, "*The Scarlet Letter* is a story of socialization in which the point of socialization is not to conform, but to consent" (xiii). This consent is a positive condition in Bercovitch's analysis, and it is solicited not only from Hester, but from Hawthorne's contemporaries and from us today. Hawthorne's most famous work is therefore "our most enduring classic because it is the liberal example par excellence of art as ideo-logical mimesis" (xiii). Again, we feel compelled logically to agree, espe-cially since Bercovitch contextualizes his argument so thoroughly in history and political theory. Then, struck by our conflicting interpretive allegiances to Berlant and Bercovitch, we perhaps question whether adjudicating this argument is the most productive way of spending our time. If the main appeal of Hawthorne's fictional works is the light they throw on our politi-cal heritage, then why not read political science instead? When all is said and done, the larger explanation for Hawthorne's continuing appeal cannot be that he writes—however well or however incisively—about American history.

In her essay "Sacvan Bercovitch, Stanley Cavell, and the Romance Theory of American Fiction" (1992), Budick directs attention to another helpful-but-partial interpretive approach when she writes, "The largest target of the New Americanists may not be the romance tradition (and its claim to be exceptional within American literature) but rather new criticism" (80). The contention among critical schools noted by Budick probably argues against Bercovitch's claim that Hawthorne's achievement has been "to rechannel indeterminacy into pluralism, conflict into correspondence, and relativism into consensus" (25). Especially in our own time, highly varied Hawthornes based on highly different interpretive strategies vie for critical ascendancy. This is true also of critics committed to exploring what Budick here calls "the romance tradition" and its claims of exceptionality.

Critical works such as Michael Davitt Bell's *The Development of American Romance: The Sacrifice of Relation* (1980), Evan Carton's *The Rhetoric of American Romance* (1985), and Edgar Dryden's *The Form of American Ro-mance* (1988) have shown how productively the critical category of ro-mance may be examined. In the naive days of New-Critical organicism, most readers were content with formulations like the following, from Rich-ard Chase's *The American Novel and Its Tradition*: "Being less committed to the immediate rendition of reality than the novel, the romance will more freely veer toward mythic, allegorical, and symbolistic forms" (13). Recent romance critics have consistently cited Chase's principles as points of de-parture for their own, more rigorous discussions of Hawthorne's work. Bell, for example, sees romance as "a highly self-conscious experimental fictional tradition that transcended solipsism by exploiting and investigating an analogous self-consciousness in the national experiment of which it was a part" (xiii). To Carton, in *The Rhetoric of American Romance*,

> American romance . . . is most profitably and challengingly approached as an imaginative expression of the conceptual (and, by implication, social and moral) tensions that inform our literary history, as an artistic enterprise that engages and transforms post-Cartesian epistemological questions, and as a creative mode that highlights the act of interpretation and suggestively exemplifies the problem of meaning in contemporary criticism. (1)

"For Hawthorne," according to Dryden, "the shaping impulse of romance is a profound experience of loss and absence . . . [of] a happy, undisturbed relation between fiction and reality, imagination and perception, and writer and reader" (32). Each of these critics enriches our understanding of what it means to read, especially what it means to read Hawthorne's fiction. At the same time, each seems to me to replace the fiction with a different philosophical construct.

Shortly before beginning to write this chapter, I read Richard H. Millington's *Practicing Romance: Narrative Form and Cultural Engagement in Hawthorne's Fiction* (1992). Having had access to the work of many predecessors, Millington sophisticatedly explains that Hawthorne's form of romance "is represented less as a literary form than as a psychological and cultural place where art happens, where writer and reader meet in a special sort of interchange" (43). By stressing transactional reading rather than historical circumstances of publication, Millington is able to resolve some elements of the critical conflict identified by Budick. Thus, Millington seems justified in observing about *The House of the Seven Gables* that "Hawthorne assigns the reader a crucial role within this drama of the cultural system: we represent the community" (115). Reading Millington's remark, we perhaps see a way to reconcile Bercovitch's political concerns with those of the generic critics. In a larger sense, however, this reconciliation is of interest primarily to professional Hawthorneans. It is doubtful that other readers are seeking such solutions when they turn to Hawthorne, or that fictional works rooted in such issues could evoke such an amazing variety of readings over so many decades.

Despite the common ground implied by the shared vocabulary in generic studies, their authors' more fundamental disagreements concerning the nature of romance and Hawthorne's practice of it seem to support Nina Baym's claim, in *Novels, Readers, and Reviewers: Responses to Fiction in Antebellum America* (1984): "The invention of a subgenre called the romance with specifically American fictional properties is a later critical development; it is a concept alien to the practice and production of the times it is now used to analyze" (271). Baym provides another reason to question long-held assumptions about Hawthorne's place in his own time and in ours when she argues that it "would have made no sense in 1850" to assume that "the most important works of American fiction are romances" (235) — rather than other forms such as historical, social, sentimental, religious, or reform novels. This line of argument is developed further in *Sensational Designs*, when Jane Tompkins explains that "editors are active shapers of the canon, whose differing aims and assumptions determine what will seem central and what peripheral" (188). Baym's and Tompkins's stimulating arguments have led to significant revaluations of what we now call Hawthorne's canonical status. As Tompkins explains: "It is not from any neutral space that we have learned to see the epistemological subtleties of Melville or Hawthorne's psychological acuity. Those characteristics have been made available by critical strategies . . ." (187). Arguments of this sort demand that we try to reimagine Hawthorne's place among his contemporaries and that we rethink our own critical strategies, as so many of the critics already cited have done.

This act of reimagining has led other critics to dispute the canonical revisions of critics like Baym and Tompkins. In *Beneath the American Renaissance: The Subversive Imagination in the Age of Emerson and Melville* (1988), David S. Reynolds writes: "The claim that women's fiction began as a relatively sparse genre and then by midcentury assumed dominance of the popular scene has no basis. The reverse, in fact, was true . . ." (338). There is much contested ground among these critics, ground that we have learned to identify with political as well as critical projects. Transcending any disagreements about exactly who read exactly what during the mid-nineteenth century, however, these critics enhance our understanding of the books of that time as rhetorical engagements between authors and readers. Even so, as I have suggested about generic studies, critical debates of this sort have grown so complex as substantially to fill the space formerly occupied by Hawthorne's works. Just as symbolic, psychological, and historical interpretations seem limited to me because they often supplant Hawthorne's fiction, so I conclude that the romance tradition—however complexly defined and historicized—can no better supply answers to why, decade after decade, both professional and general readers read and reread Hawthorne's works.

Even while I cannot fully endorse any of these critical projects, I freely acknowledge my debts to all the critics mentioned in this chapter and to the dozens of others included in my list of works cited. I would be proud to have written any of these works, especially those that I have read most recently. Although no one seems to me to have all the answers, each of these critics has helped me to look at some aspect of "Hawthorne" differently. In the end, however, I am still left with the question of why I—and so many others—should wish to look at Hawthorne again and again. To answer this question, it seems to me that we must adopt a different critical strategy, one derived from the enterprise loosely called "narratology."

According to Gerald Prince's *A Dictionary of Narratology* (1987), this concept may be simply defined as "The (structuralist-inspired) theory of narrative." Prince further explains that "Narratology studies the nature, form, and functioning of narrative (regardless of medium of representation)" and adds that "The term was proposed by [Tzvetan] Todorov" (65). Rooted in the analytical methodology proposed in Emile Benveniste's *Problems in General Linguistics* (1966; trans. 1971) and encouraged by the contemporary interest in semiology, the critical practice of narratology flourished, especially in France, during the 1970s and 1980s. Often called structuralist poetics, the method is exemplified in Todorov's *The Fantastic: A Structural Approach to Literary Genre* (trans. 1973) and *The Poetics of Prose* (trans. 1977). Gerard Genette's *Narrative Discourse: An Essay in Method* (1972; trans. 1980) and *Figures of Literary Discourse* (1966–72; trans. 1982) provide illustrations of the method even more searching and more influential than Todorov's. Roland Barthes's "Introduction to the Structural Analysis of Narratives" (1977) was also a valuable contribution to the development of narratology even though the author soon turned his interests elsewhere. Later critics, including Prince, Robin Warhol, and Wallace Martin have helped to clarify the work of the originators and to popularize the method in English.

Narratologists like Todorov and Genette differ from interpretive critics in one way because they write about the transactional activity called "narrative discourse" rather than about the more familiar fixed genres of tale and prose sketch. These critics also discuss the effects of different tenses and personal pronouns in a text rather than the effects of symbols and irony. They investigate different levels of narrative authority rather than points of view. To some extent, of course, narratology can be understood simply as a source of new critical jargon. More profoundly, narratology provides a way to slow down our reading so as to focus on individual sentences and parts of sentences, to keep track of someone writing these sentences one after another. Particularly in the case of Hawthorne, narratology permits us to examine why this sentence should follow that one, why an apparently straightforward assertion about an event that was fictional in the first place should be followed by a sentence or a paragraph questioning or problematizing the assertion.

Asking questions of this sort admittedly tends to direct critical attention away from the humanistic content of fictional works toward their technical properties as narratives. Genette typically charges in *Narrative Discourse* that criticism has historically been guilty of "concentrating almost all its attention on the statement and its contents" rather than on what he calls "the problems of narrative enunciating" (26). Refocusing attention on narrative enunciating is particularly useful in the case of Hawthorne since it helps to show how he creates interpretive uncertainty by destabilizing his texts. Despite slighting of the familiar thematic ground of interpretation, then, narratological criticism seems to me highly worthwhile. In his introduction to the paperback collection *Nathaniel Hawthorne: Selected Tales and Sketches*, even Michael Colacurcio concedes that "Perhaps the literary strategy of these tales is every bit as deep as their historical plot" (xxv). Close narratological examination confirms Colacurcio's suspicion.

Structuralist poetics naturally cannot answer all our questions about Hawthorne, and the wisest practitioners of the method have usually displayed a healthy degree of self-criticism. Genette, for example, writes in *Narrative Discourse Revisited* (1988), "I am well aware that a narrative text can be viewed from other angles (for example, thematic, ideological, stylistic)." Even so he claims that "the strongest . . . justification for the momentary hegemony of narratology seems to me to derive not so much from the importance of the object as from narratology's own degree of maturation and methodological elaboration" (8). In the eyes of many, including Wayne C. Booth, this maturation is attributable in the largest part to Genette himself. As Booth testifies in his essay "Rhetorical Critics Old and New: the Case of Gerard Genette," "[W]hen I plead for aid, the one fashionable critic who best answers my call is Gerard Genette" (128). In this respect, I agree totally with Booth.

In spite of the enormous critical debt I freely and cheerfully acknowledge, however, I have not finally developed this book as a structuralist reading of Hawthorne. The shortcomings of a purely structural approach can be seen as early as in Barthes's "Introduction to the Structural Analysis of Narratives." When Barthes writes there, "Nuclei and catalysers, indices and informants, . . . these, it seems, are the initial classes into which the functional level units can be divided," he assumes that naming is tantamount to understanding, even while conceding that "the names are of little importance" (96). Here we may see the form of critical nominalism to which structuralism—even as practiced by Genette—is most susceptible. As I agree with Booth's praise of Genette's work, so I share his reservations: "[I]t seems to me that [Genette's] analysis is . . . scientific precisely in the sense that certain rhetorical traditions became scientific: by narrowing the subject's field artificially, the critic makes possible a kind of detailed coverage that looks more complete than it is" (140). In other words, orthodox structuralist poetics can expend a great deal of taxonomic energy in an effort to bring a specious air of scientific certainty to an activity that must finally acquiesce in humanistic partiality.

That this effort was also the probable intention of the New Critics is an irony that has received considerable comment. Howard Felperin, for one, says about structuralism, in *Beyond Deconstruction*: "The hypertrophication of structures and taxonomies produced by the new poetics in the decade of the seventies bears an uncanny resemblance not only to the Byzantine scholasticism of the old historicist positivism, but to the burgeoning impressionism of the old *critique d'interpretation* they were designed to check and replace" (102). As a result of such very sensible reservations on the part of Booth and Felperin—and myself—my intentions in this book are both greater and less than those likely to be endorsed by a true structuralist. In this respect, my attenuated allegiance to structuralism resembles the affection I hold for other critical influences—the work of Fogle and Male, for example.

I have therefore felt free to borrow from other narrative theorists whenever their approaches seemed more useful to me than structuralist poetics. Mikhail Bakhtin's *The Dialogic Imagination* (trans. 1981) has provided me with several additional perspectives, as well as with a rich new vocabulary. Bakhtin's theories of "dialogism" and "heteroglossia," for example, can help us think productively about unresolved tensions in Hawthorne's work. Bakhtin's conception of the "chronotope" also seems applicable to Hawthorne. Because I understand my activity in this study to be engaging with the voices I believe I can hear speaking to me from Hawthorne's pages, my approach has been influenced not only by the structuralists and by Bakhtin, but—as my earlier citations suggest—also by the work of Wolfgang Iser. I should explain that this influence, though real, has not been total either. I do not propose to account fully for how my sense of what goes on in Hawthorne's fiction got out of the author onto the page or off the page into my head. Again, my intentions are more modest.

What I hope to show is how Hawthorne keeps me—keeps us—reading, how the language on his pages shapes our responses and expectations. Coming at Hawthorne from this direction allows us to think of him primarily as a writer—as someone who wants his work to be read all the way through, to the last word, by actual readers. The last book I intend to discuss also attempts to study Hawthorne along these lines, and so it can provide a kind of closure for this introduction. In *The Art of Authorial Presence: Hawthorne's Provincial Tales* (1993), G. R. Thompson sets up a project that I could easily adopt as my own:

> In terms of the broad questions of Hawthorne the writer, this book attempts to demonstrate the validity of four claims: (1) that he early perfected the art of the open-ended "twice-told" tale and sketch dominated by an insistent but ironic authorial presence; (2) that this skeptical authorial presence frames and foregrounds the problematic function of Hawthorne's narrators; (3) that it aesthetically contextualizes and complicates any "interpretation" of American history to be found in his works; and (4) that the "shape of Hawthorne's career" is consistent along aesthetic lines that he developed from the beginning. (3)

Even so brief a statement demonstrates Thompson's rejection of rigidly historical interpretive paradigms, his avoidance of psychological explanations, and his focus on the Hawthorne on the page rather than on some Hawthorne in his mind. This last choice also entails a tolerance for Bakhtinian open-endedness—even apparent contradiction—that would be unacceptable to such differently disposed critics as Berlant and Bercovitch. All of these initial premises seem to me promising, especially Thompson's interest in Hawthorne's narrators, in "the figured literary self as authorial construct" rather than in "the biographical subject of the author" (20). And yet even Thompson's tolerance for indeterminacy is limited. When all is said and done, he must interpret some tales, he must establish what the fiction is "about." Following the established practices of Hawthorne criticism, this activity requires contextualizing these interpretations among those that have preceded them. The consequences may be illustrated by Thompson's gloss on "The Wives of the Dead": "Colacurcio adopts, almost inexplicably, Doubleday's objections. Commenting negatively on Patricia A. Carlson's elaboration of Lang's 'grammatical suspicion' into a 'structural chart,' he offers the opinion that 'the original "insight" remains unconvincing' " (68). I cite this example from Thompson only because I greatly admire his book, although equally telling examples could easily have been drawn from other critical works I have mentioned in this chapter. Even if no other objection were raised to Thompson's argument here, all the embedded punctuation might be taken as a sign that some other approach must be available.

When all is said and done, I cannot believe that even the most exacting exegesis can explain our continuing desire to reread Hawthorne's work, and so I no longer read or write about Hawthorne in order to resolve critical disputes. Therefore, I propose to write a critical study without footnotes. This is not to deny my obligations to all the critics in my list of works cited. Even though I do not consistently quote their opinions concerning every text I discuss, I have read and greatly profited from these opinions. However, my intention is not to agree or disagree with other critics and their interpretations, but merely to describe what I see going on on the page. These transactions are what I am calling Hawthorne's narrative strategies, and it seems to me finally that they are what keeps us all coming back to and reinterpreting Hawthorne decade after decade.

These strategic elements vary in size and scope. In examining the 1837 edition of *Twice-told Tales*, the first published book to which Hawthorne attached his name, I emphasize topics closely allied with the structuralist project, including Hawthorne's use of personal pronouns, verb tenses, and levels of narration. Together with his appropriations of techniques associated with the Gothic and fantastic traditions, Hawthorne's experiments with these narrative elements allow him to create very different degrees of narrative authority. As a result, readers must cooperate energetically in the creations of these fictions, selecting their own readings from a text that remains, as Iser says, "infinitely richer than any of its individual realizations." Other localized elements of Hawthorne's narrative practices are illustrated by several narrative sketches added to the second edition of *Twice-told Tales*, works that do not substantially differ from the sketches included in the first edition—or from those included in *Mosses from an Old Manse* and *The Snow-Image*. Hawthorne's narrative sketches are alike not only in the narrative strategies they exemplify, but also in the sense that few of them would win the aesthetic approval of our contemporaries—and this despite their popularity with readers of Hawthorne's day. This paradox interests me because Hawthorne practiced many of the same narrative strategies in the sketches as in the tales of symbolism and irony canonized by modernist critics and esteemed by our contemporaries. Some of these more complex tales, including "Rappaccini's Daughter" and "Alice Doane's Appeal," can be profitably examined using vocabulary borrowed from Gerard Genette, as can Hawthorne's longer narratives *The Blithedale Romance* and *The Marble Faun*. These narrative techniques include the framing of narrative structures, tales-within-tales, dialogue, description, flashbacks, and summaries—common and uncommon varieties of mimesis and diegesis. These narrative levels are used by Hawthorne to vary the pace of his narratives, stimulate suspense, convey information, insinuate Gothic thrills, accommodate a growing popular taste for realistic representation, and create varying degrees of narrative authority.

Hawthorne also appropriated larger narrative elements from the materials provided by his own culture in order to challenge and destabilize his readers' reading. One form of appropriation involves the perennially examined topic of Hawthorne's engagement with history. While focusing on "The May-Pole of Merry Mount," the four interrelated "Legends of the Province-House," and *The House of the Seven Gables*, I hope to consider this old topic from a new perspective. In part because these texts share many narrative strategies with the works examined in the earlier chapters—including manipulations of diegetic levels—I propose that we reconsider history not as something that Hawthorne made fiction *about*, but as something that he made fiction *out of*. Two other forms of appropriation involve thematic entities and thus approach more nearly the provinces of interpretation. My emphasis, however, is not on what Hawthorne did or did not believe about transcendental romanticism and domesticity, but rather on how he raises conventional expectations in his readers and then varies and/or exploits these expectations. Just as public and private history provide Hawthorne with materials that he alters freely to suit his narrative purposes, so romantic symbols, themes, and plot structures undergo radical transformations in his fiction. Hawthorne also appropriates and transforms the domestic ideology shared by writers who were his contemporaries, such as Henry Wadsworth Longfellow and Susan Warner. In his tales, and even more so in his four great romances, Hawthorne transforms the imagery and settings of popular domestic literature in order to create original fiction.

In my last, brief chapter I present no conclusions about Hawthorne's views on love, guilt, sex, democracy, or art, but simply note resemblances between narrative techniques present in Hawthorne's last completed work of fiction, *The Marble Faun*, and the strategies that define his career overall. I willingly concede in conclusion that other readers may usefully interpret Hawthorne's works so as to uncover great truths. In the past I have often done so myself. But I do not propose to explain in this book what I consider these great truths to be nor to argue the superiority of my truths to those uncovered by other critics. The road of hermeneutics may lead others to the palace of wisdom; I no longer expect it to lead me there. I believe instead that it is more productive for me to track and analyze Hawthorne's narrative strategies, and that is what I propose to do.

# TWO

# Varieties of Narrative Authority in Hawthorne's
## *Twice-told Tales* (1837)

Nathaniel Hawthorne called his first published volume of short fiction *Twice-told Tales* (1837) in recognition of the fact that all of the pieces had already appeared in periodicals. Taken together, these previously published narratives accurately reflect the author's thematic and stylistic concerns at that stage of his writing career. Hawthorne's lifelong thematic preoccupations—secret guilt, the dangers of isolation, the influence of the past on the present—are easily recognizable in some of the better-known tales, such as "The Minister's Black Veil," "Wakefield," and "The May-Pole of Merry Mount." Surely it is significant that ideas which continued to engage Hawthorne's artistic attention even in his unfinished romances of the 1860s manifest themselves in this early work. As Q. D. Leavis observes in her landmark essay "Hawthorne As Poet," it is amazing that "The essential if not the greatest Hawthorne had so soon found himself" (35). In recognition of such thematic continuities, generations of literary critics have devoted their interpretive energies to these tales and their successors. It can also be revealing, however, to examine this collection in isolation, apart from what the stories portend thematically concerning Hawthorne's later work. Most especially in some of the tales less frequently anthologized, it is profitable to trace the obscure but ambitious writer's search for modes of narration suited to his artistic needs. Such an investigation is useful not only for what it reveals about Hawthorne, but also for what it suggests about the nature of prose narrative, particularly about the relations between author and authority.

Most commentators on Hawthorne's early fiction—including Nelson F. Adkins, Neal Frank Doubleday, J. Donald Crowley, and Nina Baym— discuss the work in the context of the young author's strategic implementation of his desire, as he wrote in the 1851 Preface to *Twice-told Tales*, "to open an intercourse with the world" (9:6). Doubleday says in summary that Hawthorne "was for the first time fully considering his relationship with the public he hoped would support his work" (74). In investigating this proposition, Doubleday and the other critics mentioned focus primarily on Hawthorne's concern with order and pacing, with his juxtapositioning of different tones and themes in the collection. Little note has been taken, however, of Hawthorne's efforts to effect this intercourse with his readers through technical means. Robert Scholes and Robert Kellogg suggest the significance of such inquiries when they identify "the essence of narrative art" with "the relationship between the teller and the audience" (240). Later critics, including Gerard Genette, Gerald Prince, and Robin R. Warhol, have refined these general observations by drawing subtle distinctions and coining new terminology. Building on these proposals, critical readers continue to investigate the basic issues, including the one identified by Scholes and Kellogg as "the problem of the authority of the narrator" (242). It should come as no surprise, then, that such matters also might concern a writer of prose fiction, especially an emerging American writer in the 1830s.

The 1837 edition of *Twice-told Tales* richly repays technical attention because it abounds in experiments with verb tenses, points of view, authorial interventions, and attributions of authority, the very elements identified by Genette and other contemporary theorists as crucial indices of narrative discourse. Five of the eighteen selections are cast in the first-person mode of narration, for example. Four of these are apparently conventional sketches presented, usually, in the present tense: "Sunday at Home," "Little Annie's Ramble," "A Rill from the Town-Pump," and "Sights from a Steeple." The fifth, "The Vision of the Fountain," recounts, in the past tense, a youthful romantic experience of a now more mature narrator. These demonstrations of romantic sensibility are interspersed throughout the volume, usually between more solemn and symbolic tales. In the four sketches, Hawthorne's narrative strategy is to pretend that a series of elaborated reactions to social and natural phenomena issue directly, in the present tense, from first-person narrators. In the *Columbia Literary History of the United States*, Michael

Colacurcio summarily, but accurately, describes these sketches as follows: "[A]dumbrating the inherited epistemology, a localized observer makes quotidian observations and arranges them in the linear pattern of the mind's well-known patterns of association" (223). As we might expect on the basis of Colacurcio's description, the organizing principles in these works are quite conventional: time in "Sunday at Home," distance in "Little Annie's Ramble," association of ideas in "A Rill from the Town-Pump," and space in "Sights from a Steeple." Despite their conventionality, however, the four sketches illustrate several facets of their author's concern with narration.

In "Sights from a Steeple," the first-person narrator never alludes directly to the facts of his writing or of anyone else's reading. He just seems to respond sensitively to the sights before him at the same time that the sights appear. Perhaps a hint of the author's presence emerges in the following rhetorical complaint: "There are broad thoughts struggling in my mind, and, were I able to give them distinctness, they would make their way in eloquence" (9:196). If so, the hint is extremely subtle, especially since the quality he claims to lack is "eloquence," the talent of oral expression, rather than literary style. The narrator of "Little Annie's Ramble" is only slightly more direct in claiming his role as a writer. The closest he comes to doing so is this sentence in the last paragraph: "Say not that it has been a waste of precious moments, an idle matter, a babble of childish talk, and a reverie of childish imaginations, about topics unworthy of a grown man's notice" (9:129). Surely the person addressed in this sentence can only be the reader, but the formulation "a babble of childish talk" allows the reader to slip into the role of listener or observer if this is more congenial. In consequence, the narrator, and author, must disavow their true function as writers, at least temporarily.

"A Rill from the Town-Pump" varies slightly from these two sketches, first of all by beginning with stage directions, and then by proceeding as a dramatic monologue cast in the first person. However, the sketch is like the first two structurally in that, when the narrator interrupts the flow of impressions, his words are identified as speech rather than writing. His similarity to the narrator of "Little Annie's Ramble" is especially clear in this sentence: "But I perceive, my dear auditors, that you are impatient for the remainder of my discourse" (9:145). Again the actual reader is addressed as a fictional listener. Perhaps the actual writer gains some measure of protection through this practice, like the author of a Gothic tale disguising his authority through the kinds of narrative distancing described by Jane Lundblad in *Nathaniel Hawthorne and the European Literary Tradition*. If so, Hawthorne's narrator must also sacrifice his claim to creative responsibility for his tale, despite his assertion of the pronoun "I."

The last of these sketches comes closest to presenting the narrator as a writer capable of deliberate choice and creativity. In "Sunday at Home," the first-person narrator follows the practice of the first three in never directly mentioning writing. He does address the reader, though, in instructions of this sort: "Suppose that a few hours have passed, and behold me still behind my curtain, just before the close of the afternoon service" (9:24). As a result of these instructions and a series of rhetorical questions, such as "Who are the choristers?" (9:25), this narrator is the most assertively present of the four as a consciously creative force. Consequently, when this narrator begins to introduce his moralized conclusion, he addresses his audience as a "gentle reader" (9:26), rather than as an observer or listener. The difference is highly significant. When the reader is encouraged to see himself—in the case of "The Vision of the Fountain," to see herself—as a reader, he/she must implicitly recognize his/her engagement with a text on a page, words produced at a previous time by a writer, not words spoken immediately by a person, real or fictional. Yet even the most assertive narrative stance adopted in these four sketches hardly approaches the creative ingenuity employed by Hawthorne elsewhere in the collection.

In "The Vision of the Fountain," Hawthorne's only first-person narrator in the collection outside the sketches tells about an unconsummated romance. First of all, he makes it easy for the reader to reject the more fanciful interpretation of the uneventful narrative, namely, the possibility that some Naiad inhabiting the fountain is to become the fulfillment of the teenaged protagonist's dreams. As a consequence, the more realistic interpretation becomes privileged. The face in the fountain surely belongs to a real girl, the reader assumes, and she will appear at the end of the tale to be joined with the young man. She does. She is Rachel, the daughter of the village squire. When the expected scene occurs, the two young people recognize each other, Rachel mirthfully, the narrator with delighted surprise. Then the narrator departs, never to return, and the narrative ends. Nothing happens: no love, no broken heart, not even a face to haunt the narrator's later years. And yet, despite the absence of incident, there is marked evidence of the narrator's presence. His voice frequently breaks into sentences to address his audience as "My sweet readers" (9:215) or as "Fair ladies" (9:219). As a result, he draws attention to the fact that these nonevents are being deliberately created on this page, right before the reader's eyes. This is not a record of supposedly actual events, or even, the narrator insists, the events of a typical "romance" (9:217). It is an exercise in narrative discourse involving a witty narrator and his specifically identified female readers/listeners. (When the tale was originally printed in *New England Magazine* for August 1835, an introductory paragraph, omitted in *Twice-told Tales*, began: "Dear ladies, could I but look into your eyes, like a star-gazer, I might read secret intelligences. Will you read what I have written? . . ." [9:623].)

The variations that Hawthorne rings on first-person narration in these selections are interesting in themselves, but they are of a different technical order from the ones discussed at greater length in this chapter. Furthermore, Chapter 3 thoroughly investigates several other first-person sketches. Because the authority in a first-person narrative is rooted in supposedly autobiographical experience, the author's relation to the narrator in such work and the narrator's to the reader entail somewhat different rhetorical forces from those under consideration here. The same might be said for the five tales purportedly retelling historical events: "The Prophetic Pictures," "The May-Pole of Merry Mount," "The Minister's Black Veil," "The Gentle Boy," and "The Gray Champion." All five are, naturally enough, recounted in the past tense by quasi-omniscient third-person narrators. Here again, the variety of technical experiment is arresting, most especially in the narrators' acceptance and/or modification of the historical sources, an issue discussed at greater length in Chapter 5.

In some of these historical fictions, Hawthorne pretends to borrow authority for a narrative by attributing its origins to a previously published source. For example, the reader is told in a footnote to "The Prophetic Pictures" that the "story was suggested by an anecdote of Stuart, related in Dunlap's History of the Arts of Design" (9:166). This claim to authenticity is moderate. The story was merely "suggested" rather than determined by its source, and the source was an "anecdote" rather than a complete narrative. Even so, fact not fancy is claimed to be its ultimate source, a claim reenforced later when the narrator says that a fictional painter in the tale executed portraits of actual participants in the early history of New England: Governor Burnet, Mr. Cooke, the wife of Sir William Phips, John Winston, and Chief Justice and Madam Oliver. Historicity obviously confers some sort of authority on the narrative. "The May-Pole of Merry Mount" also begins with the narrator's claim to historical authenticity, not in a footnote, but in an epigraph in which the narrator refers both to "the grave pages of our New England annalists" and to "Strutt's Book of English Sports and Pastimes." What could be further from a narrative flight of fancy? And yet, these claims to facticity are balanced, or undermined, by the narrator's reference in this same epigraph to "the slight sketch here attempted" and to the story's quality as "a sort of allegory" (9:54). Readers are clearly reminded before encountering a single sentence of narrative that they are reading words arranged on a page by a conscientious craftsman.

In "The Minister's Black Veil," the narrator lays claim to a measure of historical accuracy when he explains that the protagonist, Mr. Hooper, gave an election sermon during Governor Belcher's administration and that, as a consequence, "the legislative measures of that year, were characterized by all the gloom and piety of our earliest ancestral sway" (9:49). That is, the narrator proposes a fictional event to be an important link in a "real" historical sequence. Even more supportive of historical accuracy is the narrator's initial footnote with its unarguable reference to the experience of "Another clergyman in New England, Mr. Joseph Moody, of York, Maine, who died about eighty years since" (9:37). And yet, all this pretense of historicity is made to support a tale of macabre and humorous Gothicism. Clearly, history is not the only ingredient in this tale. It is precisely owing to such assertions of historical accuracy, however, that Hawthorne's narrator is liberated to enter this tale whenever he feels inclined. At one point he digresses to allude to another story by Hawthorne, "The Wedding Knell" (9:43). At several others, he editorializes on the action directly, lest the reader too readily assume that Mr. Hooper's view is the narrator's. In one telling instance, a delegation from the church find themselves tongue-tied when forced to confront Hooper and his black veil in the minister's study. Hooper makes no effort to relax them by inquiring the purpose of their visit. The narrator wryly observes: "The topic, it might be supposed, was obvious enough" (9:44–45). Here we see the narrator obviously pleased with the tale he is telling, as is often the case in this story. One other example must suffice to establish the point. Having summarized most of Hooper's subsequent life in about two pages, the narrator brings the minister to his deathbed and describes the persons observing his last moments. One is female. "Who, but Elizabeth!" the narrator exclaims (9:50), clearly pleased at his manipulation of the characters, and calling on his reader to join in his pleasure. How appropriate! the reader must observe, appropriate as only carefully contrived writing can be. This is, of course, what the narrator promises in the opening footnote when he contrasts Mr. Moody's case with the "eccentricity that is here related of the Reverend Mr. Hooper." The word *related* deliberately calls attention to the narrator's presence in the tale, as does his claim later in the note that "the symbol had a different import" in Moody's case (9:37). Here the reader encounters something other than a historical reconstruction, despite the narrator's claims to historical authority. "The Minister's Black Veil" is carefully contrived, original fiction, calculated to engage the reader's attention and to elicit admiration for the narrator's artistry, that is, for the author's.

Another tale rooted in history, "The Gentle Boy," suggests the same conclusions about Hawthorne's narrative freedom, except, of course, regarding the narrator's sense of humor. The opening sentence of "The Gentle Boy" makes claims to historical validity well beyond those advanced by the narrator's footnotes in the previous tales: "In the course of the year 1656, several of the people called Quakers, led, as they professed, by the inward movement of the spirit, made their appearance in New England" (9:68). The executions of two Quakers in 1659, the year in which the narrative opens, and the later royal decree forbidding persecution of the sect are other events intended to establish the tale in its historical matrix. More interesting in respect to Hawthorne's narrative experiments, however, is the narrator's summary of a Quaker historian's account of these events, even including several words of direct quotation:

> The historian of the sect affirms that, by the wrath of Heaven, a blight fell upon the land in the vicinity of the "bloody town" of Boston, so that no wheat would grow there; and he takes his stand, as it were, among the graves of the ancient persecutors, and triumphantly recounts the judgments that overtook them, in old age or at the parting hour. He tells us that they died suddenly, and violently, and in madness; but nothing can exceed the bitter mockery with which he records the loathsome disease, and "death by rottenness," of the fierce and cruel governor. (9:70)

Since Hawthorne's narrator treats these providential events as occurring at a historical point somewhere between the events of the tale and the time of the present writing, he creates another fictional-historical sequence, similar to that in the previous tale.

As we have also seen there, this historicity has a liberating effect on Hawthorne's narrator. Freely but evenhandedly he editorializes that the Quakers engaged in "actions contrary to the rules of decency, as well as of rational religion" (9:69), while a Puritan clergyman delivered a sermon "in which error predominated, and prejudice distorted the aspect of what was true" (9:80). As such passages illustrate, this narrator writes from a position of total control over his material, bestowing praise or blame on characters and sects whenever he deems it necessary. Early in the tale, this narrative strategy leads to his creation of an almost Keatsian tableau, intended to represent the values that the narrator is analyzing: "The two females, as they held each a hand of Ilbrahim, formed a practical allegory; it was rational piety and unbridled fanaticism, contending for the empire of a young heart" (9:85). Such contrivances can operate effectively in fiction only when a narrator is granted the editorial freedom that Hawthorne bestows here. In fact, the narrator seems to acknowledge something of this sort later when he writes:

> And now the tale must stride forward over many months, leaving Pearson to encounter ignominy and misfortune; his wife to a firm endurance of a thousand sorrows; poor Ilbrahim to pine and droop like a cankered rosebud; his mother to wander on a mistaken errand, neglectful of the holiest trust which can be committed to a woman. (9:95)

We could hardly ask for clearer evidence of an assertive narrator. Such writing demonstrates that for Hawthorne history was not a dream from which he might seek to awaken, but a paradoxically liberating source of creativity and an opportunity to explore the varied possibilities of narrative.

Historical materials also afford Hawthorne opportunities to experiment with narrative remoteness and presence in several tales cast in the third-person-omniscient mode. It is significant, first of all, that Hawthorne uses this mode both for acknowledged fiction and for supposed historical fact. It is further significant, and much more surprising, that the supposedly historical tales sometimes afford the author more opportunity for creative engagement than the purely fictional.

The contrast can be clarified by considering "The Hollow of the Three Hills" and "The Gray Champion" in terms of what Mikhail Bakhtin would call their "chronotopes." In *The Dialogic Imagination*, Bakhtin defines *chronotope* as "the intrinsic connectedness of temporal and spatial relationships that are artistically expressed in literature," and he elaborates:

> The chronotope of literature has an intrinsic *generic* significance. It can even be said that it is precisely the chronotope that defines genre and generic distinctions, for in literature the primary category in the chronotope is time. The chronotope as a formally constitutive category determines to a significant degree the image of man in literature as well. The image of man is always intrinsically chronotopic. (84–85)

"The Hollow of the Three Hills" begins with this sentence: "In those strange old times, when fantastic dreams and madmen's reveries were realized among the actual circumstance of life, two persons met together at an appointed hour and place" (9:199). Here the narrator establishes a chronotope in which the supposedly historical past merges easily into the apparently timeless world of fantasy. "The Gray Champion" has this first sentence: "There was once a time, when New-England groaned under the actual pressure of heavier wrongs, than those threatened ones which brought on the Revolution" (9:9). The date of "there was a time" is technically as unfixed as that of "those strange old times," and yet the narrator proposes this chronotope as part of a historical sequence that will later include the American Revolution and Hawthorne's own day. One consequence of this historical fabulation is that the spectral champion is proposed to be real in a sense that the witch of "The Three Hills" is not. He lives first in history, an illusion deepened by references to James II and King William, and then in fiction, whereas the witch lives only in Hawthorne's story.

As an ironic consequence, the narrator feels free to manipulate his supposedly factual material deliberately, as the narrator of the fantasy is apparently unable to do. The Gray Champion will thus come again, the narrator predicts, when historical necessity calls for his presence: "I have heard, that, whenever the descendants of the Puritans are to show the spirit of their sires, the old man appears again" (9:17). Previous narratives from history and/or legend serve Hawthorne's purposes well here: the narrator has "heard" this. Someone else has said all this before, and the narrator has found an apt context in which to retell it—admittedly with his own embellishments. The reader cannot overlook the narrator's contributions here, or his presence in this admittedly "twice-told" tale.

In "The Hollow of the Three Hills," the narrator partially evades the whole issue of authority in the first sentence by locating the tale in a purely fictional chronotope. By admitting the marvelous nature of the tale, this narrator apparently feels liberated from some of the responsibilities we might expect him to assume, such as accounting for his relation to the material. This freedom is suggested in the first paragraph when the narrator observes, "In the spot where they encountered, no mortal could observe them" (9:199). Despite this assertion that only the two women were present, the narrator still knows assuredly what happened. He has this knowledge because the events described are entirely his invention, as are the words, thoughts, and emotions of all the characters. As a result, the narrator can look at will into the soul of the younger woman, as in confident assertions of this sort: "She hesitated a moment, but the anxiety, that had long been kindling, burned fiercely up within her" (9:201). Considerable narrative authority must be assumed in such a statement. The narrator does not attempt to stretch this authority too far. When the witch conjures up the loved ones whom the younger woman left in a distant land, the narrator does not claim that they are visible. He does claim that they are audible, however, as when he states that "the conversation of an aged man, and of a woman broken and decayed like himself, became distinctly audible to the lady as she knelt" (9:201). Although this sentence connects the sounds only with the younger woman, we should recall that the witch is the only other "mortal" present. Furthermore, we should notice that the language does not stress the possibility of delusion; there is no formula such as "or so it seemed." It is not the narrator's intention to show that the younger woman is being deceived, but rather to establish that the voices carry the same degree of fictional authority as "the wind sweeping mournfully among the autumn leaves" (9:202) later in the same paragraph. It might seem that all parts of the tale are accorded equivalent authority.

There are some subtle distinctions apparent in the narrator's commitment to his statements, however, as the following passage reveals:

> Such scenes as this (so gray tradition tells) were once the resort of a Power
> of Evil and his plighted subjects; and here, at midnight or on the dim verge

of evening, they were said to stand round the mantling pool, disturbing its putrid waters in the performance of an impious baptismal rite. The chill beauty of an autumnal sunset was now gilding the three hill-tops, whence a paler tint stole down their sides into the hollow. (9:200)

In the second sentence, the narrator describes the setting confidently, on his own authority. In the first, the narrator hedges his Gothic claims. He can repeat exactly what "gray tradition tells" us, but he will not affirm on his own that the tradition is truthful. As a result, the devil worshippers can only be "said" to have met on the spot. The narrator cannot guarantee the reports, despite his apparent omniscience. He can, however, guarantee that "two persons met together" and that, in the place where they met, "Three little hills stood near each other" (9:199). The reader is clearly intended to accept information of the latter sort as reliable merely on the narrator's say-so. As Wolfgang Iser explains in his essay "Representation: A Performative Act," "[R]epresentation can only come to full fruition in the recipient's imagination . . ." (243). Examining the mixture of proposed and qualified assertion in this tale shows how active the "recipient's imagination" must be in order to evaluate the levels of narrative authority in Hawthorne's fiction.

The narrator of "Dr. Heidegger's Experiment" often adopts a mixed approach to authority also, sometimes writing entirely from his own perspective and sometimes calling on the support of external agencies. The overall rhetorical effect of the strategy is different in this tale, however. Borrowing some critical vocabulary from Tzvetan Todorov's *The Fantastic: A Structural Approach to a Literary Genre*, we might observe that "The Hollow of the Three Hills" is, finally, a tale of the "marvelous," because the reader's hesitancy between logical and supernatural interpretations of the fictional events is most likely resolved in favor of the supernatural. In "Dr. Heidegger's Experiment," on the other hand, the reader's hesitancy is never resolved but is maintained throughout the tale through the narrator's alternation of "marvelous" and logical or "uncanny" explanations. In consequence, "Dr. Heidegger's Experiment" displays the generic properties of the "fantastic."

A long descriptive paragraph offers especially clear evidence of this practice, beginning with its first sentence: "If all stories were true, Dr. Heidegger's study must have been a very curious place." While the narrator will not take responsibility for these "stories," and even adopts the indirect locution "must have been," he will affirm in the next sentence that "It was a dim, old-fashioned chamber, festooned with cobwebs, and besprinkled with antique dust." The narrator continues in this manner to describe, on his own authority, the study's bookcases, books, and bust of Hippocrates. Then he retreats into secondary testimony to write that "according to some authorities, Dr. Heidegger was accustomed to hold consultations, in all difficult cases" with this bust. He does not need the support of "some authorities" in the next sentence to describe an obscure closet and the skeleton in it, or in the next to describe a looking glass in "a tarnished gilt frame." When he wishes, in the sentence following, to suggest the possibility that the images of the doctor's dead patients may live within the looking glass, he drops the language of direct description to write, "Among many wonderful stories related of this mirror, it was fabled that . . ." (9:228). In *The Fantastic* Todorov has claimed that "If a certain apparition is only the fruit of an overexcited imagination, then everything around it is real" (168). This paragraph about Dr. Heidegger's study suggests that Todorov's proposition may be critically convertible, that a narrator's unqualified assertions of descriptive detail may lend some sort of authenticity to contingent elements of the marvelous. In any event, the insistence with which Hawthorne's narrator adheres to the fantastic here seems indisputable.

This is true even at the crucial point in the story when four elderly characters seem to have been restored to youth after drinking a magic potion created by Dr. Heidegger. As the characters prance before this same mirror in the bloom of regained youth, the narrator writes that "the tall mirror is said to have reflected the figures of the three old, gray, withered grand-sires, ridiculously contending for the skinny ugliness of a shrivelled grand-dam" (9:237). Perhaps the mirror accurately reflected such, perhaps not. The narrator takes no stand. Alfred H. Marks was among the first to connect Hawthorne's narrative deviousness in such matters with the devices characteristic of German Romantic Irony. Surely the indirection in this and similar passages may profitably be considered in that light. Even while accepting Marks's suggestions, however, we should go on to take account of how variously Hawthorne employs such devices within a single tale. In doing so, we must conclude that this narrator's relation to his own story seems very remote indeed in the paragraph devoted to the doctor's study.

Elsewhere, this narrator seems much less timid. For example, shortly after attributing all preternatural elements in the doctor's study to secondary testimony, the narrator turns to a characterization of the man himself. The first paragraph devoted to this task shows Hawthorne's narrator in a new role:

> Now, Dr. Heidegger was a very strange old gentleman, whose eccentricity had become the nucleus for a thousand fantastic stories. Some of these fables, to my shame be it spoken, might possibly be traced back to mine own veracious self; and if any passages of the present tale should startle the reader's faith, I must be content to bear the stigma of a fiction-monger. (9:229–30)

Here we see the narrator accepting responsibility for a fanciful story and, more significantly, acknowledging that his role in the creation of imaginary events, or "tales," is that of a "fiction-monger." Surely the "shame" and "stigma" he admits to, then, must be read as transparent ironies. The narrator not only admits his responsibility for this tale, as Marks cogently observes (289–90), but exalts his responsibility through an inverted apology. It is this narrator's focus on himself *as* narrator that creates the principal authority in this tale. Thus, he feels free to break in on his tale from time to time to attract the reader's attention to his efforts:

> And, before proceeding farther, I will merely hint, that Dr. Heidegger and all his four guests were sometimes thought to be a little beside themselves; as is not unfrequently the case with old people, when worried either by present troubles or woful recollections. (9:228)

The authority for these remarks resides in the narrator, not in his sources, textual or legendary. Because "I" rather than "they" is the instrumental pronoun, this narrator can describe furniture, create characters, tell tall tales, and comment sagely on old age. That is, he may perform most of the duties of an author.

"Mr. Higginbotham's Catastrophe" shows Hawthorne approaching the issue of narrative authority from a different angle. As J. Donald Crowley explains in the historical commentary to *Twice-told Tales* (9:492–96), this story was originally intended to be part of a larger structure called "The Story Teller." When first published in the *New England Magazine* for December 1834, the tale was accompanied by a portion of the projected longer work, a frame in which the narrator, an aspiring artist, is characterized and given a past. Reprinted in *Mosses from an Old Manse* as "Passages from a Relinquished Work" (10:405–21), this frame is two pages longer than the tale itself. Readers who first encountered the tale in the *New England Magazine* must surely have had their attitudes toward this narrator's authority shaped by fictional details concerning the narrator's childhood, his awesome guardian Parson Thumpcushion, his naive enchantment with show business, and his comic discomfiture as a performer. Most especially in the section entitled "The Village Theatre," in which he tells a story entitled "Mr. Higginbotham's Catastrophe" to an audience, the narrator becomes thoroughly fictionalized. In such a context, the narrator and his characters are sealed together in a purely fictionalized chronotope, a world as hermetically remote as "those strange old times." However, these factors do not operate upon a reader encountering "Mr. Higginbotham's Catastrophe" without its frame in the pages of *Twice-told Tales*, either in 1837 or today.

As C. S. B. Swann has aptly observed, the piece stripped of its frame is still "a sophisticated joke about tales and their tellers" (188). As a result, the reader cannot fail to recognize the narrator's presence in the tale. Even though this story is largely told in the past tense and in the third person, from a point of view restricted to an itinerant trader named Dominicus Pike, the narrator occasionally interrupts to call attention to himself. In the first paragraph, for example, the narrator says the following: "The pedler drove a smart little mare, and was a young man of excellent character, keen at a bargain, but none the worse liked by the Yankees; who, as I have heard them say, would rather be shaved with a sharp razor than a dull one" (9:106). The interposed remark "I have heard them say" is not absolutely essential, but it lends broader authority to this observation about the business practices of the Yankees. At the same time, it supports the narrative in which it is embedded by suggesting that the narrator is not inventing his discourse whimsically, at least not entirely, but is basing it, at least in part, on his experience in the "real" world. The narrator returns to this self-reflexive practice in the final paragraph of the tale. Having married Pike to "the pretty school-mistress" and settled Mr. Higginbotham's considerable fortune on them and their children, the narrator presents in the last sentence of the tale the "Christian death, in bed" of Mr. Higginbotham. The sentence concludes: ". . . since which melancholy event, Dominicus Pike has removed from Kimballton, and established a large tobacco manufactory in my native village" (9:120). Surely these final words are intended to function as an ethical appeal, confirming the narrator's veracity. In *Narrative Discourse* (227–37) Genette has analyzed at length the rhetorical influence of this sort of "metalepsis," the attribution of equivalent reality to fictional characters and narrators. Suffice it to say here that in this concluding passage the narrator is asserting authority through his own experience as well as through the internal coherence of his narrative.

This narrator also attracts attention to himself and his function by admitting, in the very first paragraph, that he is recounting a "story" (9:106) and by acknowledging the presence of a reader. At times this acknowledgment is metaleptical, as when he incorporates the reader into his own sphere of awareness: "With these meditations, Dominicus Pike drove into the street of Parker's Falls, which, as every body knows, is as thriving a village as three cotton-factories and a slitting-mill can make it" (9:111). The mild social satire coloring this remark probably contributes to the reader's sense of this narrator's sophistication and consequently of his authority. However, the reader's absorption into the community of what "every body knows" is even more significant in establishing a cozy relation between reader and narrator. Partly as a result, the narrator may address the reader directly later on while unknotting the central mystery of the tale: "If the riddle be not already guessed, a few words will explain the simple machinery, by which this 'coming event' was made to 'cast its shadow before' " (9:119). Obviously, it is the reader who has or has not "already guessed" what has been going on. The narrator has understood it all from the start, as he implies by presenting the narrative in the past tense, and as he directly affirms in his first and last paragraphs. That is to say, he openly exercises considerable authority in his narrative.

"David Swan" also proceeds from an acknowledged narrator. Though not fictionalized, as the narrator of "Mr. Higginbotham's Catastrophe" was originally intended to be, nor identified in the first-person singular as that narrator continued to be, this narrator is insistently present in his tale, both as spokesman for what "we"—the narrator and the reader—know and as an admitted manipulator of his fictional material. The narrator's role as spokesman is apparent in the first sentence of the tale: "We can be but partially acquainted even with events which actually influence our course through life, and our final destiny" (9:183). Because this statement is cast in the temporal mode that Wallace Martin has identified as the "gnomic present" (124), it carries the sort of rhetorical authority that leads readers to nod affirmatively, being, if not totally convinced, at least persuaded to follow the narrator to see where he is tending. At the end of eight pages, the narrator arrives at a concluding sentence cast in the same tone: "Does it not argue a superintending Providence, that, while viewless and unexpected events thrust themselves continually athwart our path, there should still be regularity enough, in mortal life, to render foresight even partially available?" (9:190). Again, a reader seems likely to respond affirmatively, or at least to say, maybe so! This agreement results not primarily from the conclusion's appropriateness to the tale, but from a sense of community that has grown out of the narrator's reasonable tone. Thomas F. Walsh has demonstrated how frequently in his early career Hawthorne organized this sort of tale around an abstract premise, but no one has investigated how this narrative strategy affects the relations among narrator, tale, and reader.

One promising approach is to consider how the narrator uses a similar tone of reasonableness to authorize his intrusions into his tale. For example, he emphasizes the fictionality of his enterprise in the second paragraph by stipulating the point at which readers may enter the tale: "We have nothing to do with David, until we find him, at the age of twenty . . ." (9:183). He draws attention to his skill by commenting on his handling of a scene involving the sleeping David Swan and a young girl: "How sweet a picture!" (9:187). He also attracts attention to himself when describing this girl's animated entrance: "Perhaps it was this merry kind of motion that caused—is there any harm in saying it?—her garter to slip its knot" (9:186). After this interpolated apology, even genteel readers could hardly object to the garter's inelegant presence in the tale, and no reader can ignore this narrator's presence. It has been obvious since his declaration of artistic control in the second paragraph: "This idea may be illustrated by a page from the secret history of David Swan" (9:183).

The final testimony to this narrator's presence lies, paradoxically, in his control over what does not happen in the tale. A rich old couple do not adopt David Swan and make him their heir, although they discuss doing so over his sleeping body. As if in recognition of some preminimalist aesthetic, the narrator comments: "While these whispers were passing, the sleeper's heart did not throb, nor his breath become agitated, nor his features betray the least token of interest" (9:186). The young girl with the garter does not awaken David and become his true love, and so he does not succeed to her father's prosperous business. About these nonhappenings, the narrator observes, "Had David formed a way side acquaintance with the daughter, he would have become the father's clerk, and all else in natural succession" (9:187). When two cutthroats do not rob and murder the boy, the narrator observes in similar fashion: "As for David Swan, he still slept quietly, neither conscious of the shadow of death when it hung over him, nor of the glow of renewed life, when that shadow was withdrawn" (9:189). The suggestion in each case is that any of these events might have taken place if it had been the will, not of Providence, but of the narrator that this should have been the case. By raising such possibilities only to foreclose them, this narrator is quite deliberate in directing his reader's attention to some preexisting written source, here not "the grave pages of our New England annalists" or "Strutt's Book of English Sports and Pastimes" but an entire genre of popular writing. This narrator could exploit the materials of popular romance— the sudden bestowal of a fortune, the accidental discovery of true love, the coincidental encounter with blood and danger—but he chooses not to do so. The effect is to remind the reader of this narrator's control over his tale, that is to say, to call attention to his narrative authority.

The narrator of "Fancy's Show Box" also considers events that do not take place. Providing another example of what Walsh calls "Hawthorne's Illustrated Ideas," the tale questions whether "guilty thoughts . . . will . . . draw down the full weight of a condemning sentence, in the supreme court of eternity" (9:220), even if the thoughts are never acted upon. The narrator quickly establishes that the question will be investigated entirely in his terms and under his direction: "Let us illustrate the subject by an imaginary example" (9:220). Next, he ostentatiously names the character who supposedly harbors the evil thoughts "Mr. Smith." Then, after introducing the show box of the title as a device to dramatize evil thoughts, he again interjects himself by writing, "We can sketch merely the outlines of two or three, out of the many pictures, which, at the pulling of a string, successively peopled the box with the semblances of living scenes" (9:222). Through such continual reminders of his presence, this narrator probably becomes more "real" to the reader than Mr. Smith does. The final, and perhaps most influential, evidence of this narrator's presence occurs near the end of the tale. By this point, the narrator has decided that Mr. Smith—and, by extension, the reader—is probably guiltless so long as the evil intentions remain unfulfilled. To clarify this judgment, the narrator essays an analogy: "Thus a novel-writer, or a dramatist, in creating a villain of romance, and fitting him with evil deeds, and the villain of actual life, in projecting crimes that will be perpetrated, may almost meet each other, half-way between reality and fancy" (9:225–26). The professed effect of this analogy is to call attention to an often-quoted Hawthornean moral: "Man must not disclaim his brotherhood, even with the guiltiest . . ." (9:226). But another effect is to emphasize the "writer" who declares himself to be both the subject and the creator of this analogy, and the creator as well of Mr. Smith, his guilty thoughts, and the whole tale. It might be observed, then, that self-avowed narrators of this sort may operate with as much freedom as they wish without sacrificing their authority.

"The Wedding-Knell" appears under two guises in *Twice-told Tales*, as a self-referential allusion in "The Minister's Black Veil"—"If ever another wedding were so dismal, it was that famous one where they tolled the wedding knell" (9:43)—and as an independent exercise in narrative authority. When examined thematically, the tale does not altogether contradict Lea Newman's claim that it is the "least effectual of stories" (322). However, we might note that in the tale Hawthorne integrates a number of narrative devices that function separately elsewhere. For example, instead of attributing rumors about his principal characters to an external "they," as in the mode of "Dr. Heidegger's Experiment," the narrator assimilates the remarks into the texture of the tale by treating them as gossip circulating in the community surrounding Mr. Ellenwood and Mrs. Dabney. He therefore remarks, when people speculate concerning this elderly couple's decision to marry, "Superficial observers, and deeper ones, seemed to concur, in supposing that the lady must have borne no inactive part, in arranging the affair . . ." (9:29). Since the major events in the tale take place in the presence of a large crowd, attributions of this sort operate organically to flesh out the fictional community as well as to introduce multiple interpretations of events. In the same way, fictional characters are used to offer varying interpretations of the apparent coincidence of the church bell's tolling as the wedding party arrives (9:30) and of the apparently inexplicable later arrival at the church of a party of mourners (9:33–34). The same may be said of the narrator's approach to interpretive morals. When he wishes to remind the reader that all significant human experiences are colored by a mixture of joy and sorrow, the narrator has a fictional character, the rector of the Episcopal church, refer to "a marriage sermon of the famous Bishop Taylor" (9:31) to convey the message. Paradoxically, this twofold internalization establishes authority by displacing it. Another significant moral, the suitability of different behavior to different ages, is conveyed through attribution to Mr. Ellenwood (9:34–35). Since some have earlier suggested that Ellenwood might perhaps be mentally unbalanced, his articulation of the moral may provide some ironic italics. Even so, the moral enters the tale.

Despite all this attention to organic coherence, an authoritative narrator is clearly present in the tale. In the first paragraph, he begins by attributing authority for his narrative to his grandmother, who, as a child, "chanced to be a spectator of the scene." Almost immediately, however, he substitutes his own authority, not only for that of the supposed eyewitness, but also for that of historical accuracy, as he writes:

> Whether the edifice, now standing on the same site, be the identical one to which she referred, I am not antiquarian enough to know; nor would it be worth while to correct myself, perhaps, of an agreeable error, by reading the date of its erection on the tablet over the door. (9:27)

Since this narrator asserts his control over the material so obviously, he feels free to enter the tale whenever necessary, as to make the following transition: ". . . with whose arrival, after this tedious but necessary preface, the action of our tale may be said to commence" (9:30). In another case, he asks rhetorically, "How shall the widow's horror be represented!" Immediately he answers, "It gave her the ghastliness of a dead man's bride" (9:34). This combination of organic attributions and obvious narrative interventions should go far in demonstrating that, even if the tale itself is not very "effectual," Hawthorne's creation of his narrator clearly is.

"The Great Carbuncle" resembles "The Hollow of the Three Hills" and "Dr. Heidegger's Experiment" in featuring a narrator who adopts a mixed

approach to authority. In this case, Hawthorne's strategy was, in all probability, thematically dictated by the subject of the tale, a quest for an enormous, preternatural gem by eight characters chosen to represent different
dimensions of human nature and society. Obviously, a satiric narrative
about a fabulous object calls for a complex narrative strategy. The narrator
speaks very confidently in some places, as when he draws a moral lesson
from the entombment of the proud Lord de Vere: "As the funeral torches
gleamed within that dark receptacle, there was no need of the Great Carbuncle to shew the vanity of earthly pomp" (9:164). Predictably enough,
the narrator is also confident when describing characters and settings. In
partial justification for the latter, he turns briefly to the first person to write
in the final sentence of the tale: "And be it owned, that, many a mile from
the Crystal Hills, I saw a wondrous light around their summits, and was
lured, by the faith of poesy, to be the latest pilgrim of the GREAT CARBUN-
CLE" (9:165). This narrator may speak about some things with authority,
that is, because he knows personally whereof he speaks.

At other times, the narrator is careful to avoid responsibility for what he
recounts. In discussing the character called the Seeker, for example, the
narrator attributes the old man's obsession with the Great Carbuncle to a
curse, but he attributes the curse to "a fable in the valley of the Saco"
(9:150). Similarly, he uses the carefully hedged locution, "It was told of
him, whether truly or not," to introduce the possibility that the scientist, Dr.
Cacaphodel, "drained his body of all its richest blood . . . in an unsuccessful
experiment" (9:151). By the same token, it may be only a "ridiculous story"
told by "His enemies" that the miserly Master Pigsnort likes to wallow "naked among an immense quantity of pine-tree shillings" (9:151). Obviously,
these strategies of attribution show considerable ingenuity, but they show
little direct claim to authority. In these matters, the fantastic definitely mod-
ulates toward the merely "uncanny." Skeptical readers may temporarily
rest easy.

In other matters, assurance is harder to come by. The narrator directly
affirms that Hannah and Matthew succeed in their quest: "For the simple
pair had reached that lake of mystery, and found the long sought shrine of
the Great Carbuncle!" (9:161). However, an event no more nor less plausible is presented as follows: "There is also a tradition that, as the youthful
pair departed, the gem was loosened from the forehead of the cliff, and fell

into the enchanted lake . . ." (9:165). Instead of hesitating between alternative supernatural and logical interpretations, this narrator alternately presents one or the other. Moreover, there is apparently no intrinsic principle of plausibility to account for these choices, only the narrator's judgment of how the material will be received. This issue of narrative credibility is illuminated by a passage occurring toward the end of the tale. The narrator says there that Hannah and Matthew liked to recount "the legend of the Great Carbuncle" during their later years, but he adds: "The tale, however, toward the close of their lengthened lives, did not meet with the full credence that had been accorded to it by those, who remembered the ancient lustre of the gem" (9:165). Perhaps it stretches Hawthorne's intentions to convert the problems that Hannah and Matthew had with their audiences into a commentary on the problems Hawthorne might anticipate from his readers.

If there is any validity to such a reading, however, it must lie in the sense that tales are neither true nor false, but only credible or incredible. In *The Fantastic* Todorov addresses this point by claiming that "literary language is a conventional language in which the test of truth is impossible" (82). Genette agrees in *Narrative Discourse Revisited*: "[F]or reasons that have been set forth a thousand times (and not only by me), I believe that there is no imitation in narrative because narrative, like everything (or almost everything) in literature, is an act of language" (42). In this light, Hawthorne and his characters might equally propose that the only useful standard for tellers of tales is credibility or incredibility. The first page of this tale lends plausibility to such conjectures. In a footnote purporting to authenticate his tale, the narrator attributes authority for its essence to "Indian tradition" and claims James Sullivan's history of Maine as supporting testimony. Calling up sources in this way might seem to deflect the reader's awareness of this narrator's authority. However, the clever verbal formulation has a rather different effect: "The Indian tradition, on which this somewhat extravagant tale is founded, is both too wild and too beautiful to be adequately wrought up, in prose" (9:149). As in "Dr. Heidegger's Experiment," a falsely modest apology serves ironically to affirm a narrator's skill. The legend cannot defy being "adequately wrought up, in prose" because the narrator proposes to do that very thing in the tale that follows. It is significant, too, that this narrator directs his readers' attention, from the beginning, to the fact that they will be reading a "somewhat extravagant tale." It hardly need be stated, therefore, that this tale is like all others in that it must have a narrator—in this case, a narrator who is very much present.

Hawthorne's narrative strategies in "Wakefield" have elicited considerable critical notice. Walsh (34) and Doubleday (152) observe how the author consistently stresses the fictionality of the whole exercise by informing the reader directly of his creative intentions. In "The Unity of Hawthorne's *Twice-told Tales*," Crowley encapsulates this promising train of thought when he writes that Hawthorne "makes the donnee of the tale the very process by which he seems to invent it before the reader's eyes and even with the reader's help" (43). By shifting critical emphasis from Hawthorne to his narrator, and by considering how narrative strategies affect this narrator's authority, we can profitably approach this final and most challenging example. It is clear from the first sentence that this narrator will be assertively present in the tale: "In some old magazine or newspaper, I recollect a story, told as truth, of a man—let us call him Wakefield—who absented himself for a long time, from his wife" (9:130). Here the narrator claims "a story" already published as original authentication for his narrative, but he also implies his own authority by identifying himself in the first-person singular. Another possible sign of this authority is the narrator's observation that the original account was "told as truth," implying, perhaps, that writing is not identical to fact but must be shaped by a writer's intentions. When he parenthetically interposes the words "let us call him Wakefield," however, there is no need for a tentative "perhaps." Even more aggressively than the narrator who calls his character Mr. Smith, this narrator is announcing his control over his material.

Later passages confirm this presence. At one point, the narrator promises that his narrative will convey "a pervading spirit and a moral, even should we fail to find them, done up neatly, and condensed into the final sentence" (9:131), thus effectually establishing that the reader is encountering not life but writing, "sentences," created deliberately. This literariness is emphasized also when the narrator admits to altering his source material. After raising the rhetorical question "What sort of a man was Wakefield?" the narrator observes, "We are free to shape out our own idea, and call it by his name" (9:131). Actually, "our" idea can only mean the narrator's. That this is the case is demonstrated in the first sentence of the next paragraph when the narrator begins to dramatize his premises: "Let us now imagine Wakefield bidding adieu to his wife." If the first-person plural pronoun does not clearly establish the narrator's influence here, the verb "imagine" must. The following sentence is even more striking: "It is the dusk of an October evening" (9:132). When a narrator feels free to switch tenses for dramatic effect, we cannot fail to recognize his presence. As a result of such passages, the narrator can risk his most outrageous intervention in the narrative. Just after summarizing the passage of ten years in a brief paragraph, the narrator writes: "Now for a scene!" (9:137). He then goes on to dramatize a meeting between Wakefield and his wife in two lengthy paragraphs presented, unapologetically, in the present tense.

The cumulative effect of all these technical flourishes is to establish a narrative voice that affords Hawthorne unusual thematic possibilities. Because this narrator exercises his control so authoritatively, he is empowered to pronounce gnomically on a wide variety of issues. Sometimes these remarks pertain solely to the case of Wakefield, as when, on the first morning of the self-imposed exile, Wakefield passes the end of the street on which his wife lives. The narrator observes: "At that instant, his fate was turning on the pivot" (9:134). Some of his other comments on Wakefield's conduct are even more pointed, such as his calling the deluded man a "crafty nincompoop" and the quest a "long whim-wham" (9:135). Such commentary on a fictional character's behavior may proceed only from a narrative eminence at which the narrator's control of the material is unquestionable. Most decisive of all is the narrator's judgment, stated as Wakefield climbs the steps of his former dwelling to rejoin his wife: "Stay, Wakefield! Would you go to the sole home that is left you? Then step into your grave!" (9:139). There can be no doubt in these cases that the reader is encountering a narrator's "sentences" rather than a mirror of life.

This narrator also feels qualified to speak about "life" as the reader knows it. The tale is laced with gnomic utterances such as "It is perilous to make a chasm in human affections; not that they gape so long and wide—but so quickly close again!" (9:133). The supposed moral of the tale is couched in a similar tone:

> Amid the seeming confusion of our mysterious world, individuals are so
> nicely adjusted to a system, and systems to one another, and to a whole,

that, by stepping aside for a moment, a man exposes himself to a fearful risk of losing his place forever. Like Wakefield, he may become, as it were, the Outcast of the Universe. (9:140)

This disturbing sentiment may seem plausible to most reasonable readers. However, as is the case with "David Swan," there is no necessary connection between the moral and the tale. The same reasonable reader might draw another, equally plausible, moral from Wakefield's experience. In the same way, the narrator's moral about the "fearful risk of losing [one's] place forever" might be drawn from dozens of other narratives. The moral is primarily part of the narrator's discourse, an opinion he feels called upon to articulate before the tale ends. At an earlier point, the narrator feels such moral urgency that he states a principle without even pretending any dramatic relevance:

Would that I had a folio to write, instead of an article of a dozen pages! Then might I exemplify how an influence, beyond our control, lays its strong hand on every deed which we do, and weaves its consequences into an iron tissue of necessity. (9:136–37)

These dark truths about "real life" are interpolated solely on the basis of the narrator's authority, not for their actual or putative relations to the case of the fictional Wakefield.

Here is the peculiar success of "Wakefield." Hawthorne develops a narrator so clearly present in the words on the page that he becomes a rounded fictional character with attitudes and dispositions, a sense of humor, and opinions about morality, society, love, marriage, and "real life." C. S. B. Swann claims that "at least one moral of . . . 'Wakefield' is related to the author's authority over his readers. When Hawthorne uses 'we' or 'us' in this story, it always means you, gentle reader, and myself, the author. It is never the editorial 'we' " (195). This authority is used to establish a relation with the reader similar to that animating Hawthorne's more mature work. In this respect, we can see that "Wakefield" contributes substantially to the development of the sophisticated narrative strategies of Hawthorne's later career—the voice used in the "Custom-House" sketch, for example, and Miles Coverdale's tone in *The Blithedale Romance*.

Each of these tales must have contributed in some way to Hawthorne's increasing grasp of the possibilities that narrative in the larger sense held out individually to him as a writer. In this respect, each must be viewed as successful, if only as an artistic experiment. For my purposes here, the tales have been arranged in order to foreground the issue of narrative authority. It would be a mistake, however, to use this technical element—or some other one—to classify the narratives in *Twice-told Tales* according to a putatively evolutionary taxonomy of narrative sophistication. Q. D. Leavis's remark bears repeating: "The essential . . . Hawthorne . . . soon found himself" (35) and continued along the literary paths he had discovered. Or, as G. R. Thompson writes, "[T]he 'shape of Hawthorne's career' is consistent along aesthetic lines that he developed from the beginning" (3). Hawthorne experimented with subtly different forms of narrative authority in the 1830s, and he continued to do so. His narrative strategies did not evolve uninterruptedly toward a Jamesian sort of organic perspective or toward some metafictional sort of game-playing. Rather, Hawthorne incorporated varieties of narrative authority and other strategies of narration into his fiction throughout his career, certainly into all of his completed romances. What is more, he did so even within single works, and within single paragraphs. In Hawthorne's longer works, as in *Twice-told Tales*, the narrator's shifting perspectives demand subtly varying responses from the reader. We cannot help choosing among the possibilities that Hawthorne's narrators propose, problematize, question, retract, and suggest. From our almost limitless choices arise our almost limitless interpretations. We may conclude, therefore, that Hawthorne's first published collection of tales previewed not only the themes of his later fiction but also many of the narrative strategies.

THREE

# Narrative Voice in the Sketches

The 1837 edition of *Twice-told Tales* contained eighteen pieces of short fiction ranging from richly ambiguous tales such as "The May-Pole of Merry Mount" and "Wakefield" to fictional sketches such as "Sights from a Steeple" and "Little Annie's Ramble." Surprisingly, the book makes no taxonomic distinctions among these fictional forms. Readers today are likely to be amazed that Hawthorne published these pieces side by side with no sign that one sort of fiction was more congenial to his sensibility than the other, or that "The Minister's Black Veil," for example, might be of a higher aesthetic order than "Sunday at Home." This is almost certainly not how a modern reader would have edited the collection. In *The Shape of Hawthorne's Career*, Nina Baym says about this issue, "In all probability a critic of today, given the same opportunity, would choose almost none of the works that Hawthorne selected" (69). In *Hawthorne's Early Tales: A Critical Study*, Neal Frank Doubleday offers a similar judgment: "The selection of pieces does not very well conform to our notions today about what his best work is" (74).

In 1842 Hawthorne had a chance to adopt different editorial principles when he prepared a second, two-volume edition of *Twice-told Tales*, with contents expanded to thirty-nine selections. In the expanded edition, however, Hawthorne followed the same editorial strategy. Among the tales he added were some that are highly esteemed today, such as "Lady Eleanore's Mantle," "The Ambitious Guest," and "Endicott and the Red Cross." But Hawthorne also chose to reprint quite a few fictional sketches, including "The Toll Gatherer's Day," "The Haunted Mind," "The Sister Years," "Snow-flakes," "Chippings with a Chisel," "Night Sketches," and "Foot-prints on the Sea-shore." If we are aware that in choosing to reprint the latter pieces Hawthorne passed over tales such as "Roger Malvin's Burial," "My Kinsman, Major Molineux," and "Young Goodman Brown," his attachment to these fictional sketches seems all the more striking. So does his continuing practice of interspersing sketches among the more solemn and symbolic short stories without distinguishing them generically or aesthetically. Hawthorne added "The Toll-Gatherer's Day" to the works printed in 1837 to help give volume 1 of the 1842 edition a length comparable to that of volume 2, which was composed entirely of previously uncollected pieces. As was typical of his practice, Hawthorne inserted this sunny sketch between the grisly Gothic tale "The Hollow of the Three Hills" and a fanciful tale of young love, "The Vision of the Fountain." Readers convinced of Hawthorne's artistic distinction cannot help feeling that the sketches pose some sort of literary problem. J. Donald Crowley addresses this issue in his essay "The Unity of Hawthorne's *Twice-told Tales*" when he says that the make-up of both editions "has had embarrassing implications for most Hawthorne scholars, given the fact that, among other pieces in the two volumes, Hawthorne selected what are to modern taste such obviously inferior and disappointing ones . . ." (36).

Because critical consensus is rare, we should take these modern negative judgments seriously. We should also take seriously the different judgment of Hawthorne's contemporaries, whose praise of the sketches focused, as Crowley explains in the historical commentary to the *Centenary Edition* of *Twice-told Tales*, "primarily on the spiritual character of the man, his sensibilities and singular mode of consciousness . . ." (9:511). These differing historical evaluations of the sketches demonstrate that critical judgments are not so much statements of fact as observations authorized by particular intellectual paradigms, by what Grant Webster has called "critical charters" in *The Republic of Letters: A History of Postwar American Literary Opinion*. As Webster explains, "A charter . . . is a set of literary values which relies on a grant of intellectual authority, is embodied in a document, organizes a critical community, and is limited in time and function . . ." (10). Webster continues: "Functioning as it does as the intellectual world within which the critic operates, the critical charter defines the questions an individual critic can ask and hence limits the literature he can talk about effectively" (25). Or, as R. S. Crane earlier observed, "[T]he immediate context of any statement [in criticism] is the precise question (often not explicitly formulated at all) to which it is an intended answer" (178–79). Crane's and Webster's observations help to account for the "embarrassing implications" of Hawthorne's sketches. Hawthorne's contemporaries often valorized the genteel spiritual atmosphere suffusing his sketches, revealing their commitment to an aesthetic charter often dismissed condescendingly by critics today.

It is equally probable that the disposition toward Hawthorne's sketches shared by Baym, Doubleday, Crowley, and others consists of answers worked out in response to questions authorized by a different charter, the organic/objectivist understanding of prose fiction. This critical charter arose originally in Henry James's observations on fiction and flowered in the writing of the American New Critics, most influentially in the seminal textbook *Understanding Fiction* (1943, 1959), by Cleanth Brooks and Robert Penn Warren. One crucial element of this charter is the assumption that any piece of prose fiction is an autotelic organism that must be analyzed in terms of what Brooks and Warren call "the total structure . . . a set of organic relationships . . . the logic of the whole" (xiii), without reference to the personality or intentions of its author. Another crucial assumption is evident in James's contention in "The Art of Fiction" that a work of fiction—in this case the novel—is a "personal, a direct impression of life" (29). Brooks and Warren show their agreement by calling a short story "an attempt, however modified and limited, to make sense of experience, to understand how things hang meaningfully together" (526). This last verbal formula vividly demonstrates the conflation of thematic and technical assumptions common to James and the New Critics, the theory their ally Mark Schorer calls "Technique as Discovery." In practice, this conflation assures that certain technical devices—most especially those involved in point of view, or what Brooks and Warren call "focus of narration"—privilege certain sorts of themes. Brooks and Warren again speak succinctly to the point in describing the sort of organic unity most to be admired: "There is conflict and tension present, and the structure involves almost as much of vindictive opposition as of genial conspiracy. . . . [But] some sort of resolution, however provisional and marginal, must be implicit in the tensions of the fictional structure, if the unity is to be achieved . . ." (xviii).

We need not go beyond these basic premises to envision the sort of fictional work that would elicit positive answers to the questions authorized by this critical charter: a Jamesian/Joycean/Young-Goodman-Brownian tale of paradox and irony that issued from a consistently maintained point of view or "focus of narration"—in other words, just what the sketches in the 1842 collection are not. Thomas Kent has observed, in *Interpretation and Genre: The Role of Generic Perception in the Study of Narrative Texts*, "[A] genre may be disparaged because it is not on a high enough hierarchic level in a certain period of history to ensure that it will be meaningful or important" (72). A historical shift in critical charters has most probably brought about the diminished hieratic standing of Hawthorne's sketches today. Without readopting the values of Hawthorne's contemporaries, however, it is possible to get outside the critical charter of modernist organicism and subject these sketches to a different form of interrogation. The resulting answers might help us to guess why "Snow-flakes" and "Foot-prints on the Sea-shore" might continue to appeal to the author of "Wakefield" and "The May-Pole of Merry Mount."

We might begin to counter the negative view by recognizing that some modern readers have been favorably disposed toward some of Hawthorne's sketches. Mary Van Tassel has plausibly concluded, in "Hawthorne, His Narrator, and His Readers in 'Little Annie's Ramble,' " that "the sketch form worked well for Hawthorne" (168). In "The Literary Sketch in Nineteenth-Century America," Thomas H. Pauly has argued that because "Fully one-third of [Hawthorne's] short works are sketches . . . contemporary criticism has overlooked [a] vital complement to his tales" (495) in dismissing them. To redress this oversight, I intend to de-emphasize the subject matter of the sketches, genteel or otherwise, and to defer questions about how consistently these subjects echo or contrast with the subjects of the tales. In terms of a passage quoted earlier from Gerard Genette's *Narrative Discourse*, instead of "concentrating almost all its attention on the statement and its contents," my approach will be to focus instead on "the problems of narrative enunciating" (26). In practice this approach involves asking questions like: Who can speak on the page? To whom? About what? Why should the reader believe what the narrator says? To what degree is this credence possible?

A narratological critical strategy is at least consistent with Hawthorne's own description of the sketches in his 1851 preface to *Twice-told Tales*: "They are not the talk of a secluded man with his own mind and heart, (had it been so, they could hardly have failed to be more deeply and permanently valuable,) but his attempts, and very imperfectly successful ones, to open an intercourse with the world" (9:6). Genette writes similarly in *Narrative Discourse Revisited*: "[T]he main point of *Narrative Discourse*, beginning with its title, reflects the assumption that there is an enunciating instance— the narrating—with its narrator and its narratee, fictive or not, represented or not, silent or chatty, but always present in what is indeed for me, I fear, an act of communication" (101). In Chapter 2 we have seen the amazing variety of technical experiment by which Hawthorne sought to achieve this rhetorical relation in his early tales. The same is true of the sketches Hawthorne produced during this same period. In fact, freed from the obligation to create rounded characters and coherent plots, Hawthorne experimented with all sorts of narrative strategies in these sketches, some of which he never used again. From this perspective, the sketches can be seen to represent not feeble concessions to the taste of his times nor, conversely, heartfelt expressions of Hawthorne's deepest convictions, but innovative approaches to basic literary problems. It would therefore be unsurprising if the sketches continued to hold some appeal for their author, quite apart from their subject matter, as evidence of his earlier wrestling with his craft. His decisions to reprint them are thus understandable narratologically as well as professionally.

When "The Sister Years" was originally published, without authorial attribution, it carried the subtitle "Being the Carrier's Address, to the Patrons of the Salem Gazette, for the First of January, 1839." In the context of the fuller title, we can see that the author's relation to his audience is being dramatized through the characters of the Carrier Boy, who speaks in the first person, and the reader of a specific publication. Although such a reader may have been legitimately identified when the sketch first appeared, this identity has obviously been fictionalized in the 1842 *Twice-told Tales*. The narrator, of course, is fictional all along. This narrator begins to offer a narrative compact in his first sentence:

> Last night, between eleven and twelve o'clock, when the Old Year was leaving her final foot-prints on the borders of Time's empire, she found

herself in possession of a few spare moments, and sat down—of all places in the world—on the steps of our new City Hall. (9:334)

Here the pronoun *our* establishes that the narrator will speak in the first person and that the reader will be assigned the role of accomplice. This complicity is probably reenforced for readers of the *Gazette* by the ironic parenthetical remark "of all places in the world," which suggests a shared sense of Salem's cosmic insignificance as well as the security required to joke about it. The highly compressed time frame conveyed by the phrase "last night" probably contributes to this rhetorical intimacy also. By pretending that the events described in the sketch all took place so recently, the narrator also must pretend that they happened nearby, in the reader's vicinity. All of these forces come together in the last two sentences of the sketch, when the narrator purportedly addresses the reader of the *Salem Gazette* directly:

> The Carrier Boy can only say further, that, early this morning, she filled his basket with New Year's Addresses, assuring him that the whole City, with our new Mayor, and the Aldermen and Common Council at its head, would make a general rush to secure copies. Kind Patrons, will not you redeem the pledge of the NEW YEAR? (9:342)

When the sketch has been transferred into book form, however, this rhetorical community must be redefined. The reader is now confronted by the second volume of *Twice-told Tales*, not a newspaper. The year is 1842 (or 1994), not 1839. The date is probably not January 1, and the place is probably not Salem. Still, in reprinting the sketch Hawthorne must have expected to establish some sort of rhetorical community with the reader. Perhaps this confidence arose in the author's recognition of how fictionalized the whole situation was in the first place. We should recall, as Hawthorne probably did, that the sketch was not actually written on the morning of January 1 and that it was not written by a delivery boy. It should probably go without saying, furthermore, that the female personifications of the old and new years did not meet and speak as the narrator claims. Since the narrative specifications supposedly validating the sketch during its original appearance lose their force when the piece is republished between "The Ambitious Guest" and "Snow-flakes" in the 1842 *Twice-told Tales*, we must then ask, what does take place between the narrator and the reader of the sketch in 1842, or today in the *Centenary Edition*?

For one thing, this reader immediately recognizes the purely fictional quality of the whole enterprise. The phrase "last night" has, in this context, a distancing effect similar to that of "once upon a time." Neither formula could seriously be used to introduce a record of actual experience in a book, at least so long as the narrator exists in the present tense, as he does in locutions like: "The Carrier Boy can only say further . . ." (9:342). In the same way, the reader probably understands Salem to be a locale deliberately chosen by a storyteller as the unlikely site of cosmic happenings rather than as one of the unchangeable circumstances of actual events. In consequence, the narrator's profession of his Salem roots paradoxically reenforces the sense that this sketch is imaginary. Even if the geographic details were taken to establish the narrator's character as a local colorist, the reader is surely aware that such a role is another sign of literariness. Finally, this reader sees the transparent allegory of the Sister Years as merely an opportunity for a writer to advance his ideas and not as a pretense that the events of the sketch are "real," either literally or symbolically.

The narrator of "The Sister Years" comes to be, for later readers of this sketch, a writer who makes artistic choices and exploits artistic possibilities. This writer-narrator gives further definition to his character in the second paragraph when he contrasts pessimistic expectations toward the New Year advanced by "A few dismal characters . . . here and there about the world" with his own optimism: "I have faith in her; and should I live to see fifty more such, still, from each of those successive sisters, I shall reckon upon receiving something that will be worth living for" (9:335). It is clear that although this narrator is capable of mild irony—toward his supposed hometown, for example, or toward the custom of female travellers to carry "a very capacious band-box" (9:334)—he is certainly not bitter or jaundiced. He is unillusioned, perhaps, but not disillusioned, the sort of decent narrator who speaks, as Hawthorne suggests in the 1851 preface, in "the style of a man of society" (9:6).

This socially aware literary man of 1842 is an even more effective narrator than the Carrier Boy of 1839. Above all, he is more likely to understand and appreciate social satire. When the Sister Years discuss fashion, fads, beauty, ambition, and politics, the gentle criticism implicit in their remarks seems perfectly consistent with this sophisticated character. Furthermore, when the mild bite of these comments is softened and displaced through their attribution to the fictional sisters, we are reminded that the narrator is a writer as well as a man of society. In this double role, he can also essay slightly more pointed commentary as when he has the Old Year say,

> There has indeed been a curious sort of war on the Canada border, where blood has streamed in the names of Liberty and Patriotism; but it must remain for some future, perhaps far distant, Year, to tell whether or no those holy names have been rightfully invoked. (9:337)

This position is hardly subversive, but it is mildly controversial, and so it may more safely be attributed to a fictional character than to the author, real or putative. We should recall, though, that the final authority behind this report is assumed to reside in the narrator, however displaced through fictional attribution. The narrative strategy employed here also allows Hawthorne to shift his focus by alternating the more remote voice of, say, the New Year with the narrator's, a voice closer to Hawthorne's own. As the sketch draws to a close, for example, the narrator speaks again in his own voice, outside of quotation marks. The purpose is to enunciate a typically Hawthornean sentiment about the relations of time and eternity: "But she, in the company of Time and all her kindred, must hereafter hold a reckoning with Mankind" (9:341). The voice taking responsibility for this proposition is not that of the Old Year, the antecedent of the pronoun "she," nor her allegorical sister. Significantly, and despite the probable assumptions of his contemporaries, it is not Hawthorne's voice either. That is to say, the true author can adopt the same distancing technique used by his own character, the fictional author, elsewhere in the sketch when speaking through the voices of the Sister Years or of the Carrier Boy.

Finally, we suspect that no one is really fooled and that Hawthorne is glimpsed behind the curtains the whole time. In other words, "The Sister Years" is not a particularly effective work of fiction, as critics like Baym, Crowley, and Doubleday would agree. And yet, the sketch is just as much a part of the 1842 *Twice-told Tales* as "Lady Eleanore's Mantle." Doubleday explains that one motive behind Hawthorne's decision to reprint his sketches was that "He intended to offer a variety of his pieces, in temper as well as in genre." Another was that "he intended to offer fairly obvious, unsubtle pieces" (80). Still another motive probably was, as Hawthorne wrote to Evert Duyckinck on 24 January 1846 about a similar project, the considerable difficulty involved in "collecting my vagrant progeny" (16:139) from their original magazine sources. In other words, whatever Hawthorne could lay his hands on at the time had a good chance for inclusion. Looking closely at "The Sister Years" suggests still another reason. Like Hawthorne's other sketches, the piece represents the author's engagement with what Genette calls "the problems of narrative enunciating." Since Hawthorne's more complex fictions demonstrate a comparable interest in these problems, the appearance of both narrative types in *Twice-told Tales* makes narratological sense.

"Foot-prints on the Sea-shore" resembles Hawthorne's other sketches in being overlooked by today's public and professional readers of Hawthorne. For example, in his popular study *Nathaniel Hawthorne: The Man, His Tales and Romances* (1989), Edward Wagenknecht totally ignores "Foot-prints on the Sea-shore" and the rest of the sketches. Lea B. Newman's extremely valuable book, *A Reader's Guide to the Short Stories of Nathaniel Hawthorne* (1979), excludes all of Hawthorne's fictional sketches on the ground that they lack "an identifiable narrative pattern" and so cannot stand up to the sort of close scrutiny usually accorded those pieces of Hawthorne's short fiction called "tales" (xi–xii). These modernist judgments predictably conflict with those of Hawthorne's contemporaries. F. O. Matthiessen notes, for example, Herman Melville's "many pencillings" in his text of "Foot-prints," but Matthiessen also concludes that "Without Melville's emphases it would hardly be possible to discern anything fresh in Hawthorne's description of an eventless day . . ." (209–10). We should begin by seconding Matthiessen's view and recognizing how little "Foot-prints" offers thematically in the way of irony and paradox, resolved or otherwise. A first-person narrator recounts, or narrates, going for a walk, deliberately alone, during which he looked at the sea and shore, climbed some rocks, viewed three girls and later some fishermen from a distance, ate a lunch of "bread and water, and tuft of samphire, and an apple" (9:462), meditated on weighty subjects, and finally joined the girls and fishermen for dinner on the beach. The descriptions are often lively and the reflections sometimes provocative, but if this piece of fiction merits analysis, it must be on account of its manner, not its matter.

One striking facet of this manner is the narrator's frequent, un-Jamesian, shifts in verb tense from present to past and back to present. The present tense is used in this sketch sometimes to indicate the narrator's habitual dispositions, as in, "When . . . the yearning for seclusion becomes a necessity within me, I am drawn to the sea-shore . . ." (9:451). Sometimes the narrator uses the present to create a sense of immediately occurring action, as in, "Dinner being over, I throw myself at length upon the sand . . ." (9:459). Curiously, the former use of the present is intended to denote typical experience and the latter a unique event. More curiously still, uniqueness is sometimes also the effect intended in this narrator's use of the past tense, as in, "Another day, I discovered an immense bone, wedged into a chasm of the rocks; it was at least ten feet long . . ." (9:457). Since many contemporary theorists of narrative accept Emile Benveniste's proposition that narrative may be distinguished from other forms of discourse primarily by its constant reliance on the past, aorist, and past-perfect tenses (205–15), this narrator's eccentric use of tenses seems to raise questions concerning the very "nature of narrative," to borrow a phrase from Scholes and Kellogg. Such questions would probably underline the sketch's patent fictionality.

Some theorists—for example, Genette in *Figures of Literary Discourse* (137–43)—reject Benveniste's distinctions as more useful linguistically than critically. Whichever side of this debate one adopts, the following passage surely demands some sort of investigation:

> On the day of my last ramble, (it was a September day, yet as warm as summer,) what should I behold as I approached the above described basin but three girls sitting on its margin, and—yes, it is veritably so—laving their snowy feet in the sunny water! These, these are the warm realities of those three visionary shapes that flitted from me on the beach. Hark! their merry voices, as they toss up the water with their feet! They have not seen me. I must shrink behind this rock, and steal away again. (9:457)

Here the narrator begins in the definite past of a specific occasion, the September visit. Then he moves into the generalized present of "it is veritably so," claiming the perception to be as valid in the *now* of this writing, or reading, as in the *now* of the dramatized experience. Then again, in order to simulate his emotional reactions, he shifts to the present associated with immediate experience, even employing a deictic of immediate presence: *this*. There is, as a result, an almost cinematic quality to this passage, the illusion of montage, or perhaps of double exposure. A reader must be a willing participant to absorb such shifts, but even a willing participant is forced to make constant choices about what to accept and what to reject.

Thinking about the reader of this sketch raises other technical questions regarding this narrator's shifting use of the personal pronouns *I*, *we*, the indefinite *one*, and *you*. Following Benveniste, some theorists have recognized the third-person singular pronoun as the ideal narrative instrument, since it seems to create a favorite narrative illusion: the total effacement of the author. In this sketch, different authorial intentions necessitate the creation of a different fictional illusion and consequently of different syntactic patterns. Hawthorne's peculiar strategy is suggested in the first sentence of the sketch when the narrator states his premise: "It must be a spirit much unlike my own, which can keep itself in health and vigor without sometimes stealing from the sultry sunshine of the world, to plunge into the cool bath of solitude" (9:451). The narrator's aim here is surely to establish with the reader a community of spirits who occasionally seek solitude, an association not likely to be rejected by the actual reader of this piece of fiction. This postulated reader is the receptive consciousness analyzed by Gerald Prince in his essay "Introduction to the Study of the Narratee." More schematically, Prince defines the term, in *A Dictionary of Narratology* as: "The one who is narrated to, as inscribed in the text. There is at least one (more or less overtly represented) narratee per narrative, located at the same DIEGETIC LEVEL as the NARRATOR addressing him or her" (57). Having established common rhetorical ground with this entity in "Foot-prints," the narrator ventures forth, on behalf of the reader/narratee, to encounter experiences and reflect upon them. This community of more-or-less-actual listener/reader and purely fictional speaker/writer is strengthened later by the shift of pronoun in sentences of this sort: "When we have paced the length of the beach, it is pleasant, and not unprofitable, to retrace our steps, and recall the whole mood and occupation of the mind during the former passage" (9:453–54). After all, by shifting to "we," the narrator merely recognizes syntactically what he has been assuming for some time, presumably without objection from the reader/narratee who has advanced thus far in the sketch. Parenthetically, we might also note how the phrase "former passage" testifies, through punning, to the fictionality of the experience. This open admission of fictionality may explain why it is unnecessary in this case to simulate the author's disappearance.

This narrator also uses second-person pronouns unconventionally, and for similar reasons. By using *one* or *you* interchangeably, this narrator blurs distinctions between the general and particular, a frequent goal of narrative syntax according to Tzvetan Todorov in *The Poetics of Prose* (100–01). Significantly, these uncommon usages often occur in "Foot-prints" in relation to topics not at all uncommon, another "inorganic" practice. For example, the narrator tells the reader that it is "pleasant" to write in the sand: "With your staff, you may write verses—love verses, if they please you best—and consecrate them with a woman's name" (9:454). In a sense, this "you" is a word used to refer to human beings in general, the collective identity usually called "one," as Todorov explains. Anyone may write in the sand in this manner. However, in another sense, this "you" implies a more restricted group when the sentence concludes with the phrase "consecrate them with a woman's name." We might ask, is this syntax gender-coded? Are the narrator and the reader exclusively male? When we examine the next sentence, we discover that the answer is, not necessarily! The narrator here returns to the generalized "you." He at least lifts the restrictions of gender when he continues: "Here, too, may be inscribed thoughts, feelings, desires, warm outgushings from the heart's secret places, which you would not pour upon the sand without the certainty that, almost ere the sky has looked upon them, the sea will wash them out" (9:454–55). Anyone in Hawthorne's potential reading audience, irrespective of gender or condition, might recognize "the heart's secret places," might fill the role of the narratee called "you."

As I have noted, the narrator employs such technical experiments in the service of some fairly conventional subject matter. In fact, it is possible that familiar ideas function in the sketch as another source of community between author and reader. For example, the narrator goes on to propose that "one," or the reader, or "you" might also draw pictures or "write your name in the sand," and he observes that in either case the sea would naturally wash away all evidence of this human intervention. Despite the self-reflexive pun suggested by the word *write*, the lesson to be drawn is hardly original: "The sea will have swept over it, even as time rolls its effacing waves over the names of statesmen, and warriors, and poets." And yet, the narrator pretends to a sort of originality for the lesson when he concludes: "Hark, the surf-wave laughs at you!" (9:455). Syntactically, the narrator includes himself among those who must ultimately be frustrated by time when he writes about its "effacing waves" in the continuous mode of the gnomic present. The narrator includes the narratee, male or female, more forcefully still through the direct address conveyed through his use of the second person. A sense of fictional community is clearly the effect intended.

Through techniques such as direct address to the narratee, Hawthorne's narrator can be seen to engage in the sort of "transition from one narrative level to another" that Genette considers, in *Narrative Discourse* (234), to be the essence of metalepsis. It should be obvious from the examples cited so far concerning tenses and pronouns that Hawthorne's narrative abounds in such transitions and that Hawthorne's reader must repeatedly adjust his or her relation to the narrator to accommodate these shifts. The result of these adjustments is also metaleptical in Genette's sense, creating an illusion of equivalent reality for the narrator and the reader. The reader is thereby absorbed into this work, along with the narrator, the three girls, and the fishermen, as elements of the narrator's "diegesis." This final concept from Genette's *Narrative Discourse* refers to the continuous encompassing "voice" that narrates or simulates actions, scenery, characters, thoughts, and linguistic transactions. Understood in this sense, the term *diegesis* is coextensive with Hawthorne's sketch. The term may in fact be seen as synonymous here with fiction—the fiction that a voice is speaking on the page. It is the creation of this diegetic fiction, rather than the "attempt . . . to understand how things fit together" called for by Brooks and Warren, that motivates this early work by Hawthorne. Reading "Foot-prints on the Sea-shore" with these premises in mind serves to redirect attention from its conventional themes to its more interesting narrative devices. Since these devices also appear in more complex fictions like "Rappaccini's Daughter," this critical attention may be well spent.

Another arresting narrative experiment is "The Haunted Mind," first published in *The Token and Atlantic Souvenir*, a gift book released in the fall of 1834 and dated 1835. In this, his only piece of fiction cast in the rare second-person mode of narration, Hawthorne examines, with considerable ingenuity, the experience of suddenly awakening from sleep at two o'clock in the morning. The rhetorical strategy of the sketch consists of pretending that the author, the reader, the narrator, and the sleepless "you" are equally familiar with the experience and the emotions it provokes. The first sentence of the sketch clearly implies that this occasion has the same psychological dimensions for everyone: "What a singular moment is the first one, when you have hardly begun to recollect yourself, after starting from midnight slumber!" (9:304). This illusion of typicality is furthered by the sketch's consistent adherence to present tense or perfect progressive verb forms, as in the opening sentences of the second paragraph:

> If you could choose an hour of wakefulness out of the whole night, it would be this. Since your sober bedtime, at eleven, you have had rest enough to take off the pressure of yesterday's fatigue; while before you, till the sun comes from "far Cathay" to brighten your window, there is almost the space of a summer night; one hour to be spent in thought, with the mind's eye half shut, and two in pleasant dreams, and two in that strangest of enjoyments, the forgetfulness alike of joy and woe. (9:305)

Again, the "you" of the first sentence is intended to function as the grammatically typical "one," in the sense that all of us would make this moment our choice. In the same way, the hours between the "sober bedtime of eleven" and the current two o'clock should be assumed to have the same restorative effect on any metabolism; all of us will "have had rest enough" by this time. Furthermore, "there is almost the space of a summer night" between now and morning, no matter who the reader may be. Not to belabor the point any further, the experiences recorded in the sketch are proposed as easily recognizable by most human beings.

The assertion of typicality is a frequent rhetorical strategy in Hawthorne's sketches. As he explains in his 1851 preface, "Every sentence, so far as it embodies thought or sensibility, may be understood and felt by anybody, who will give himself the trouble to read it, and will take up the book in a proper mood" (9:6). Sometimes, as in "The Haunted Mind," this effect is created by describing supposedly universal human experiences and responses; sometimes, as in "Night Sketches," by assembling supposedly complete catalogues of representative human types. In either case, the purpose is to elicit the reader's conviction that the feelings and activities represented are familiar and, consequently, the reader's complicity in the judgments later to be expressed by the narrator. In "The Haunted Mind" this strategy is particularly ingenious because the emotions that the narrator proposes as universal can be understood upon analysis to be nothing of the sort. Hawthorne first rhetorically suborns his reader's involvement in the sketch through use of this highly eccentric point of view and then projects a purely private vision as if it were the reader's own.

In his essay "Toward a Rhetoric of Poetics: Rhetor as Author and Narrator," John T. Kirby proposes that "when the narrative is spun out in the second person . . . typically, the narratee is both made identical with the reader and thrust as a character into the very text" (10). This is clearly the rhetorical intention behind Hawthorne's use of the second person here, and his narrative strategy is even more complex than Kirby's proposition might suggest. Consider the sketch's fourth paragraph, in which the sleepless character, having looked out the window at a snowy street and "frosty sky" (9:305), seeks relief from the physical and emotional chill by climbing back into his snug bed, an action easily attributable to most of us. Once back in bed, he engages in a flight of fancy that is hyperbolic but not necessarily implausible: "You speculate on the luxury of wearing out a whole existence in bed, like an oyster in its shell, content with the sluggish ecstasy of inaction, and drowsily conscious of nothing but delicious warmth, such as you now feel again" (9:306). Thus far, the paragraph recounts behavior that might be expected of most human beings, whether narrator, narratee, reader, or fictional "you." Having carefully established that warmth and inaction might be welcome to all, the narrator then writes: "Ah! that idea has brought a hideous one in its train" (9:306). Subsequent reflection might show that this development is not inevitable, but most readers are unlikely to engage in such reflections immediately. Since these sentences smoothly follow one another in a paragraph devoted to the experience of "you," Hawthorne's rhetorical pretense is that some hideous idea necessarily follows the fancy of spending life in bed as surely as the warm bed follows chilliness. He offers no opportunity to demur or even to question the proposition. And, what is the idea?

> You think how the dead are lying in their cold shrouds and narrow coffins, through the drear winter of the grave, and cannot persuade your fancy that they neither shrink nor shiver, when the snow is drifting over their

little hillocks, and the bitter blast howls against the door of the tomb. (9:306)

Although this macabre speculation would probably not occur to nine persons out of ten, the narrator has accorded it psychological normality by locating it in this rhetorical context of simple association. He has projected a personal experience—or merely a Gothic literary convention—as if it were universal, confident that the reader will not notice the imposture.

As was the case in several tales discussed in Chapter 2, Hawthorne's narrator is definitely controlling his reader, a fact further exemplified in the sentence of comment that concludes the paragraph: "That gloomy thought will collect a gloomy multitude, and throw its complexion over your wakeful hour" (9:306). Unchallenged narrative authority colors this whole paragraph, most notably here in the predictive "will" and the assured phrase "your wakeful hour." This authority distinguishes "The Haunted Mind" as much as its experimental use of the second person. This authority also justifies the narrator's melancholy assertion in the following paragraph that "the depths of every heart" are filled with Sorrow, Disappointment, Fatality, and Shame, which will parade before the sleepless imagination (9:306–07). In the paragraph that follows, the narrator's control over his material has become so unquestionable that he adopts an imperative verb to dismiss the allegorical figures he has just conjured up: "Pass, wretched band!" (9:307). Only a narrator very sure of his control would dare exploit such a device. It is, from an organic perspective, practically an affront to the reader. And yet, the strategy is successful, as is clear when the next paragraph opens smoothly in the second person as if the narrator had never intruded: "By a desperate effort, you start upright, breaking from a sort of conscious sleep, and gazing wildly round the bed, as if the fiends were any where but in your haunted mind" (9:307).

This return to the second person's sleepless situation marks a clever psychological transition in the sketch. Apparently feeling that he has exhausted all the macabre possibilities of the material, the narrator begins to alter his tone to prepare for the emotional uplift with which Hawthorne preferred to end sketches. Therefore, after "start[ing] upright" in the first sentence of the paragraph, the fictional "you" searches the room, in the sentences that follow, seeking out familiar objects to dissipate the sombre atmosphere.

Gradually, the desired effect takes place: "Throughout the chamber, there is the same obscurity as before, but not the same gloom within your breast" (9:308). It is noteworthy that this positive mood swing is accomplished purely by assertion. The narrator determines that "you" will now feel better, the character obediently does, and the way is cleared for happier night thoughts. These flow abundantly in the next, penultimate paragraph: "pervading gladsomeness and beauty . . . the merriment of children . . . the sunny rain of a summer shower . . . the brightest of all rainbows . . . the tuneful feet of rosy girls" and so forth (9:308–09). Readers in our culture, inoculated against sentimentality by exposure to New-Critical orthodoxy, might well reject such images. However, as Nina Baym has demonstrated in *Woman's Fiction: A Guide to Novels by and about Women in America, 1820–1870* and in *Novels, Readers, and Reviewers: Responses to Fiction in Antebellum America*, Hawthorne's contemporaries were firmly ensconced in the domestic culture of nineteenth-century America, a situation I will explore at greater length in Chapter 7. Such readers might well find in the conventionally uplifting words that conclude the sketch—". . . the entrance of the soul to its Eternal home!" (9:309)—evidence of what Crowley calls the "spiritual character of the man, his sensibilities and singular mode of consciousness" (9:511). Historical circumstances aside, the narrator seems to feel that he has rung all the changes possible on his chosen subject, negative and positive, and thus may conclude with a satisfied exclamation point.

This satisfaction must be attributed not only to the rich variations the narrator has played on his material, but also to his sense of control over the reader. Perhaps the most striking evidence of the latter occurs at the crucial moment when the narrator assures the fictional "you" that there is "not the same gloom within your breast." In the very next sentence, the narrator adds a new and very significant dimension to this fictional character, who is intended to represent the reader's experience:

As your head falls back upon the pillow, you think—in a whisper be it spoken—how pleasant in these night solitudes, would be the rise and fall of a softer breathing than your own, the slight pressure of a tenderer bosom, the quiet throb of a purer heart, imparting its peacefulness to your troubled one, as if the fond sleeper were involving you in her dream. (9:308)

When we recall that this sketch was originally submitted to *The Token*, a gift book aimed at a primarily female reading audience, this establishment of an exclusively male "you" must be recognized as an especially bold stroke on the narrator's part. It can only be that Hawthorne felt such confidence in the rhetorical illusion of universal experience created by this narrator that he could allow the narrator to write about himself—or, more properly, to write about himself and Hawthorne—without fear of discovery and without objections from his readers. This narrator seems to feel in total control of his sketch, and this feeling is largely a consequence of the narrative technique employed. As Van Tassel observes in her discussion of "Little Annie's Ramble," Hawthorne's sketches allowed him "to vary his tone from moment to moment, to work in a bright, light-hearted vein, and to experiment with different narrative techniques" (168). Even though Hawthorne never used precisely this second-person narrative technique again, therefore, this "experiment" would be worth keeping and worth publishing a second time.

Another avenue for possible reclamation of Hawthorne's sketches may be glimpsed behind Michael Colacurcio's reminder in *The Province of Piety* that "It would be grotesque" to condemn one of them, "Night Sketches," for "failing to deliver what it cannot on premise have" (490). Colacurcio would be even more helpful if he did not go on to treat the sketch as an analogue of Hawthorne's deeper thoughts about fantasy, solipsism, and domestic happiness. Despite his commitment to historicism, Colacurcio may thus be seen to follow a critical methodology similar to that of Crowley, who interpreted the sketch in "The Unity of Hawthorne's *Twice-Told Tales*" (55) as dramatizing a conflict between adventure and safety, and that of Hyatt H. Waggoner, who, in his essay "Art and Belief," interpreted "The speaker's night walk in the rain . . . [as] emblematic of man's journey through life" (180). Despite disagreements about their findings, critics who interpret narratives such as "Night Sketches" from within a critical charter focused on organicism must treat the works as successful or unsuccessful efforts to satisfy James's criteria. By these standards, Hawthorne's sketches are usually judged failures today. As I hope the three preceding discussions have suggested, I believe that a more productive approach lies in considering the sketches as purely literary performances, exercises in narrative discourse undertaken by an aspiring author eager to test the capacities of his chosen literary instrument. Writing about another sketch, "Sights from a Steeple,"

Jeffrey H. Richards argues that "fiction, at least in the form of the sketch, can be nothing more than a stage trick rendered as prose. There is no authorial self-revelation, nor any masking of self" (40). Inspecting "Night Sketches" from this narratological perspective, without recourse to modernist critical assumptions, shows Richards's remark to be true in several senses.

We must, first of all, relinquish our expectations of a plot filled with agonistic tension, either between characters or within the protagonist. Waggoner accurately describes what passes for plot in "Night Sketches" as follows: "The vehicle is a brief walk out into a rainy winter night after a day spent in a warmly cheerful and lighted room, and then an implied return to the fireside" ("Art and Belief" 179). In place of an Aristotelian plot, then, Hawthorne must have chosen to rely on some other narrative strategy to compel his reader's attention. In fact, his choice was the creation of a controlling narrative voice. In narratological terms, we may say that Hawthorne has chosen to emphasize diegesis over mimesis. The sketch easily supports such an assumption. Having decided to take the walk mentioned by Waggoner, the narrator treats his leave-taking with mock-heroic irony. He records "fearful auguries" which stimulate a desire to skip the walk and spend "such an evening of sluggish enjoyment as the day has been." Should this happen, he reports, he would "go to bed inglorious" (9:427). Since the walk can only be his idea, and since abandoning the project of walking around in a cold rain can hardly be regarded as a serious moral defect, the hyperbole of the narrator's discourse must be the primary information communicated. When, therefore, he turns to apparently more serious matters in his next sentence, it would be unwise to take the pronouncement as a univocal revelation of the author's deepest thoughts:

> The same shivering reluctance, no doubt, has quelled, for a moment, the adventurous spirit of many a traveller, when his feet, which were destined to measure the earth around, were leaving their last tracks in the home-paths. (9:427)

Though the topic is serious enough, the diegetic voice enunciating it emanates from the same narrator responsible for the ironic sentence previously recorded. The point is not that the narrator is ridiculing all enterprise or, conversely, defending adventurousness. Rather, we should suspect that

Hawthorne is as engaged in developing a literary voice capable of different sorts of utterance as in weighing the real-life merits of action and contemplation.

The literary signature established by hyperbole and verbal irony is soon confirmed when this narrator calls a large mud puddle "a certain Slough of Despond." Literary allusion is not the only confirmation; the narrator continues his sentence to say that the puddle is "ankle-deep, leg-deep, neck-deep." Again, hyperbole signals a primarily literary discourse. The narrator therefore goes on to embroider his literary figure: "Should I flounder into its depths, farewell to upper earth!" (9:428). Since there is no necessity for this fictional narrator to walk into this fictional puddle, the danger is assuredly slight. He may avoid disaster if he chooses, and he does so choose by means of another patently literary modulation of his diegetic voice. Having devoted a paragraph to his interior monologue on the hypothetical dangers of the mud puddle, the narrator begins to simulate immediately occurring action, in part by using several exclamation points:

> Pshaw! I will linger not another instant at arm's length from these dim terrors, which grow more obscurely formidable, the longer I delay to grapple with them. Now for the onset! And lo! with little damage, save a dash of rain in the face and breast, a splash of mud high up the pantaloons, and the left boot full of ice-cold water, behold me at the corner of the street. (9:428)

From a narratological viewpoint, it is significant that this simulation is presented, like the embracing diegesis, in the present tense rather than in the past customary in narrative. By the same token, the narrator's invitation to the reader to "behold" him standing on the corner departs from Jamesian conventionality in shifting metaleptically from the diegetic level on which the walk is supposedly taking place to the extradiegetic level on which communication between the narrator and the reader supposedly occurs. We should begin to grasp that any action occurring in "Night Sketches" involves Hawthorne, the practicing writer, rather than Hawthorne, the fictional persona.

Hawthorne advertises his technical virtuosity again in the following paragraph when the harshness of the wintry winds becomes the topic. Again an exclamation point signals that something noteworthy is happening on the page: "See, at this moment, how [the winds] assail yonder poor woman, who is passing just within the verge of the lamp-light!" Having noticed in passing the metaleptical force of the verb *see*, we should attend closely to what follows. First a blast of wind blows the woman's umbrella inside out. Then another blows her cloak across her eyes. Then "a third takes most unwarrantable liberties with the lower part of her attire" (9:429). The passage furnishes some matter for a discussion of genteel literary standards, but far more for an examination of this narrator's participation in his narrative. Just as there was no real puddle earlier, now there is no wind, no woman, and thus no "lower part of her attire." The narrator is creating all these elements right before the reader's eyes and—as this passage suggests—taking considerable pleasure in the activity.

One other passage must suffice to illustrate this narrator's active presence. A later paragraph begins with an implied command for the reader's alertness, albeit without an exclamation point: "Here is a picture, and a pretty one." A young couple are supposedly also out in the nasty weather on their way to a ball or a reception. The narrator admiringly describes their clothing and intimates that they are hurrying toward good times. Then he reaches for another exclamation point to say, "But, ah! a most lamentable disaster." The two lovers slip into "a confluence of swollen floods, at the corner of two streets," wetting their clothing and spoiling their evening's entertainment. The narrator exclaims his sympathy: "Luckless lovers!" Then he makes his most purely literary remark of the whole narrative: "Were it my nature to be other than a looker-on in life, I would attempt your rescue" (9:430). A modernist reading of the sketch would pounce on the sentence as a manifestation of the "true" Hawthorne revealed as "a person in retirement" (9:6) in the preface to *Twice-told Tales* and elsewhere. A narratological reading of the sentence would see in it the form of metalepsis, described in Genette's *Narrative Discourse* (234–37), in which a narrator superimposes his mimetic and diegetic activities. Here the metalepsis involves the spectator/narrator's plea of helplessness when he is the only agency empowered to act. As in the case of the poor woman earlier, the narrator is responsible for bringing the lovers out on this supposedly miserable night. He is the one who made them fall into the icy water. He is the one who could deliver them if he wished. But, for his own, extradiegetic, reasons he chooses not to save them. During his night's walk, he wishes to encounter representative human types, young and old, male and female, proletarian and genteel, happy and unhappy. The role assigned to the young lovers by the narrator is to fall into the nasty water wearing their best clothes. This they do.

With the narrator's relations to his characters thus clarified, we can examine his last significant encounter. In the penultimate paragraph of the sketch, the narrator reaches the outskirts of the town and sees a solitary man carrying a lantern. Both this lantern and the narrator's reluctance to go beyond the town's limits have attracted analysis of what they reveal about the "real" author behind the sketch—for example, Waggoner's gloss of the episode in *Hawthorne: A Critical Study* (34–38) as a thematic precursor of Robert Frost's "Acquainted with the Night." A narratological reading would focus primarily on the narrator's discourse. Having said that he will not follow the solitary man, the narrator begins his last paragraph with this sentence: "This figure shall supply me with a moral, wherewith, for lack of a more appropriate one, I may wind up my sketch" (9:432). Arlin Turner's modernist reading of the passage observes, "There follows a conventional statement bearing no relation to the rest of the sketch" (53). In a Jamesian sense, Turner's judgment is plausible, as the following quotation will perhaps show: "And thus we, night-wanderers through a stormy and dismal world, if we bear the lamp of Faith, enkindled at a celestial fire, it will surely lead us home to that Heaven whence its radiance was borrowed" (9:432). In the light of a different critical charter, we can see that the pressing questions are not how conventionally genteel this moral may be, how inconsistent it is with the rest of the sketch, or, conversely, how consistent with other Hawthornean pronouncements elsewhere. The narrative function of the moral is not to provide what "The Art of Fiction" requires—"a personal, a direct impression of life"—but rather is to end Hawthorne's tale. Of course, we need not conclude that the moral is itself specious or deliberately misleading; we merely need to see it for what it truly is: something else the narrator says, part of the texture of language that constitutes his fictional personality.

This brings us to the final point at which narrative theory can throw light on "Night Sketches." Throughout, I have been referring to the narrator as a personality and to his sentences as what he "says." But, of course, this is the greatest fiction about written diegesis. No one is really saying anything to anyone. In *The Fantastic*, Todorov plausibly observes that "the sentences of a literary text . . . are not true assertions, for they do not satisfy one essential condition: the test of truth. . . . Truth is a relation between words and the things that the words designate; now, in literature, these 'things' do not exist" (82). The narrator of "Night Sketches" provides strong support for Todorov's remark. Wallace Martin explains, in *Recent Theories of Narrative*: "[W]hen a character speaks, the words are not a substitute for, or representation of, something else. The language of the character *is* the character, just as the words you and I speak *are* ourselves, in the eyes of others" (51). In "Night Sketches," as in his other narrative sketches, Hawthorne wrote down sentences at some previous time in such a manner as to create the illusion that a narrator is speaking directly to a reader in the present of the reading experience. When a narrative is couched in the present tense and the first-person singular, as many of these sketches are, the illusion can become very powerful. It remains an illusion, however, as Walter Ong has persuasively argued in "The Writer's Audience is Always a Fiction." In *The Art of Authorial Presence*, G. R. Thompson explains how Hawthorne created a corresponding fiction of himself on the pages of his early works. In Hawthorne's sketches particularly, how such fictional speakers are created is at least as significant as what they say, probably more so.

Reading the sketches in terms of their contents can provide us supporting evidence for preselected critical theses concerning what Hawthorne "really thought" about society, sex, art, American history, and a variety of other subjects. The great variety of these theses suggests that each of them can be sustained only by selecting carefully from among Hawthorne's narrators' remarks. This suggestion might in turn lead us to question the propriety of thematic readings. Simply analyzing the activities of Hawthorne's narrators, on the other hand, can help us to understand the sketches as exercises in narrative discourse rather than as organic representations of the writer's ideology. It would be very surprising indeed if the author who experimented so ingeniously to create these illusions dismissed them as lightly as many critics do today.

# FOUR

# Narrative Levels and Narrative Authority

As we have seen in Chapter 3, the almost total ascendancy in America of the modernist aesthetic, typified by the opinions of Henry James, succeeded during much of this century in privileging authorial impersonality as the standard by which to evaluate fiction critically. These critical assumptions were challenged during the 1960s when American writers such as John Barth, Donald Barthelme, and Robert Coover began producing what has been called metafiction, surfiction, and fabulation—all self-referential narrative modes foregrounding some sort of authorial presence. This fiction often signalled its departures from Jamesian organicism by interweaving complexly related—or apparently conflicting—levels of narrative, as in Robert Coover's story "The Babysitter" and John Barth's "Lost in the Funhouse." As Raymond Federman explains in the *Columbia Literary History of the United States*, "As of 1968, fiction offers texts that are analogous to language, that reflect upon their own movement, and that function beyond social reality and subjectivity, or rather function between social reality and subjectivity in order to undermine the illusory relationship between the two" (1155). Largely as a result of these narrative experiments, many readers began to view authorial invisibility, not as an inherent principle of value, but as a historically determined (and possibly outmoded) critical preference.

Fewer readers have recognized similar challenges to the doctrine of impersonality posed by sophisticated fiction written at the other historical end of the modernist ascendancy. In fact, in the decades before Henry James's "The Art of Fiction" (1884), many American writers explored metafictional modes of narrative involving significant elements of authorial intervention and self-referentiality. Thomas Bangs Thorpe's "The Big Bear of Arkansas" (1841, 1854), for example, frames the incredible narrative of a bear hunter named Jim Doggett within another narrative attributed to an unnamed, but equally fictional, genteel narrator who is much concerned about the technical accuracy of his own narrative. Edgar Allan Poe's "The Balloon-Hoax" (1844) is the narrative of a fictional trans-Atlantic crossing, which includes the narrative diary entries of fictional aeronauts named Monck Mason and Harrison Ainsworth, the whole being framed within a fictionalized newspaper account, complete with protestations of scrupulous journalistic authenticity. After the analyses in Chapters 2 and 3 of Hawthorne's narratological practices in *Twice-told Tales*, it should come as no surprise if I claim that Hawthorne should be viewed as another of these experimental writers.

Like Thorpe and Poe—and like Barth and Coover—Hawthorne found the manipulation of narrative levels a very fruitful source of experiment. To begin, we should note what Gerard Genette says about such levels in his *Narrative Discourse*: "[A]ny event a narrative recounts is at a diegetic level immediately higher than the level at which the narrating act producing this narrative is placed" (228). In other words, when a narrator tells us about the actions of fictional characters who live in a fictional world—the narrator of "Rappaccini's Daughter" telling us about Signor Pietro Baglioni, for example—he is the diegetic narrator of a diegetic narrative. When one of this narrator's fictional characters, Baglioni, tells a tale about Alexander the Great, Baglioni becomes a metadiegetic narrator and his tale a metadiegetic narrative. It is also possible, according to the ingenuities of structuralist poetics, to have an extradiegetic narrator, who exists apart from the diegetic narrative, as in the fictional critical essay framing "Rappaccini's Daughter." Finally, a narrative may elide the differences among any of these levels of diegesis by means of metalepsis, as when the diegetic narrator claims actually to have met a fictional character, or when the events of a fictional narrative are claimed to have some restraining or liberating effect on their narrator. Like his contemporaries in the 1840s, Hawthorne seems to have been fully aware of such metafictional possibilities, even if ignorant of the Gallic subtleties and the cumbersome vocabulary with which we must describe them.

"Rappaccini's Daughter" proves to be an excellent introductory illustration. This tale was first published in the *United States Magazine and Democratic Review* in December 1844 under the title "Writings of Aubépine," with "Rappaccini's Daughter" as its subtitle. It later appeared in the 1846 edition of Hawthorne's *Mosses from an Old Manse*, minus the first two paragraphs of the original version and the "Aubépine" title. (Several anthologies intended for college students, including *American Poetry and Prose*, edited by Norman Foerster [1957], and *The Romantic Movement in American Writing*, edited by Richard Harter Fogle [1966], have reprinted the story in this form.) In the 1854 edition of *Mosses*, the paragraphs were restored and the "Aubépine" title was revived but reduced to a subtitle, as it usually is today. As J. Donald Crowley explains in the historical commentary to the *Centenary Edition* of *Mosses* (10:523), these additions and subtractions were probably dictated by changes in the political climate which made Hawthorne's complimentary references in the introductory paragraphs to John L. O'Sullivan, a prominent Democratic politician, more and less dangerous. For our purposes, however, the political implications of these paragraphs are less significant than their narratological functions.

As many will easily recognize, *aubépine* is French for *hawthorn*. Thus, we may understand the original title and later subtitle of "Rappaccini's Daughter" as a thinly veiled reference to its author. The introductory paragraphs of the story intensify this self-referentiality. Adopting a fictionalized editorial voice, Hawthorne discusses the literary efforts of this Aubépine with the same mild irony he employs toward his own work in the introductory sketch to *Mosses*. In "The Old Manse," for example, Hawthorne explains how he selected the material for the collection as follows:

> With these idle weeds and withering blossoms [the "few tales and sketches" written during Hawthorne's residence in the Manse], I have intermixed some that were produced long ago—old, faded things, reminding me of flowers pressed between the leaves of a book—and now offer the bouquet, such as it is, to any whom it may please. These fitful sketches, with so little of external life about them, yet claiming no profundity of purpose,—so reserved, even while they sometimes seem so frank,—often but half in earnest, and never, even when most so, expressing satisfactorily the thoughts which they profess to image—such trifles, I truly feel, afford no solid basis for a literary reputation. (10:34)

About Aubépine, Hawthorne's extradiegetic narrator says in a similar tone:

[H]e generally contents himself with a very slight embroidery of outward manners,—the faintest possible counterfeit of real life,—and endeavors to create an interest by some less obvious peculiarity of the subject. Occasionally, a breath of nature, a rain-drop of pathos and tenderness, or a gleam of humor, will find its way into the midst of his fantastic imagery, and make us feel as if, after all, we were yet within the limits of our native earth. (10:92)

This narrator also attributes several of Hawthorne's own tales to Aubépine under invented French titles: *Le nouveau Père Adam et la nouvelle Mère Eve*, for example, and *Roderic; ou le Serpent à l'estomac*. He also identifies "The ensuing tale" as "a translation" of Aubépine's *Beatrice; ou la Belle Empoisonneuse* (10:92–93).

In the third paragraph of the tale, we depart from the extradiegetic narrator's immediate rhetorical situation—in the editorial world of the 1840s—to enter a much more exotic chronotope: "A young man, named Giovanni Guasconti, came, very long ago, from the more southern region of Italy, to pursue his studies at the University of Padua" (10:93). The time and place of the tale are so distinctly remote from the world inhabited by Hawthorne and his readers that all sorts of Gothic improbabilities may be expected to take place. Even the characters' names serve to distance this fictional material. Sandwiched as they are in *Mosses*, between the undeniably Anglo-Saxon Young Goodman Brown and Mrs. Bullfrog, Giovanni, Lisabetta, Pietro Baglioni, and Beatrice and Giacomo Rappaccini might be characters from another world. And they are from another world—the world of literature. Therefore, the narrator may introduce an allusion to Dante in his first diegetic paragraph, suggesting that a former inhabitant of Giovanni's dwelling had been condemned to the Inferno. The allusively named Beatrice is soon compared to "one of those beings of old classic fable, that lived upon sweet odors" (10:102). Later she experiences "a pure delight from her communion with the youth, not unlike what the maiden of a lonely island might have felt, conversing with a voyager from the civilized world" (10:112). In an environment delineated so emphatically as belonging to the world of literature, Hawthorne hardly needs to identify Miranda and *The Tempest*. After all, as Edwin Haviland Miller reports in *Salem*

*Is My Dwelling Place*, Hawthorne read aloud to Sophia "a dozen or more of Shakespeare's plays in what must have been lengthy sittings on cold winter nights" during their second winter in the Manse (224), when he was writing "Rappaccini's Daughter." The author might understandably assume Shakespearean allusions to be as accessible to his readers as to his wife.

By a simple process of association, literary allusions to another pair of lovers also enter the tale. Many critics following the suggestions in Fogle's *Hawthorne's Fiction: The Light and the Dark* have argued that Giovanni and Beatrice are anticipated by Adam and Eve. When Giovanni first looks carefully out his window at Rappaccini's garden, the narrator asks, "Was this garden, then, the Eden of the present world?" (10:96). After several other passing allusions to the story of the Fall, the narrator says about Giovanni and Beatrice: "They stood, as it were, in an utter solitude, which would be made none the less solitary by the densest throng of human life" (10:125). The imaginative reverberations of this biblical story for Hawthorne should be evident not only in the author's personal experience as a new husband— Miller entitles a chapter devoted to this period in Hawthorne's life "Eden in Concord" (208–25)—but also in other tales such as "The New Adam and Eve" (also contained in *Mosses* and mentioned, under a French title, in the opening paragraphs of "Rappaccini's Daughter").

Aesthetic allusions of other sorts also serve to establish the tale's richly imaginative chronotope. At one point, for example, the narrator presents Giovanni's fantasy of "basking in the Oriental sunshine of [Beatrice's] beauty" (10:110), thereby connecting Beatrice with the kind of literary temptress discussed in Luther S. Luedtke's *Nathaniel Hawthorne and the Romance of the Orient*. As critics developing the suggestions in Frederick I. Carpenter's "Puritans Preferred Blondes" (1936) have also remarked, the narrator is probably anticipating the exotic beauties in Hawthorne's romances—Hester, Zenobia, and Miriam. Another aesthetic allusion that may be thought to anticipate *The Marble Faun* is the narrator's description of Lisabetta's expression as "not unlike a grotesque carving in wood, darkened by centuries" (10:108). In addition to the temporal distancing established by the word *centuries*, the narrator can take advantage of the powerfully resonant *grotesque* as well as the imaginative conception of artistry in general. We might say the same about Baglioni's description of the silver vial containing the supposed antidote to Rappaccini's poisons: "It was wrought by the hands of the renowned Benvenuto Cellini, and is well worthy to be the love-gift to the fairest dame in Italy. But its contents are invaluable. One little sip of this antidote would have rendered the most virulent poisons of the Borgias innocuous" (10:119). By layering "the most virulent poisons of the Borgias" onto the infamous Cellini, and Cellini onto the fictional world of Rappaccini's garden, Hawthorne has established an almost incalculable imaginative distance between the quotidian nineteenth-century world in which this tale opens and Renaissance Padua.

This is even more true of Hawthorne's most complex allusion, a tale told by one of the inhabitants of Padua, Dr. Baglioni. This metadiegetic narrative recounts a story from Sir Thomas Browne's *Pseudoxia Epidemica (or Vulgar Errors)*, which Lea Newman identifies as the probable source for "Rappaccini's Daughter" (258). As Baglioni recounts this story: an "Indian prince . . . sent a beautiful woman as a present to Alexander the Great. She was as lovely as the dawn, and gorgeous as the sunset; but . . . [she] had been nourished with poisons from her birth upward, until her whole nature was so imbued with them, that she herself had become the deadliest poison in existence" (10:117). Giovanni immediately denies the relevance of the story, calling Baglioni's narrative "A childish fable," but Baglioni is insistent: "That old fable of the Indian woman has become a truth, by the deep and deadly science of Rappaccini, and in the person of the lovely Beatrice!" (10:118–19). By this point in Hawthorne's tale, readers cannot share Giovanni's naive view and cannot help but recognize the parallels suggested between this "fictional" metadiegetic beauty and the "real" diegetic Beatrice. In this respect, the twice-told tale borrowed from Thomas Browne typifies Hawthorne's use of metadiegetic narratives. As we have seen, Hawthorne goes to considerable lengths in "Rappaccini's Daughter" to achieve the atmosphere of imaginative distance that he will later call for in the prefaces to his romances. A remote time, a foreign location, Italian names, rich artistic and literary allusions—all combine to establish Hawthorne's diegetic narrative in a chronotope in which "love and horror" (10:105) can flourish without, as he says in the preface to *Blithedale*, "exposing them to too close a comparison with the actual events of real lives" (3:1). Even so, Hawthorne is characteristically careful not to ask too much credence from his readers. His narrator does not interpret Giovanni's experience in the obviously fanciful light provided by Thomas Browne; Baglioni does. Loving Beatrice may or may not prove deadly to Giovanni. Baglioni claims that Beatrice is poisonous, and perhaps Thomas Browne's narrative points in the same direction, but the diegetic narrator never goes on record one way or the other. For this reason, readers are free to think whatever makes "Rappaccini's Daughter" a more attractive work of fiction to them.

Hawthorne's metadiegetic narrative thus serves the same purpose in this tale as his characteristic use of what an approving F. O. Matthiessen called "the device of multiple choice" in *American Renaissance* (276) and an annoyed Yvor Winters called "the formula of alternative possibilities" in *Maule's Curse* (170). Just before speaking to Beatrice for the first time, Giovanni is looking down into the garden from his window when he sees "A small orange-colored reptile, of the lizard or chameleon species . . . creeping along the path, just at the feet of Beatrice." Soon "a drop or two of moisture from the broken stem of the flower [in Beatrice's hand] descended upon the lizard's head. For an instant, the reptile contorted itself violently, and then lay motionless in the sunshine." One might assume that a poisonous flower that can kill a lizard on contact has no ill effect on Beatrice. Such an assumption certainly accords with events elsewhere in the tale, and yet Hawthorne's narrator will not vouch for its validity. It is possible, the narrator says, that "Giovanni's draughts of wine had bewildered his senses," and it is probable that "at the distance from which he gazed, [Giovanni] could scarcely have seen anything so minute" (10:102–03). As Carol Marie Bensick exhaustively establishes in *La Nouvelle Beatrice* (1–11), no one can be certain exactly what happened, on the basis of the narrator's direct statements. And yet, what reader can doubt that the lizard died, that the flower had something to do with it, and that the flower has no ill effects on Beatrice? At the end of this scene, the floral bouquet that Giovanni has tossed down to Beatrice seems "to wither in her grasp" as she "vanish[es] beneath the sculptured portal," but the narrator refuses to confirm this marvelous occurrence, insisting that "there could be no possibility of distinguishing a faded flower from a fresh one at so great a distance" (10:104). Concerned even so, Giovanni "resolved to institute some decisive test that should satisfy him, once for all, whether there were those dreadful peculiarities in [Beatrice's] physical nature, which could not be supposed to exist without some corresponding monstrosity of soul." The narrator explains Giovanni's reasoning as follows: "His eyes, gazing down afar, might have deceived him as to the lizard, the insect, and the flowers. But if he could witness, at the distance of a few paces, the sudden blight of one fresh and healthful flower in Beatrice's hand, there would be room for no further question" (10:120–21). If there is "room for no further question," however, there is room for no further fiction. The second bouquet of flowers does wither, but it withers in Giovanni's hand, not Beatrice's.

What this all goes to show thematically has attracted an enormous expenditure of critical energy, as Newman demonstrates in *A Reader's Guide to the Short Stories of Nathaniel Hawthorne*, and as every annual *MLA International Bibliography* confirms. These thematic disagreements are perfectly understandable and perfectly in keeping with the indirection of Hawthorne's narrative strategies in this tale. According to the narrator, "There is something truer and more real, than what we can see with the eyes, and touch with the finger" (10:120). Hawthorne's practice in "Rappaccini's Daughter" illustrates that there is also a "truer and more real" level of fictional discourse than that marked by any single diegetic level. When it suits his purposes, Hawthorne has his extradiegetic narrator lie and say that this story was written by someone else, or he has his diegetic narrator say "truly" that the young man is named Giovanni. Elsewhere, a lizard dies, but Beatrice cannot be absolutely established as responsible; flowers wither in a poisonous hand, but the hand belongs to Giovanni rather than to Beatrice. No wonder readers are hard put to decide what, exactly, the truth is.

In one of his most outrageous acts of self-referentiality, Hawthorne offers at one point in this tale to settle at least something for sure. Approximately one-fourth of the way through the tale, Giovanni is dining with Baglioni when the latter warns him against trusting Doctor Rappaccini. Suddenly, the diegetic narrator intervenes to say on his own authority: "The youth might have taken Baglioni's opinions with many grains of allowance, had he known that there was a professional warfare of long continuance between him and Doctor Rappaccini, in which the latter was generally thought to have gained the advantage" (10:100). Provided with enough information, Giovanni "might" have been able to evaluate Baglioni's judgment. The narrator offers his readers an unimpeachable source of validation: "If the reader be inclined to judge for himself, we refer him to certain black-letter tracts, on both sides, preserved in the medical department of the University of Padua" (10:100). By metaleptically validating the truth of his diegesis through this reference to an extradiegetic library, the narrator might seem to engage in the kind of diegetic gamesmanship practiced by Poe in "The Balloon-Hoax." Since, however, the diegesis in Hawthorne's tale has been acknowledged from the outset to be one of Aubépine's "fictions," this validation cannot take place. The result of the metalepsis is to intensify the level of fictionality rather than to lessen it, a consequence assured by the narrator's ostentatious use of the metaleptical term "reader." It would seem then that Hawthorne's use of an extradiegetic device in this case serves the same purpose as his metadiegetic use of Browne's *Pseudoxia Epidemica* elsewhere in the tale. Both forms of diegetic manipulation serve to convey elements of the author's imaginative construction to his readers without compromising the authority of his diegetic narrator.

Hawthorne engaged in such narrative practices long before writing "Rappaccini's Daughter," and he continued to use them long afterwards, on through the romances he wrote during the next decade. For illustration, let us turn to a very early example. Nelson F. Adkins first demonstrated in "The Early Projected Works of Nathaniel Hawthorne" (121–28) that "Alice Doane's Appeal" must have had a complicated artistic gestation before its first appearance in *The Token and Atlantic Souvenir* for 1835. Perhaps for this reason, the tale has been interpreted from highly diverse perspectives. Some critics have focused on how Hawthorne treats the psychosexual elements of incest and Oedipal revenge first identified by Frederick C. Crews in *The Sins of the Fathers: Hawthorne's Psychological Themes*. Historical critics following in the footsteps of David Levin have thematized the story in the context of other tales, such as "Young Goodman Brown," which focus on the problems posed for the New England Puritans by "specter evidence." Dennis G. Coffey speaks for another, more narratologically disposed, group of readers when he calls the tale "a story about how to write a story" (230). G. R. Thompson, the most narratologically disposed reader to date, even rejects the evolutionary theory proposed by Adkins to construct an excellent reading in which "the historical is dialogically played off against the literary" (201). One might go beyond Thompson's formulation to suggest that "Alice Doane's Appeal" can also be understood as a story "about" different levels of diegesis.

On the principal diegetic level, an unnamed first-person narrator presents a narrative, in the past tense, about escorting two unnamed young women to Gallows Hill in order to read them a metadiegetic narrative, "one of a series written years ago, when my pen, now sluggish and perhaps feeble, because I have not much to hope or fear, was driven by stronger external motives, and a more passionate impulse within, than I am fated to feel again" (11:269). This metadiegetic narrative concerns an unnamed wizard, a brother and sister named Leonard and Alice Doane, and a mysterious foreigner named Walter Brome, who bears an uncanny resemblance to Leonard and who seems to be sexually attracted to Alice. In the course of this metadiegetic narrative—which is sometimes summarized by the diegetic narrator and is sometimes represented directly—Leonard Doane narrates a meta-metadiegetic adventure to the wizard, which includes Leonard's retelling of a real or imaginary experience from his childhood. When the two young women respond indifferently to these interlocking stories, the fictional narrator creates a different metadiegetic narrative on the spot: "With such eloquence as my share of feeling and fancy could supply, I called back hoar antiquity, and bade my companions imagine an ancient multitude of people, congregated on the hill side . . ." (11:278). Throughout the diegetic tale, furthermore, the fictional narrator comments directly on his own immediate rhetorical relation to the two young women comprising his listening audience as well as on his rhetorical intentions as author of the narrative about Alice and Leonard Doane.

The diegetic narrative opens in a style similar to what we have seen in Hawthorne's sketches. The story begins: "On a pleasant afternoon of June, it was my good fortune to be the companion of two young ladies in a walk" (11:266). The first four paragraphs then go on to describe the local vegetation, postulate the two young women's "feminine susceptibility . . . [to] melancholy associations" (11:268), establish a hilltop prospect of contemporary Salem, and develop this setting into the occasion for "a wondrous tale of those old times" (11:269), the Puritan world of 1692. These paragraphs echo Hawthorne's technique in the sketches also by asserting a more general applicability for the fictional narrator's imaginative projections than is probably warranted. Thus, after leading the two young women to this isolated, gloomy setting and noting the mixture of "mirth" and "gloom" with which they react to it, this narrator observes, "With now a merry word and next a sad one, we trod among the tangled weeds, and almost hoped that our feet would sink into the hollow of a witch's grave" (11:268). Surely this cannot be the hope of the two female characters, who have otherwise given no signs of morbid dispositions. One might recall the supposedly natural progression in "The Haunted Mind," from a desire to stay warm in bed to a meditation about "how the dead are lying in their cold shrouds and narrow coffins, through the drear winter of the grave" (9:306). Hawthorne's intention in both cases is the same: to suborn his readers into accepting purely Gothic contrivances as if they represented perfectly normal psychological reactions.

The early paragraphs of "Alice Doane's Appeal" differ somewhat from comparable passages in the sketches in that the fictional narrator unabashedly asserts his character as a writer. In lamenting his fellow townspeople's conviction that "we are not a people of legend or tradition," for example, the narrator explains that "Till a year or two since, this portion of our history has been very imperfectly written." According to Colacurcio, in *The Province of Piety* (88, 552), the narrator is most probably referring here to an actual historical publication, Charles Upham's *Lectures on Witchcraft* (1831). Whether the reference supposes a real or a fictional text, however, the next sentence must be understood to apply beyond this immediate context:

> Recently, indeed, an historian has treated the subject in a manner that will keep his name alive, in the only desirable connection with the errors of our ancestry, by converting the hill of their disgrace into an honorable monument of his own antiquarian lore, and of that better wisdom, which draws the moral while it tells the tale. (11:267)

Clearly this sentence is intended to apply equally to the author of the Salem history (whether Upham or a purely fictional historian), to the fictional narrator of the metadiegetic tale, and to the author of "Alice Doane's Appeal." However, Hawthorne is not so much proposing himself as a reliable historian of the Salem witch trials—or of Cotton Mather's responsibility for the witch hysteria, or of the unreliability of spectral evidence—as he is asserting his responsibility for the language of this tale, whether or not grounded in historical events.

We should note that when the fictional narrator begins his fifth paragraph with the sentence "I had brought the manuscript in my pocket" (11:269), he is not introducing a historical account but a narrative that "draws the moral while it tells the tale," that is, the metadiegetic narrative that provides a title for Hawthorne's story. In this light, we should also note the directness with which the fictional, diegetic narrator asserts his own presence: "I read on. . . . I brought forward the personages who were to move among the succeeding events" (11:270). This assurance also permits him to make assertions of this sort: "The central scene of the story was an interview between this wretch [the wizard] and Leonard Doane . . ." (11:271). Unlike the actual author of "Alice Doane's Appeal," this fictional author may begin and end his narrative at any point he chooses, freely dispensing with contextualizing elements such as the pleasant June afternoon and the charming young companions. Instead, he may introduce only those elements designed to intensify his Gothic tone: "the wizard's hut," "a mouldering fire," "a tempest of wintry rain," "a night attack by the Indians," "a secret sympathy between his [Leonard's] sister and Walter Brome," and the "distempered jealousy" that "maddened" Leonard (11:271). Since this metadiegetic narrative is admittedly an invention, there is no need for the diegetic narrator to pretend that these Gothic prodigies are grounded in a realistic matrix.

Hawthorne may therefore freely introduce extreme—even operatic—emotions into this tale without establishing psychological plausibility and without resorting to the elaborate alternative possibilities he introduces elsewhere. This is true whether the fictional narrator is summarizing his story or representing it directly within quotation marks. For example, in the first paragraph intended to represent the metadiegetic narrative directly, Leonard tells the wizard, within quotation marks, "But my soul had been conscious of the germ of all the fierce and deep passions, and of all the many varieties of wickedness, which accident had brought to their full maturity in him [Walter]" (11:271). Because Hawthorne's diegetic narrator assumes responsibility for this implausible speech through the representational quotation marks, Hawthorne is free to indulge in the broadest Gothic effects of unspeakable passion and wickedness. In the following paragraph, Hawthorne has the fictional narrator say, this time in summary: "Leonard Doane went on to describe the insane hatred that had kindled his heart into a volume of hellish flame" (11:272). Hawthorne, we may assume, would never introduce such blatant theatricality in a tale emanating from a narrative perspective nearer to his own.

The fictional narrator's distinction from Hawthorne, the careful author, is suggested in several ways. For one thing, the narrator can conceive of no better way to get across the idea that Walter and Leonard might have been long-lost brothers than to have Leonard further confess a memory, or perhaps a "delusion," to the wizard who may be responsible for all his problems. This narrative, within Leonard's narrative, within the diegetic narrator's narrative, within Hawthorne's narrative, is presented as follows:

> Methought I stood a weeping infant by my father's hearth; by the cold and blood-stained hearth where he lay dead. I heard the childish wail of Alice, and my own cry arose with hers, as we beheld the features of our parent, fierce with the strife and distorted with the pain, in which his spirit had passed away. As I gazed, a cold wind whistled by, and waved my father's hair. Immediately, I stood again in the lonesome road, no more a sinless child, but a man of blood, whose tears were falling fast over the face of his dead enemy. But the delusion was not wholly gone; that face still wore a likeness of my father. . . . (11:273)

As in some examples previously cited, both the vocabulary and the imagery are lushly Gothic. As also in the previous examples, psychological consistency is hardly even an issue. No wonder the tale has elicited such conflicting thematic interpretations!

Even the diegetic narrator seems somewhat unsure about what it all adds up to in the paragraph that follows:

> Such was the dreadful confession of Leonard Doane. And now tortured by the idea of his sister's guilt, yet sometimes yielding to a conviction of her purity; stung with remorse for the death of Walter Brome, and shuddering with a deeper sense of some unutterable crime, perpetrated, as he imagined, in madness or a dream; moved also by dark impulses, as if a fiend were whispering him to meditate violence against the life of Alice; he had sought this interview with the wizard, who, on certain conditions, had no power to withhold his aid in unraveling the mystery. The tale drew near its close. (11:273–74)

The second sentence in this paragraph, especially, almost parodies the technique of alternative possibility that so distressed Yvor Winters. The third sentence is also somewhat misleading. The metadiegetic narrative is not really nearing its close. Actually, it continues, interruptedly, for six more paragraphs. The first contains an elaborate description of Salem "glittering in icy garments" (11:274) that might have appeared in one of Hawthorne's sketches. In the next paragraph, the narrator explains the rhetorical intentions behind this passage: "By this fantastic piece of description, and more in the same style, I intended to throw a ghostly glimmer round the reader so that his imagination might view the town through a medium that should take off its every day aspect, and make it a proper theatre for so wild a scene as the final one" (11:274). Of course the term *reader* is richly ambiguous here. The diegetic narrator declares that he composed this prose narrative many years ago for some anticipated "reader." Within the principal diegesis, he is reading this narrative to young women from whom he hopes to elicit responses similar to those of his desired "reader." And, naturally, there is some actual reader—however this entity might be defined by Wayne C. Booth, Gerald Prince, or Robin R. Warhol—namely, the person holding a text of "Alice Doane's Appeal" right this minute.

Only the last two classes of readers ever encounter the narrator's story, at least as far as we can tell, and so only these two kinds of readers need work out their responses to his self-reflexive narrative. When the narrator finally tries to bring closure to his metadiegetic narrative by assembling Alice, Leonard, and a crowd of ghosts including Walter Brome in the graveyard, the two young women work out an ambivalent response: "The ladies started; perhaps their cheeks might have grown pale, had not the crimson west been blushing on them; but after a moment they began to laugh" (11:277). Despite the narrator's creative efforts, his "reader," the two young women, cannot accord his Gothic monstrosity enough credence to validate it as a successful piece of fiction. We may suppose that the actual author anticipated a more favorable response from *his* "reader."

The basis for Hawthorne's confidence may be glimpsed in the first two sentences of the paragraph immediately following the young women's mixed responses:

We looked again towards the town, no longer arrayed in that icy splendor of earth, tree and edifice, beneath the glow of a wintry midnight, which, shining far through the gloom of a century, had made it appear the very home of visions in visionary streets. An indistinctness had begun to creep over the mass of buildings and blend them with the intermingled tree tops, except where the roof of a statelier mansion, and the steeples and brick towers of churches, caught the brightness of some cloud that yet floated in the sunshine. (11:278)

In other words, the "fantastic piece of description" of "trees . . . hung with diamonds and many-colored gems" represented earlier (11:274), within quotation marks, as part of this narrator's metadiegetic narrative must be granted a "reality" equivalent to that of the description beginning with the second sentence. Moreover, this equivalency is to take place despite the fact that the first description has been clearly represented as fiction and the second is being proposed as the actual setting in which the diegetic narrator will operate for the remainder of the tale. Thus, although the voice we encounter here is attributed to the diegetic narrator, the controlling force behind it can only belong to the extradiegetic Hawthorne, the creator of all the settings, all the actions, all the words in "Alice Doane's Appeal."

This actual Hawthorne is equally responsible for the last metadiegetic narrative by which his diegetic narrator seeks to move the imaginations of his fictional audience of two. The narrator first explains his strategy: "Though it was past supper time, I detained them a while longer on the hill, and made a trial whether truth were more powerful than fiction" (11:278). This "truth" is conveyed through two summary paragraphs of historical narrative recounting the emotions purportedly experienced by victims of the Salem witch trials and by their accusers. The thematic issues raised by critical commentary on these paragraphs are thoroughly treated by Melinda Ponder in her discussion of the tale in *Hawthorne's Early Narrative Art* and by Thompson. The issues of particular interest to me, however, are primarily nonthematic. At one point, for example, the narrator suddenly shifts to the imperative mood, to command metaleptically: "See! the whole crowd turns pale and shrinks within itself, as the virtuous emerge from yonder street" (11:278). (One might weigh in passing the deictic force of the word *yonder*.) Also significant, it seems to me, is the narrator's use—in a "truthful" "historical" narrative—of details like the inner thoughts of the woman who "almost believed her guilt"; the emotions of the mother who "groaned inwardly"; and the contents of the silent prayers uttered by the "ordained pastor" (11:279). Because he is willing to avail himself freely of all such narrative materials, Hawthorne both resembles and transcends his diegetic narrator. The latter must attempt these various strategies serially.

His first—Gothic—effort, we recall, produces a mixture of fear and laughter in his audience. The results of his second—historical—effort are more consistent with his desires: "But here my companions seized an arm on each side; their nerves were trembling; and sweeter victory still, I had reached the seldom trodden places of their hearts, and found the well-spring of their tears" (11:279–80).

Hawthorne's strategy is more inclusive than his narrator's. His tale includes the Gothic *and* the historical, the diegetic *and* the metadiegetic, the realistic *and* the sentimental. After the narrator has moved his listeners to tears, for example, the subsequent actions of the three are presented in the sort of language Hawthorne uses in his sketches—and in the opening paragraphs of this tale: "We slowly descended, watching the lights as they twinkled gradually through the town, and listening to the distant mirth of boys at play, and to the voice of a young girl, warbling somewhere in the dusk, a pleasant sound to wanderers from old witch times" (11:280). Because of such stylistic interweaving, Hawthorne's reader is confronted with a narrative both more complex and more imaginatively assimilable than any of its constituent parts. This actual reader is thus placed rhetorically in the situation analyzed in Wolfgang Iser's essay "Representation: A Performative Act":

> The aesthetic semblance can only take on its form by way of the recipient's ideational, performative activity, and so representation can only come to full fruition in the recipient's imagination; it is the recipient's performance that endows the semblance with its sense of reality. And so representation causes the recipient to repeat the same performance out of which it arose, and it is the repeat of this performance that initiates and ensures the transfer from text to reader of what is to be represented. (243)

Although it is beyond Iser's sphere of inquiry to consider what part diegetic layering might play in the recipient's performative act, it seems clear on the basis of "Alice Doane's Appeal" that the site of the transaction is as likely the mind of the reader as the printed text. In any case, the primary site is most probably not the historical past of New England, or the thematic entity called "what Hawthorne really thought," but a narratological territory called "how Hawthorne gets his stories told."

Herein we can see the probable attraction of metadiegetic narratives to

Hawthorne. Since writers such as Irving, Poe, and Longfellow made a great success out of gleaning the rich Gothic harvests of continental romantic narrative, we might imagine Hawthorne's desire to do the same. At the same time, we might imagine a writer of Hawthorne's psychological and ethical subtlety hoping to reserve sufficient narrative authority to address contemporary moral issues in other tales. By shifting narrative responsibility for the exotic to another diegetic level in tales such as "Rappaccini's Daughter" and "Alice Doane's Appeal," Hawthorne can spin narratives of witchcraft, incest, murder, broad comedy, poison, love, and magic without sacrificing his claims to other fictional territory. If any hardheaded reader should level charges of exaggeration or imaginative indulgence, Hawthorne can disavow responsibility. These practices, so useful to Hawthorne in his shorter fiction, also figure prominently in his fully developed romances.

In *The Scarlet Letter*, Hawthorne uses metadiegetic narrative devices only indirectly. In Chapter 2, for example, Hester Prynne eases the psychological stress of her public humiliation by thinking back over her earlier life (1:57–58). Realistically, what she remembers can be understood as narrative exposition crucial to the reader's understanding of how Hester came to be the mother of an illegitimate child. In another sense, what she recalls—an ancient family, an unprotected, beautiful young girl, a twisted but preternaturally powerful older man—can be seen as elements of Gothic romance that are implanted in the reader's imagination without invoking the narrator's complete authority or misdirecting the realistic emphasis of his narrative.

Another interesting passage, appearing in the prefatory "Custom-House" sketch, might almost be called "paradiegetic." Here, Hawthorne's narrator explains that "the main facts of [Hester's] story are authorized and authenticated by the document of Mr. Surveyor Pue" (1:32), a local historian and Hawthorne's predecessor in the customhouse. Later, in the romance proper, the narrator sometimes uses Pue's account to authenticate a diegetic event. When Dimmesdale's partisans deny his confession of adultery and the presence of any mark on his chest, the narrator uses Pue's manuscript to dispute their pious version of what happened during the final scaffold scene: "The authority which we have chiefly followed—a manuscript of old date, drawn up from the verbal testimony of individuals, some of whom had known Hester Prynne, while others had heard the tale from contemporary witnesses—fully confirms the view taken in the foregoing pages" (1:259–60).

The surveyor's manuscript also contains eye witnesses' recollections of Hester as "a very old, but not decrepit woman, of a stately and solemn aspect." In this character, she would "go about the country as a kind of voluntary nurse, and doing whatever miscellaneous good she might; taking upon herself, likewise, to give advice in all matters, especially those of the heart" (1:32). This is what Pue recorded, the narrator claims, because this is what people actually remembered. Therefore, Hester cannot leave New England permanently in *The Scarlet Letter*. Nor can she and Dimmesdale grow old together in happily married bliss. According to the narrator, these possibilities are foreclosed not because of Aristotelian probability but because of the preexisting structure set down in Pue's account. Thus, while Lauren Berlant and Sacvan Bercovitch can explain Hester's return to New England plausibly in terms of political thematics, a narratological standpoint allows us to claim with equal plausibility that Hester returns because Surveyor Pue's metadiegetic narrative says that she returned.

As Hawthorne's reliance on Surveyor Pue demonstrates, diegetic manipulation can provide an author advantages beyond its legitimation of Gothic implausibilities. A particularly striking example appears in Hawthorne's next romance, *The House of the Seven Gables*, in which Chapter 13 consists entirely of a metadiegetic narrative entitled "Alice Pyncheon," composed and read by the diegetic character Holgrave. This episode figures prominently in Hawthorne's manipulations of historical authority in that romance, however, and so I will postpone discussion until my fifth chapter and turn instead to Hawthorne's following book.

In *The Blithedale Romance*, there are two metadiegetic narratives. The first appears in Chapter 13, which carries the title "Zenobia's Legend." In this case, a narrative told by a diegetic character, Zenobia, is preceded by eight introductory paragraphs that set the scene for her recitation. The metadiegetic narrative follows, without surrounding quotation marks, preceded by the offset title, "THE SILVERY VEIL," and followed by four paragraphs detailing the effect of Zenobia's narrative on the other diegetic characters. The second metadiegetic narrative constitutes Chapter 22 of the romance and is neither a supposedly written account like Holgrave's nor a recitation like Zenobia's. Rather, this narrative, entitled "Fauntleroy," recounting the backgrounds of Zenobia, Priscilla, and the character previously called Old Moodie, comes from the fictionalized narrator, Miles Coverdale, partly on the authority of Moodie/Fauntleroy and partly on the basis of his own conjectures and his expertise as a writer.

In one respect, both of these metadiegetic narratives resemble Holgrave's "Alice Pyncheon" more than they do Surveyor Pue's account. That is to say, neither determines the shape of Coverdale's diegetic narrative. More in the manner of Hester's flashback during the first scaffold scene, both of the metadiegetic narratives in *Blithedale* explain events in the realistic world of the diegetic present in terms of a decidedly Gothic metadiegetic past. This narrative device is, in fact, the source of Henry James's objection to the book in his 1887 study of Hawthorne. While James applauds Hawthorne's occasional success in making us "feel beneath our feet the firm ground of an appeal to our own vision of the world, our observation" (137), he objects to the presence of such Gothic elements, however indirectly they may be introduced:

> The portion of the story that strikes me as least felicitous is that which deals with Priscilla and with her mysterious relation to Zenobia—with her mesmeric gifts, her clairvoyance, her identity with the Veiled Lady, her divided subjection to Hollingsworth and Westervelt, and her numerous other graceful but fantastic properties—her Sybilline attributes, as the author calls them. Hawthorne is rather too fond of Sybilline attributes. . . . (136)

James's strictures clearly identify the problems Hawthorne faced in creating romances, the difficulty of balancing the need for the realistic, the psychologically plausible—"every-day Probability"—with the exciting freedom offered by the Gothic/romantic narrative mode—"an atmosphere of strange enchantment" (3:1). In the preface to *Blithedale*, from which these quotations are taken, Hawthorne laments the absence of a literary "atmosphere" in the light of which such balances might be struck: "In its absence, the beings of imagination are compelled to show themselves in the same category as actually living mortals; a necessity that generally renders the paint and pasteboard of their composition but too painfully discernible" (3:2). Perhaps such conflicting impressions might be the final result, perhaps not. By examining Hawthorne's use of metadiegetic narratives in this romance, we might be able to decide.

To begin with "Zenobia's Legend," we should first consider some of Coverdale's remarks toward the end of the previous chapter. First of all, he laments, as Hawthorne did in the preface, that "real life never arranges itself exactly like a romance" (3:104). He then goes on to acknowledge his own interventions in his diegetic narrative by commenting on his handling of the just-concluded scene between Zenobia and Westervelt: "Other mysterious words, besides what are above-written, they spoke together; but I understood no more, and even question whether I fairly understood so much as this" (3:104). Despite such demurs, however, readers have already listened to words attributed to Zenobia and Westervelt and have inevitably absorbed these words somehow into an explanation of the relations between these two diegetic characters. The element of uncertainty introduced through Coverdale's self-doubts surely subtilizes the explanation, but it does not lead readers to conclude that Coverdale has entirely invented a nonexistent relationship: that, for example, Zenobia and Westervelt are virtual strangers who have passed the time of their real or imaginary walk discussing the possibility of equality between the sexes or of socialistic reform. Coverdale's self-professed involvement in his narrative thus limits the possible responses of his readers very effectively. Similarly determined possibilities are offered to the readers when the diegetic narrative turns at the beginning of Chapter 13 to the "occasional modes of amusement" (3:106) popular at Blithedale. Since Coverdale professes some sort of narrative continuity between the subject matter of Chapter 13 and "the incident narrated in the last chapter" (3:106), readers are free to assume that Coverdale is coloring his description of the frolics and of Zenobia's metadiegetic narrative with his usual tone of slightly jaded irony. However, readers cannot conclude that the members of the commune never engaged in any sort of recreation or that Zenobia did not tell the ensuing story. In this respect, Coverdale functions effectively on the author's behalf, even when he purports to turn the narrative over to Zenobia.

Sounding very much like Hawthorne in his preface, Zenobia first proposes that the festivities turn from the masquerades based—alternatively—on "history or romance" (3:106) to story-telling:

Our own features, and our own figures and airs, show a little too intrusively through all the characters we assume. We have so much familiarity with one another's realities, that we cannot remove ourselves, at pleasure, into an imaginary sphere. Let us have no more pictures, to-night; but, to make you what poor amends I can, how would you like to have me trump up a wild, spectral legend, on the spur of the moment? (3:107)

Zenobia's proposed metadiegetic narrative is described in advance not only as "a wild, spectral legend" but also as "a fanciful little story" and "a ghost-story." It thus assuredly resembles the "theatre, a little removed from the highway of ordinary travel," that Hawthorne desires in his preface. As a result, in Zenobia's metadiegetic narrative Hawthorne may allow "the creatures of his brain [to] play their phantasmagorical antics, without exposing them to too close a comparison with the actual events of real lives" (3:1). Readers like Henry James might prefer their fiction straight, without the "extravagance" and "absurdities" that Coverdale recognizes in Zenobia's handling of her narrative (3:107), but Hawthorne is hardly a writer suited by nature to deliver straight fiction. Furthermore, even if, as Coverdale says, this metadiegetic narrative is "[f]rom beginning to end . . . undeniable nonsense," from Hawthorne's point of view a work of fiction is not "necessarily the worse for that" (3:108).

Like Coverdale, and like Hawthorne, Zenobia prefaces her narrative with some discussion of technique in order to acknowledge her own presence: "It is essential to the purposes of my legend to distinguish one of these young gentlemen from his companions; so, for the sake of a soft and pretty name, (such as we, of the literary sisterhood, invariably bestow upon our heroes,) I deem it fit to call him 'Theodore' " (3:109). Zenobia also directly comments on the contents of her narrative, as when she says about a rumor that the Veiled Lady was "the daughter of one of our most distinguished families!" that "the above-mentioned fable could not hold its ground against Theodore's downright refutation" (3:109). The result of Zenobia's narrative technique here is the introduction of a Gothic possibility, that a noble lady is in thrall, and the rejection of the possibility as unrealistic. Her narrative subsequently raises and rejects a series of other plot developments: that "the veil covered the most beautiful countenance in the world" (3:109), that "the face was the most hideous and horrible," that "It was the face of a corpse; it was the head of a skeleton; it was a monstrous visage, with snaky locks, like Medusa's, and one great red eye in the center of the forehead" (3:110). Since it later turns out that the veil conceals merely "a pale, lovely face" (3:114), all of these Gothic possibilities must be considered merely tonal rather than structural. Zenobia will allow none of these potential plot developments to reach fulfillment; they enter her narrative primarily to create Gothic reverberations in the imaginations of her hearers—and of Hawthorne's readers. If they foreshadow for the latter audience some subsequent events involving Priscilla, so much the better from Hawthorne's point of view!

Zenobia signals her presence in the metadiegetic narrative in ways familiar to readers of Hawthorne's own narratives. At one point the legend requires that Theodore gain admittance to the Veiled Lady's dressing room, even though her inaccessibility has been definitely established earlier. Zenobia merely says, "How he managed it, I know not, nor is it of any great importance to this veracious legend" (3:110). Here is a technique familiar from Hawthorne's practice in "The Artist of the Beautiful." In that story the narrator needs at one point to account for a sudden recurrence of creative energy in his central character, Owen Warland, but confesses himself unable to do so. He merely says, "How it awoke again, is not recorded" (10:466). In both cases, the narrator's profession of ignorance has the ironic effect of establishing the narrator's presence as the only reliable source of testimony. A similar device appears as the dressing room episode concludes. Zenobia says, "Theodore was alone. Our legend leaves him there" (3:114). Since Zenobia promised at the outset to "trump up a wild, spectral legend on the spur of the moment," one might assume that she could, if she wished, explain how Theodore gained entrance to the dressing room or what happened to him after the Veiled Lady disappeared. After all, Zenobia is supposedly making this story up as she goes along. Even so, Zenobia seems to be constrained by some sort of preexisting aesthetic—if not the limitations imposed by Aristotelian probability, then by the narrative ethic adopted by "the literary sisterhood." In any case, "our legend" seems to have a force of its own, not only as it limits Zenobia's freedom as narrator, but also as it affects us as readers.

Evidence of these limits clearly surfaces within the metadiegetic narrative when the Veiled Lady promises Theodore happiness ever after if he can only make an act of unquestioning love: "Theodore, thou shalt be mine, and I thine, with never more a veil between us! And all the felicity of earth and of the future world shall be thine and mine together" (3:113). Surely

all readers are attracted in some degree by such a prospect, but all readers—
even those with a less disillusioning romantic past than Zenobia's—realize
that such promises are seldom fulfilled in the world of "every-day Probability" (3:2). Even so, this metadiegetic narrative has indirectly introduced the
possibility of ideal love into the supposedly realistic world of imperfect
lovers such as Hollingsworth and Coverdale. In the same way, Zenobia's
metadiegetic depiction of the magician holding the Veiled Lady in thrall
allows Hawthorne to Gothicize Westervelt as a wizard and Priscilla as a
mesmeric medium without resorting to diegetic marvels that might offend
readers interested solely in the realistic. Such readers can rest contentedly
in the uncanny. Westervelt is probably just a showman of some sort, and
Priscilla is probably just a young girl with some sort of mild extrasensory
perception. In this sense Zenobia's narrative shadows Coverdale's rather
than actually explaining it. While we are free to connect Priscilla with the
Veiled Lady, there apparently was no Theodore in Priscilla's past. Though
the Veiled Lady and Priscilla both showed up "amid a knot of visionary
people, who were seeking for the better life" (3:114), only the Veiled Lady
was transported there magically. Priscilla arrived in a wagon driven by Hollingsworth, who delivered her in response to a request from her father, Old
Moodie. On the other hand, Priscilla is billed as the Veiled Lady when she
appears on stage at the end of Chapter 23, but it is Hollingsworth—not
Theodore—who rescues her from the clutches of Westervelt.

The shadows and parallels between Zenobia's and Coverdale's narratives
are reenforced by the other significant metadiegetic narrative in *Blithedale*,
Chapter 22, entitled "Fauntleroy." As was the case with "Zenobia's Legend,"
Coverdale introduces the metadiegetic narrative with some discussion of
the narrative technique used. He concludes Chapter 21, devoted to his interrogation of Old Moodie, by explaining first that a bottle of wine loosened
the man's tongue enough to provoke a confession: "His communications
referred exclusively to a long past and more fortunate period of his life, with
only a few unavoidable allusions to the circumstances that had reduced him
to his present state" (3:181). As in the case of Holgrave's story about Alice
Pyncheon, the interrelated factors of a remote past and a supposedly explanatory function seem appropriate justification for a metadiegetic narrative.

The narrator's admitted interventions also show the similarities between this case and those we have previously considered. Coverdale's introductory remarks conclude: "But, having once got the clue, my subsequent researches acquainted me with the main facts of the following narrative; although, in writing it out, my pen has perhaps allowed itself a trifle of romantic and legendary license, worthier of a small poet than of a grave biographer" (3:181). Apparently we are going to encounter some measure of fictionality even if the material has been derived originally from "real life." Appropriately, the metadiegetic narrative begins in the next chapter on a note that might well be characterized as exhibiting "legendary license": "Five-and-twenty years ago, at the epoch of this story, there dwelt, in one of the middle states, a man whom we shall call Fauntleroy; a man of wealth, and magnificent tastes, and prodigal expenditure" (3:182). Narrative signals abound. The inverted sentence structure leading to the verb phrase *there dwelt*, the indefinite locale signified by "one of the middle states," the explicit reference to "this story"—all testify to the initiation of a fictional narrative. These signs are surely confirmed by the narrative metalepsis, "whom we shall call Fauntleroy." Like Zenobia's decision to call her character Theodore and Hawthorne's decision elsewhere to call his character Wakefield, Coverdale's choice here attests to his narrative freedom.

Perhaps this freedom justifies him in his leanings toward Gothic exoticism. Coverdale's choice of diction seems to translate Fauntleroy's wealth beyond the bounds of realistic narrative: *magnificent, prodigal* in the first sentence and *palace, princely,* and *splendor* later in the paragraph. Even while bracketing this vocabulary with qualifications suggesting the merely uncanny—"His home might almost be styled a palace" (3:182), for example—Coverdale manages to introduce into the realistic context of saloon and village hall the sort of Gothicism that Hawthorne longed for in his preface. This is the effect also of the realistic device by which the now-impoverished Fauntleroy later tells his daughter tales of his former life "Instead of . . . fairy tales" (3:186). Other listeners to these displaced fairy tales are, of course, Hawthorne's readers.

Coverdale's literary tone at the outset of his metadiegetic narrative also serves to justify the occurrence of bizarre coincidences within the decidedly realistic environment into which Fauntleroy's rapidly declining fortunes reduce him. In several paragraphs of realistic narration Coverdale quickly establishes the remarried and rewidowed Fauntleroy in a sordid urban dwelling located within a decayed gubernatorial mansion. His companion is the daughter identified first as his "younger child" but in the very next paragraph as Priscilla (3:185–86). If Coverdale had imitated the narrator of "Ethan Brand" (11:94) by writing "the Priscilla of our tale," he could hardly have signaled more forcefully his introduction of a narrative coincidence. Nevertheless, he continues to conduct his narrative as if it were all perfectly plausible. When mentioning the Sybilline abilities to which James objected in Priscilla, Coverdale attributes all testimony regarding them to Fauntleroy's superstitious Irish neighbors. According to these neighbors—but not necessarily Coverdale or Hawthorne—Priscilla was a "ghost-child," and only the neighbors claimed that "Hidden things were visible to her . . . and silence was audible." Parenthetically, Coverdale the alleged realist must interject, "at least, so the people inferred from obscure hints, escaping unawares out of her mouth" (3:187). By means of such indirection, however, the preternatural is insinuated into Hawthorne's contemporary romance.

Coverdale next introduces Westervelt into his metadiegetic narrative, not by name but through the neighbors' claim that he was "a wizard . . . [t]he boundaries of [whose] power were defined by the verge of the pit of Tartarus, on the one hand, and the third sphere of the celestial world, on the other" (3:188). Coverdale himself feels that such superstitions are "all absurdity, or mostly so" (3:188–89). In other words, he claims to prefer not to include the preternatural in his narrative at all. Truth compels him to do so, however, at least in the form of mesmerism: "Its nature, at that period, was even less understood than now, when miracles of this kind have grown so absolutely stale, that I would gladly, if the truth allowed, dismiss the whole matter from my narrative" (3:189). Again, the realistic world of "every-day Probability" affords space to the romantic world of literature. Coverdale's handling of Zenobia follows similar lines. She is first called Fauntleroy's "forsaken child," but within the same paragraph has been specifically identified as Zenobia (3:189). Like Hester Prynne, Zenobia found herself early in life without a mother's guidance, and also like Hester she grew into a romantic heroine, "Passionate, self-willed, and imperious" (3:189). As in the case of her sister Priscilla, Zenobia's more exotic behavior enters Coverdale's narrative only through indirect testimony: "There were whispers of an attachment, and even a secret marriage, with a fascinating and accomplished, but unprincipled young man" (3:189). Need we ask what this young man's name was, or whether he had a gold band around his teeth, or whether he visited Fauntleroy in the decayed governor's mansion? Coverdale will leave those questions to his readers' discretion.

Coverdale then assumes a less coy tone to say directly that "A portion of Zenobia's more recent life is told in the foregoing pages," that is, in the twenty-one previous chapters of this book. Equally direct is the announcement "And Priscilla followed her to Blithedale" (3:190). Here there is no suggestion that Priscilla was magically transported or that a heartless Theodore played a part in her previous life. What *actually* happened, according to Coverdale, is that Priscilla followed Zenobia to Blithedale—as the diegetic narrative elsewhere establishes. In this same tone of direct assertion, Coverdale begins the following paragraph with the sentence "One evening, months after Priscilla's departure, when Moodie (or shall we call him Fauntleroy?) was sitting alone in the state-chamber of the old Governor, there came foot-steps up the staircase." Just as surely as the metadiegetic Fauntleroy is the same as the diegetic Moodie, Coverdale asserts, these footsteps belong to Zenobia. Then Coverdale abandons the pose of realistic reporter to resume the role of active narrator. In one of the most peculiar sentences in a very peculiar narrative, Coverdale thus says,

> The details of the interview that followed, being unknown to me—while, notwithstanding, it would be a pity quite to lose the picturesqueness of the situation—I shall attempt to sketch it, mainly from fancy, although with some general grounds of surmise in regard to the old man's feelings. (3:190)

As when Zenobia claimed ignorance concerning the behavior of Theodore in her metadiegetic narrative, so Coverdale does not know for sure what transpired between two characters in his own narrative. He does know that they met, however, either because Moodie told him so or because his "subsequent researches" uncovered the meeting. Neither source can supply reliable testimony for the dialogue that Coverdale proceeds to quote between Zenobia and Moodie. Coverdale provides these speeches purely on his own narrative authority. This same confidence permits Coverdale to attribute to Moodie an uttered aside containing a piece of information crucial to Hawthorne's narrative overall: "True; my brother's wealth, he dying intestate, is legally my own. I know it; yet, of my own choice, I live a beggar . . ."

(3:192). This absurd exclamation clearly violates Jamesian standards of narrative organicism. No matter how implausibly, however, the fact of the uncle's intestate death is still conveyed, thus helping readers to understand that Hollingsworth might see Priscilla as a potential heiress.

By means of Coverdale's metadiegetic narrative, Hawthorne has developed his characters, fleshed out developments in his plot to this point, supplied information crucial to later plot developments, and insinuated considerable Gothic shading. It is, however, time to move on. Therefore, Coverdale ends the chapter as follows: "But, while the man of show thus meditated—that very evening, so far as I can adjust the dates of these strange incidents—Priscilla—poor, pallid flower!—was either snatched from Zenobia's hand, or flung wilfully away!" (3:193). That "so far as I can adjust the dates" is particularly effective, I think. The same Coverdale who blandly invented internal thoughts for Old Moodie begins to scruple over the precise dating of clearly Gothic occurrences. However qualified or ironized by the author's stylistic ingenuity, narrative content has still been dispatched, and Hawthorne's readers cannot help but receive it, each in terms of his or her interpretation of the book to this point. In *The Implied Reader*, Wolfgang Iser approvingly cites George Poulet's proposal that "books only take on their full existence in the reader" (292). If we make adequate allowance for the many possible books being read by Hawthorne's many possible readers, we may see that completing this rhetorical transaction is the strategic force behind Hawthorne's manipulations of narrative levels in *The Blithedale Romance* and elsewhere.

In *The Marble Faun*, Hawthorne's last completed romance, metadiegetic narratives-within-narratives are often used, as in *Blithedale*, to introduce Gothic marvels without compromising the diegetic narrator's authority. Miriam, for example, explains her earlier relations with her mysterious model by telling her friends "with a strange air of seriousness over all her face, only belied by a laughing gleam in her dark eyes" that she has bartered her soul to him in return for some "long lost, but invaluable secret of old Roman fresco-painting" (4:34). Readers are hereby exposed to a much more spooky account of these characters' pasts than the narrator is willing to essay. Because this account is untrue, there is nothing to prevent Miriam from offering another one, and she does. Her next explanation is that "she had entered into controversy with him, hoping to achieve the glory and satisfaction of converting him to the Christian faith . . . and had even staked her own salvation against his . . ." (4:34). So far, unfortunately, Miriam must report that she has been the less effective disputant. Neither of these plots is the one that Hawthorne is developing, and yet both shadow the principal narrative in some way. Miriam does have some sort of obligation to the model, and she seems both oppressed by and unable to terminate the bond. Although these metadiegetic narratives do not really account for what has happened to these characters previously, they are, then, not totally false or unrelated to the narrator's principal diegesis.

We see the same technique at work later in Chapter 17 when the four main characters go to the Coliseum at night. Kenyon first comments on the historical and aesthetic dimensions of the scene in language that might have been drawn from Hawthorne's notebook—but was not—and then recounts an episode from Benvenuto Cellini's autobiography. As Kenyon recalls, in the present tense, Cellini writes that "a necromancer of his acquaintance draws a magic circle, (just where the black cross stands now, I suppose,) and raises myriads of demons. . . . Those spectres must have been Romans, in their lifetime, and frequenters of this bloody amphitheatre." As Hawthorne discovered earlier in connection with the silver vial of "Rappaccini's Daughter," the very mention of Cellini can add mysterious reverberations to any scene. Here too the effect is powerful and immediate. Hilda responds, "I see a spectre, now!" (4:156). This spectre is, of course, the model. Although *The Marble Faun* does not establish that this character is a demon, or the ghost of an ancient Roman, he might as well be in terms of his evil influence on Miriam.

Hawthorne pursues a similar strategy in the chapter entitled "Miriam's Studio" by exploiting the metadiegetic narrative properties of some of Miriam's paintings. Interestingly enough, these are not even finished works, merely sketches for paintings based on biblical narratives: "Jael, driving the nail through the temples of Sisera"; Judith with the head of Holofernes; "the daughter of Herodias, receiving the head of John the Baptist in a charger" (4:43–44). Miriam physically murders no one during the present action of *The Marble Faun*, and, since she is presented as morally pure, seems also to have murdered no one before. Even so, since "the artist's imagination seemed to run on these stories of bloodshed, in which woman's hand was crimsoned by the stain" (4:44), the sketches contribute an equally crimsoned tone to Miriam's characterization. They also imply as early as Chapter 5 that someone will probably be murdered in the diegetic narrative, that the victim will probably be a man, and that Miriam will probably be implicated. Therefore, metadiegetic narratives—in keeping with the book's focus on art and artists, visual narratives—shadow and help explain the principal narrative.

Miriam's sketches, like her fanciful accounts of her past and Kenyon's paraphrase of Cellini, are highly economical narrative structures, each easily contained within a single paragraph. More extensive metadiegetic narratives appear throughout Chapters 25–27, set in Monte Beni, the rural estate of Donatello. These serve to develop the symbolic connection between Donatello and the fauns of classical antiquity which colors the romance from the first through the last chapter—and which provided a title for the American edition. In Chapter 25 Kenyon observes some old frescoes "representing Arcadian scenes, where Nymphs, Fauns, and Satyrs, disported themselves among mortal youths and maidens . . ." (4:225), and remarks a resemblance between a recurring figure in the frescoes and Donatello (4:227). The narrator will not say, of course, that Donatello actually *is* a faun or even that he is descended from one, and yet readers encountering Donatello and the faun within the same paragraph, and even within the same sentence, carry away some notion along these lines. This association is greatly strengthened in the next chapter, entitled "The Pedigree of Monte Beni." Even while withdrawing behind Kenyon's worldly sophistication and his own irony, the narrator here confirms Donatello's symbolic relation to a faun by means of several related metadiegetic narratives. Especially toward the beginning of the chapter, the narrator is careful to qualify his anecdotes with the sort of vocabulary identified by Todorov in *The Fantastic*. As if in a sophisticated mathematical equation, the narrator manipulates plusses and minuses, affirmations and denials: "a romancer . . . written record . . . Tradition . . . mythical . . . romantic . . . story, or myth . . . prehistoric . . . Arcadia . . . Golden Age . . ." (4:231–34). The narrator even weighs the competing authorities of fancy and documented history when Kenyon gets access to "many chests of worm-eaten papers and yellow parchments, that had been gathering into larger and dustier piles ever since the Dark ages." As it turns out, "the information afforded by these musty documents was so much more prosaic than what Kenyon acquired from [the butler] Tomaso's legends, that even the superiour authenticity of the former could not reconcile him to its dulness" (4:236). Readers are therefore presented with the "superiour" authority of metadiegetic legends. Typical is one that Tomaso heard from his grandfather about "a Lord of Monte Beni . . . who used to go into the woods and call pretty damsels out of the fountains, and out of the trunks of old trees" (4:238). This is all we learn of this story, but, in a Jamesian sense, the donnee for a more elaborate preternatural narrative is clearly present. In the next chapter, entitled "Myths," Donatello provides the donnee for a similar, also undeveloped, metadiegetic narrative: "It is said that a Faun, my eldest forefather, brought home hither, to this very spot, a human maiden, whom he loved and wedded." Kenyon calls this story "a most enchanting Fable," but Donatello elides epistemological distinctions by asking, "And why not a fact?" (4:243–44). As was true of the stories represented by the frescoes in Chapter 25, man and nature, the natural and the preternatural intersect in these brief narratives. They do so, moreover, in an atmosphere not of "fact," but of mystery and eroticism, the same atmosphere that Hawthorne elaborates for his diegetic narrative.

A more extended metadiegetic narrative quickly follows the previous example, another "sweet old story" narrated by Donatello to Kenyon. The narrator first explains that Donatello's "myth" is set "a century ago, or a thousand years, or before the Christian epoch," a chronotope closely resembling *once upon a time*. There and then, a human knight and a "woman or sprite" fell in love. Since this female lived within the fountain, she probably was a sprite, perhaps the fulfillment of a youthful fantasy created in "A Vision of the Fountain." In any event, the two lovers were completely happy until the young man came to the fountain one day to "wash off a bloodstain." The two were never innocently happy again. The nymph disappeared into the fountain with a bloodstain on her brow, and the hero "mourned for her, his whole life long" (4:244–46). Nymphs and knights are not assimilable within the chronotope of Hawthorne's narrative, but this chronotope can contain Miriam and Donatello, lovers who briefly enjoy a blissful, uncivilized communion like that depicted in the metadiegetic narrative and who also share bloodstained guilt. Even though Donatello and Miriam enact these passions in Italy rather than in the "broad and simple daylight" of the author's "dear native land" (4:3), Hawthorne was probably wise to transfer these Gothic and marvelous intonations to the historically remote chronotope of Donatello's metadiegetic narrative.

In this respect, Donatello's story about the nymph and the bloodstained knight typifies Hawthorne's use of metadiegetic narratives in *The Marble Faun*. Like Miriam's sketches and Kenyon's anecdote about Cellini, this internalized narrative enables Hawthorne to insinuate romantic intonations and Gothic thrills into his ongoing narrative without offending the growing popular taste for realistic representation or compromising the authority that his narrator will need to develop the love plot involving Hilda and Kenyon. In the process, Hawthorne brings thematic complication to his narrative without introducing excessive plot complications into the diegesis. Moreover, by extending and withdrawing narrative assurances as he does, Hawthorne requires that we choose among the narrative options he offers. On the basis of our personal and philosophical predilections, we almost certainly will make these interpretive choices. Whichever interpretation we adopt, however, we will be forced to ignore or explain away considerable evidence to the contrary. For these reasons, *The Marble Faun*, like Hawthorne's other fiction, remains continually open to interpretation.

# FIVE

# Narrativity and Historicity

For most Americanists, even to connect the terms *fiction* and *history* is to conjure up the spirit of Nathaniel Hawthorne. A clear statement of this proposition appears, for example, at the beginning of Michael Davitt Bell's *Hawthorne and the Historical Romance of New England* (1971):

> Nathaniel Hawthorne was one of the most historically minded of our major novelists. From his first tales to his final unfinished romances he turned again and again to history—particularly to the early history of his native New England, which provided the material for his greatest novel and for many of his best tales. (vii)

In a similar spirit, Michael Colacurcio plainly says in *The Province of Piety* (1984), "On the face of it nothing would seem more self-evident than the fact that Hawthorne is in some primary way an historical writer" (14). Frederick Newberry reaffirms this position throughout *Hawthorne's Divided Loyalties* (1987), as when he writes: "As a serious historian/artist, Hawthorne recognized that the historical record was more complex than popular ideology would have it" (23–24). Of course, each of these critics understands the nature of Hawthorne's fictional historiography somewhat differently. Colacurcio devotes nearly seven hundred pages to contextualizing Hawthorne's early short fiction within a vast array of historical documents. Bell traces Hawthorne's mythopoeic engagement with the historical entity that Bell calls "The Matter of New England" (ix). Newberry is interested primarily in how Hawthorne treated America's historical relations with England. The critics are alike, however, in approaching Hawthorne's work according to some scale of "historicity," that is, by comparing and contrasting the words Hawthorne wrote in his fiction to words written by other writers, principally historians. I would propose on the contrary that the key issue should be "narrativity," or the uses to which Hawthorne puts documentary history while writing fiction.

As we have seen in Chapter 2, in *Twice-told Tales* Hawthorne sometimes pretends to borrow authority for a narrative by attributing its origins to a previously published, historical source. In "The May-Pole of Merry Mount," for example, the narrator refers both to "the grave pages of our New England annalists" and to "Strutt's Book of English Sports and Pastimes" in an epigraph vouching for the tale's authenticity. In the same epigraph, however, the narrator identifies the tale as "a sort of allegory" (9:54). Readers are thus forewarned that they will encounter a narrative constructed from historical materials, not unmediated history. The narrator's intervention, or pre-vention, in the epigraph also puts readers on notice that this narrator will be a major figure in what is to follow. Further evidence appears when the narrator interrupts his tale after five pages to digress into historical background. Significantly, he proceeds with his historical essay only after alerting readers to his intentions: "Meanwhile, we may discover who these gay people were" (9:59). Then, having devoted four substantial paragraphs to the promised discovery, the narrator again deliberately addresses his readers to express his intention of returning to the narrative: "After these authentic passages from history, we return to the nuptials of the Lord and Lady of the May. Alas! we have delayed too long, and must darken our tale too suddenly" (9:62). The narrator's concession to necessity here is, of course, purely rhetorical, but its effect is real. Because he is free to break in upon the narrative to plead his helplessness, the purportedly helpless narrator is ironically shown to be the only force controlling the tale.

Throughout the tale the narrator enters less directly by means of editorial comment, and it is unnecessary to use the first-person singular or plural to inform the reader that these are the narrator's opinions, not Strutt's or those of a New England annalist. Surely it is the narrator alone who asks about the colonists' celebration of a funeral, "But did the dead man laugh?" (9:61). He is obviously responsible too for such summary judgments as this: "The future complexion of New England was involved in this important quarrel" (9:62). Such subtle considerations are hardly necessary, however, since "The May-Pole" affords us the most striking and outrageous instance of

Hawthorne's manipulations of history. Just after returning to the narrative from his extended historical essay, and after reminding his readers of exactly what he has been doing and why, Hawthorne's narrator recounts the Puritans' attack on the colonists. At the outset, Endicott, the "Puritan of Puritans," shouts at the colonists' clergyman: "Stand off, priest of Baal! . . . I know thee, Blackstone." Immediately, the narrator addresses the reader in a footnote to explain the following: "Did Governor Endicott speak less positively, we should suspect a mistake here. The Rev. Mr. Blackstone, though an eccentric, is not known to have been an immoral man. We rather doubt his identity with the priest of Merry Mount" (9:63).

This passage seems to me crucial in understanding both Hawthorne's use of history in his fiction and the limitations of the critical tradition within which it has usually been discussed. For example, Bell (123) exemplifies the traditional approach in writing a long footnote in which he identifies the historical William Blackstone as "an Anglican cleric who lived at the future site of Boston during the 1620's," discusses Blackstone's fictional character in John Lothrop Motley's novel *Merry-Mount; A Romance of the Massachusetts Colony* (1849), and reports Terence Martin's discovery that Blackstone was misidentified as Claxton in the 1835 version of the tale. In his much more extended discussion in *The Province of Piety* (268–77), Colacurcio layers this historical Blackstone onto Caleb Snow's *History of Boston*, onto Strutt's *Sports and Pastimes*, onto theological disputes about surplices and other high-church symbols, and onto agreements and disagreements with a host of Hawthorne's critics—this last by means of twenty-seven of his own footnotes (606–10). Relying on Colacurcio's discussion, Newberry deals expeditiously with the issue in his text, concluding simply that "Hawthorne knew from several historical sources that the Reverend Blackstone had nothing to do with the antics of Merry Mount" (30), and then using only two of his own footnotes (235–36) to refer readers to Snow, Colacurcio, and G. Harrison Orians. What all this commentary goes to show is that some parallels exist between what happens in Hawthorne's tale and what some historians say happened in New England in the 1620s, and that, further, some of Hawthorne's events have no historical precedents or may even conflict with such reports. Surely these are not the correct answers—or even the correct questions. The effect of Hawthorne's footnote is radically imaginative; historicity cannot be the operative principle involveu. ᴛ.лis narrator has too easily drifted from history to fiction and back to accord history such influence at this point.

Putting aside quibbles about the historicity of Blackstone's presence in the tale, we should be able to see that there is also no valid aesthetic reason for Hawthorne not to call this priest Blackstone—or Foxe, or Laud, or Smith. This is, after all, a fictional account. In other words, the problem is narratological rather than historiographic. If Hawthorne had named his character according to ordinary historical or fictional practices, Blackstone would have disappeared into the organic web of his narrative, as Michael Colacurcio or Henry James would—for different reasons—probably recommend. By raising the whole bogus issue of historicity, especially against himself, Hawthorne makes this disappearance impossible. In consequence, readers must recognize that Hawthorne's narrator controls the supposedly historical Blackstone and Endicott as much as the purely fictional Edith and Edgar. This narrator alone conjured up these figures, just as another narrator conjures up Young Goodman Brown. The narrator alone gives life to these characters, and he can eliminate them at any time. This is, ultimately, the very nature of fictional narrative, whether rooted in the world of "once upon a time" or in supposedly historical materials. This is also the rationale behind Hawthorne's approach to the interrelated issues of historicity and narrativity throughout his career.

In 1967 Robert H. Fossum could reasonably lament that the four fictional works from the second edition of *Twice-told Tales* that Hawthorne called "Legends of the Province-House"—"Howe's Masquerade," "Edward Randolph's Portrait," "Lady Eleanore's Mantle," and "Old Esther Dudley"—were often ignored even by those attempting to analyze Hawthorne's overall career as a writer. To redress this failing, Fossum made a very strong case for considering the four tales together as Hawthorne's ironic consideration of the contending political values involved in the American Revolution of 1776. Fossum's proposal has been conscientiously fulfilled by a whole series of critics, including Julian Smith (1969), Margaret V. Allen (1971), P. L. Reed (1976), Nina Baym (1976), Evan Carton (1980), Michael Colacurcio (1984), Frederick Newberry (1987), and Emily Miller Budick (1989). The consensus of these critics is that the framing device by which Hawthorne enclosed the four tales investigates the same political ambiguities as the tales themselves, thus making the entire series a crucial illustration of Hawthorne's engagement with American history. Reading these four tales consecutively demonstrates the cogency of this interpretive direction. I would propose, however, that further light can be thrown on all these issues by refocusing attention from the themes of the tales to their technical, narratological structures. That is to say, history is indisputably Hawthorne's subject, but history is also one of the narrative elements by which he constructs his fiction. Without impugning the sincerity of the author's political concerns as an American citizen, we may profitably turn our attention to his concerns as a practicing writer who was trying to solve some of the rhetorical problems intrinsic to writing fiction.

One of these problems is acknowledged in the first sentence of the first tale, "Howe's Masquerade," when Hawthorne's narrator tries to establish his firsthand relation to the materials of the tale. He says, in the first person, that, while walking down Washington Street last summer, his eye was caught by a sign advertising the inn currently housed in a historic building, and this reminded him "of a purpose, long entertained, of visiting and rambling over the mansion of the old royal governors of Massachusetts" (9:239). Such an introduction seems intended to introduce a historic sketch about the building and its more famous inhabitants in which the narrator's authority will be founded in some sort of personal experience, however remote in time from the circumstances in which colonial history occurred. Since the narrator has already fictionalized the occasion for his narration to some degree in order to make it seem a coincidence, a historical sketch of this sort might be fictionalized to a greater or lesser degree depending on the author's confidence in the intrinsic appeal of his materials. He might, in other words, produce a localized version of "My Visit to Niagara." Instead of developing his experiences in this possible narrative direction, after three paragraphs devoted to descriptions of the old building and predictable contrasts of the past and present, the narrator introduces another narrator who is supposedly possessed of "historical reminiscences" (9:243). This old man, who will be identified in the next tale as Bela Tiffany, is then very briefly characterized in a prelude to his account of the story that gives Hawthorne's tale its title: a masquerade ball given by Sir William Howe to show his defiance of the Revolutionary army then besieging Boston. After Tiffany's account of how the rebellious colonists transvalued the masquerade to serve their own political purposes, Hawthorne's narrator resumes the narra-

tive about his visit to the Province-House in the last paragraph. For purposes of narratological classification, we might say, reassuming the vocabulary of Chapter 4, that Hawthorne's unnamed but fictional narrator relates
an extradiegetic narrative during which another fictional character, named
Bela Tiffany, relates a diegetic narrative about events occurring at the time
of the American Revolution.

As historical critics including Colacurcio and Newberry have noted,
Hawthorne's narrative problematizes the authority of Tiffany's narrative.
From this perspective, questions of narrative authority are inseparable from
questions of Hawthorne's ideological commitment. From a narratological
perspective, questions of narrative authority simply involve how the author
moves readers from the first sentence to the last. It is therefore interesting
that while discussing the substance of Tiffany's story, Hawthorne's narrator
blithely establishes a synonymy among the terms *historical reminiscences*,
*memory, tradition, gossip*, and *legend*. When discussing his own intervention
in the transmission of this story, the narrator evinces a similar indifference
to what might elsewhere be considered scrupulous historiographic accuracy:

> He [Tiffany] professed to have received it, at one or two removes, from an
> eye-witness; but this derivation, together with the lapse of time, must have
> afforded opportunities for many variations of the narrative; so that, de-
> spairing of literal and absolute truth, I have not scrupled to make such
> further changes as seemed conducive to the reader's profit and delight.
> (9:243)

The former effect probably is the motive for structuring the colonists' anti-
masquerade as a historical procession of governors, beginning with Endicott and concluding with Howe. As Colacurcio has observed in *The Province
of Piety*, "Regular history properly goes one way—forward" (424). On the
other hand, "delight" is the more probable object of the Gothic effects of
this procession, as when "some of the spectators fancied that they had seen
this human shape suddenly moulding itself amid the gloom" (9:252) and
when the experienced, sophisticated politician-soldier Howe responds to
the colonist who is enacting Howe's own role with "a look of wild amaze-
ment, if not horror, while he recoiled several steps from the figure and let
fall his sword upon the floor" (9:253). Somewhere in the transference from

eyewitness to Tiffany, to the narrator, to the reader, someone has granted equivalent status to verifiable events such as political succession and to superstitious beliefs in specters, physical misperceptions occasioned by dim light, and literary effects derived from the Gothic tradition.

The indirection by which Hawthorne establishes narrative authority in this tale makes it very difficult to determine who is responsible for blurring these lines of authority. It might be the original witnesses. It might be Tiffany. It might be Hawthorne's narrator. For example, Hawthorne's narrator should probably take responsibility for all editorial interpolations into Tiffany's story, as when he parenthetically comments, about a metaphor in which the gaiety of Howe's guests is related to a dying lamp flame, that it is "an ominous comparison" (9:245). At such times, the narrator is admittedly managing his narrative. In the penultimate paragraph of the tale—the final paragraph of Tiffany's diegetic narrative—a slightly different relation of narrator to narrative governs the following sentence: "But superstition, among other legends of this mansion, repeats the wondrous tale that, on the anniversary night of Britain's discomfiture, the ghosts of the ancient governors of Massachusetts still glide through the portal of the Province-House" (9:254). Apparently Tiffany is responsible for this Gothic heightening of the historical circumstances, since the next, and final, paragraph of the tale begins: "When the truth-telling accents of the elderly gentleman were hushed, I drew a long breath and looked round the room . . ." (9:255). Despite the editorializing implied in the phrase *truth-telling*, the narrator confesses himself impressed by Tiffany's diegetic narrative overall and by its concluding spookiness in particular. Presumably the narrator—and probably Hawthorne—would like to find the reader in the same state of mind.

"Edward Randolph's Portrait" reveals a similar narrative strategy. The tale, first of all, has considerable basis in American history, as Colacurcio—and before him John P. McWilliams, Jr.—has exhaustively shown. Edward Randolph *was* an unpopular representative of the crown in Massachusetts during the 1670s. Thomas Hutchinson *was*, in a sense, Randolph's successor as acting governor of Massachusetts in the 1770s, and Hutchinson *did* write an excellent history of the colony, mentioned even in the opening paragraph of "My Kinsman, Major Molineux." A peacekeeping force of British troops *were* quartered at Castle William in Boston during Hutchinson's administration, and so forth. On the other hand, the Gothic properties possessed by the portrait of Edward Randolph, which gives the tale its title, are substantiated only by a "wild legend" (9:267). Furthermore, Bela Tiffany's diegetic narrative concerning Hutchinson and this portrait has, according to Hawthorne's narrator, "a tinge of romance approaching to the marvelous" (9:258). The narrator—and, by extension, Hawthorne—is thus picking and choosing among a variety of narrative materials, including documented history.

This practice is consistent with the program outlined in the tale's extradiegetic frame. This time, Hawthorne's fictionalized narrator says, again in the first person, that he deliberately returned to the Province-House in January in hopes of "snatching from oblivion some else unheard-of fact of history" through another encounter with Tiffany (9:256). The narrator now seems unconcerned that Tiffany's memory may be unreliable or that the old man may have embroidered the "fact of history" with Gothic embellishments. In fact, loosening Tiffany's tongue by means of a hefty whiskey punch might seem calculated to elicit such a heightened narrative. The result of the punch and the narrator's flattering interest was that Tiffany "overflowed with tales, traditions, anecdotes of famous dead people, and traits of ancient manners, some of which were childish as a nurse's lullaby, while others might have been worth the notice of the grave historian" (9:258). The narrator does not specify which categorization best describes the following diegetic narrative, but he does admit, as we have seen, that "a tinge of wild romance approaching to the marvellous" colors it.

Questions of historiographic accuracy also arise within the tale. As a respected historian, Lieutenant-Governor Hutchinson might have been expected to understand the current crisis in the light of earlier colonial resistance to heavy-handed British authority. He is blinded to such historical lessons primarily by the obligations of his office, as Julian Smith has argued (35–36), but Hutchinson's narrow conception of historiography also gets in the way. He dismisses as mere "legends" the historical anecdotes that have given his niece, Alice Vane, fearful premonitions, countering them with his own "antiquarian researches" (9:261). On the basis of the collection of tales entitled "Legends of the Province-House," a reader might expect Hawthorne to be more confident of the authority of legends than Hutchinson seems to be. The author of "Roger Malvin's Burial" and "The

Prophetic Pictures" might also be thought sympathetic to Captain Lincoln's report from "our annals" that "the curse of the people followed this Randolph wherever he went, and wrought evil in all the subsequent events of his life, and that its effect was seen likewise in the manner of his death." To Hutchinson, however, "These traditions are folly, to one who has proved, as I have, how little of historic truth lies at the bottom" (9:262). The issue is ultimately decided in Lincoln's favor years later when he stands by Hutchinson's bedside across the sea and watches the dying man as he "gasped for breath, and complained that he was choking with the blood of the Boston Massacre" (9:269). Readers resistant to the fantastic might question the accuracy of Lincoln's testimony about Hutchinson's dying moments, but they must totally reject Hutchinson's unquestioning confidence in the superior force of authenticated history.

The relative merits of these differing interpretive strategies must have deeply engaged Hawthorne's interests as a writer, since he has the characters examine them for one-third of the twelve pages comprising Tiffany's diegetic narrative. Thematically, this extended debate exposes the dangerous historical precedent that Hutchinson seems intent on following by tyrannically ignoring the colonists' rights. Narratologically, it allows Hawthorne's narrator to introduce nonhistorical Gothic materials for which he need take no responsibility. Even Tiffany is somewhat distanced from these issues since Captain Lincoln lays claim to most of the narrative authority. In a long paragraph, presented in indirect discourse, Lincoln retells "some of the strange fables and fantasies" associated with Randolph's portrait. According to Lincoln's testimony, filtered through Tiffany, "One of the wildest, and at the same time best accredited accounts . . . stated it to be an original and authentic portrait of the Evil One, taken at a witch meeting near Salem." This incredible rumor is supported, he adds, by the testimony of "confessing wizards and witches, at their trial, in open court." If Hutchinson or the reader should find this probably hysterical testimony equally incredible, Lincoln relates another belief that "a familiar spirit, or demon" lives within the portrait and has emerged to give royal governors, such as Shirley, fair warning at "seasons of public calamity," such as the present (9:260). Again, a thematic function is well served and, again, Hawthorne is free to introduce a series of Gothic events as Lincoln authenticates these superstitions. Narrative authority is here established at a great distance from

Hawthorne: "[S]ervants of the Province-House had caught glimpses of a visage frowning down upon them. . . . The oldest inhabitant of Boston recollected that his father . . . had once looked upon [the portrait], but would never suffer himself to be questioned as to the face which was there represented" (9:260–61). In the latter case, particularly, we should note the complexity with which Hawthorne establishes narrative authority: the author creates a narrator, who passes on the testimony of the fictional Bela Tiffany, who recounts the testimony of Captain Lincoln, who reports the testimony of Boston's oldest inhabitant, concerning the testimony of his father, concerning a painting he saw once. Perhaps for these reasons, Tiffany admits that "it was impossible to refute [these legends] by ocular demonstration." Perhaps for these same reasons, he can say that they "had grown to be articles of popular belief" (9:260). This sort of belief is impossible for Hutchinson the historian, who explains that "too implicit credence has been given to Dr. Cotton Mather, who . . . has filled our early history with old women's tales, as fanciful and extravagant as those of Greece or Rome." Again a reader may suspect that the future author of *Tanglewood Tales* might consider a narrative that rivaled those of Greece and Rome a more noteworthy achievement than the sort of historical writing that has left Hutchinson incapable of understanding what is really going on. This is at least the suspicion of Alice, who responds, "And yet . . . may not such fables have a moral?" (9:262).

The answer to Alice's question may still seem to be in doubt when the narrator resumes direct control of Hawthorne's narrative in the last paragraph of the tale. There he first asks to see the fabled portrait and, being told that it has disappeared, then speculates that "some curious antiquary may light upon it . . . in some out-of-the-way corner of the New England Museum" (9:269), thus allowing us to evaluate its magical properties for ourselves. A number of readers have viewed the narrator's return to the present here—and similar framing gestures in the other three tales—as evidence that Hawthorne felt uneasy about the success of his narrative execution in the "Legends." John Caldwell Stubbs observes more helpfully in *The Pursuit of Form*: "The whole elaborate framework of the Province House is presented facetiously. It calls attention to the artifice of the tales" (32–33). In fact, we may see that Hawthorne's "artifice" consists largely of his ingenious shifts among so many levels of narrative authority. In the process,

Hawthorne frees himself to give this "historical action" a more engaging "treatment" than it might receive from a historian, especially a historian like Hutchinson, who would search for Edward Randolph's portrait to discover "how little of historic truth lies at the bottom" of the legend that a demon resided within. Hawthorne's structuring of this tale and its frame suggests not that he felt insecure in his fictionalizations of history, but rather that he agreed with Aristotle's view in *Poetics* IX that poetry is "a more philosophical and a higher thing than history" (Bate 25).

The next "Legend," "Lady Eleanore's Mantle," lends further support to this conjecture. First of all, Hawthorne's narrator establishes his presence more forcefully here than in the two earlier tales. Again, the fictionalized motive is the narrator's return to the Province-House to extract another historical account from Tiffany, in this case, "one of the oddest legends which he had yet raked from the store-house, where he keeps such matters" (9:273). Again, the narrator acknowledges his own interventions in the narrative process, admitting that the ensuing tale has been heightened by "some suitable adornments from my own fancy," rather than from Tiffany's (9:273). In a fictional advance over the two previous frame narratives, the narrator then allies himself with "the ingenious tale-teller [as] the humble note-taker of his narratives" (9:271), which have by now brought considerable "public notice" to the bar in the historic building operated by Thomas Waite and supposedly frequented by Tiffany and the narrator. (The Historical Collation of the *Centenary Edition* reveals that in the periodical version, the narrator even testified that the first two narratives were published in the *Democratic Review* [9:626–27].) The narrator also signals his presence when he says about another fictional habitué of the bar, "In another paper of this series, I may perhaps give the reader a closer glimpse of his portrait" (9:273).

Because it is established so forcefully, the narrator's presence may continue to color this tale. When Lady Eleanore walks over Jervase Helwyse's prostrate body and a narrative voice observes that "never, surely, was there an apter emblem of aristocracy and hereditary pride, trampling on human sympathies and the kindred of nature" (9:276), the reader can only attribute the editorial judgment to the narrator. It must also be the narrator who says about the ball that Colonel Shute gives in Lady Eleanore's honor, "What a pity that one of the stately mirrors has not preserved a picture of the scene . . ." (9:277), since Tiffany was perfectly willing to describe a similar ball in "Howe's Masquerade." The narrator may also balance the conflicting claims of Todorov's marvelous and uncanny when he says about "that mighty conqueror—that scourge and horror of our forefathers—the Small-Pox!" that "We cannot estimate the affright which this plague inspired of yore, by contemplating it as the fangless monster of the present day" (9:283). Surely it is the narrator, rather than Tiffany, who then follows up the suggestions of Gothic horror with a brief historical sketch for the rest of the paragraph. At other times, this narrator chooses to withdraw to the sort of narrative distance familiar from "Edward Randolph's Portrait." Thus he, or perhaps Tiffany, says that "many traditionary anecdotes" are the primary sources for our conception of Lady Eleanore's character (9:275). A similar indirection is used to make Dr. Clarke responsible for a prediction about Lady Eleanore—"See, if that nature do not assert its claim over her in some mode that shall bring her level with the lowest" (9:276)—even though the narrator was responsible for the editorial about "hereditary pride, trampling on . . . the kindred sympathies of nature" earlier on the same page.

In other words, when it suits this narrator's purpose—or, rather, when it suits Hawthorne's purpose—the narrator is willing to withdraw into the wings to let Tiffany assume narrative authority for the tale. This is especially prudent in the final sentences of the diegetic narrative:

> A remarkable uncertainty broods over the unhappy lady's fate. There is a belief, however, that, in a certain chamber of this mansion, a female form may sometimes be duskily discerned, shrinking into the darkest corner, and muffling her face within an embroidered mantle. Supposing the legend true, can this be other than the once proud Lady Eleanore? (9:288)

Since Lady Eleanore would probably be over one hundred years old at the present time of the "Legends," this "belief" seems highly unlikely, and since Eleanore was obviously on the point of death during her last encounter with Helwyse, we can hardly "suppose" that any story about her continuing punishment might be "true." As Alice Vane said in the other tale, however, "such fables [may] have a moral" even if unsupported by historical documentation, and so Eleanore's cursed existence into the present may be credited as carrying an undeniable narrative truth.

For this reason, when the tale returns to the extradiegetic barroom, the narrator, who demanded to see Edward Randolph's portrait in the previous tale, does not require any material confirmation for Tiffany's account. Although he admits that "skeptics . . . might demand documentary evidence, or even require him to produce the embroidered mantle," the narrator is content to "repose perfect confidence in the veracity" of Tiffany, despite an obviously ironic disclaimer about how "scrupulous" the old man is "to settle the foundation of his facts" (9:288). In this light we may see that these concluding paragraphs are intended to illustrate a lesson about reading narrative as well as a lesson about the dangers of pride. When asked how drama may be accepted as true if the audience is aware of the dramatic conventions at work, Samuel Johnson said that "It is credited with all the credit due to a drama" (Bate 215). Through his narrator, Hawthorne makes a similar point in "Lady Eleanore's Mantle." The story is "true" whether it happened or not. Thus, readers may profitably engage with the materials of narrative—irrespective of historical documentation—whether filtered through a Hawthorne-like narrator, Bela Tiffany, the fictional Dr. Clarke, or Cotton Mather. In the concluding sentence of "Lady Eleanore's Mantle," the narrator admits as much when he raises the prospect of a further historical narrative to be filtered through an old loyalist: "Perchance the public—but be this as its own caprice and ours shall settle the matter—may read the result in another Legend of the Province-House" (9:289).

The freedom of readers to choose what they will and will not read is an inescapable consideration for the practicing writer, but so too is the writer's freedom to choose his narrative materials. Such considerations are responsible for the powerful sense of an author's presence behind all these tales. In particular, this sense carries over from the concluding sentence of "Lady Eleanore's Mantle" to the first sentence of the following and final tale, "Old Esther Dudley." Even though a month actually intervened between the original publication of these two sentences in the *Democratic Review*, Hawthorne writes as if Thomas Waite had, during the interim, left the scene of the extradiegetic narrative only momentarily "to provide accommodations for several new arrivals" (9:289). Especially when encountering the final two "Legends" in *Twice-told Tales*, readers may easily experience the illusion that turning a page corresponds exactly to the passage of fictional time. The narrator therefore begins "Old Esther Dudley" by saying, "Our host having resumed the chair, he, as well as Mr. Tiffany and myself, expressed much eagerness to be made acquainted with the story to which the loyalist had alluded" (9:290). In addition to being introduced to still another historical redaction, readers also receive the information that the diegetic narrative in this tale will be filtered through a fictional character other than Bela Tiffany. Hawthorne's narrator takes account of the effects of this difference by noting that the emotions of the unnamed loyalist "appeared to me more excitable than those of a younger man." Perhaps, then, readers may expect a more emotional account than the three supposedly supplied by Tiffany. The narrator confirms such suspicions by adding that "At the pathetic passages of his narrative, [the old loyalist] readily melted into tears" (9:290). Perhaps readers should expect to do the same.

These preliminary remarks suit "Old Esther Dudley" organically, since the title character, Sir William Howe, and John Hancock all behave like characters out of sentimental romance. When Howe expresses a desire to confront the now-victorious rebels face to face, he cries out his defiance while "hardly repressing his tears of rage" (9:292). Later on, Esther cries out, "Wretch, wretch that I am" with "such a heart-broken expression" that "tears gushed from" John Hancock's eyes (9:301). Hawthorne's narrator withholds total support for this emotional indulgence, however, by observing in advance that "this ancient person's intellect would wander vaguely, losing its hold of the matter in hand," perhaps introducing historical implausibilities as a result. As in "Howe's Masquerade," then, readers may wonder just who stands behind what elements of the narrative, a quandary only complicated by the narrator's explanation that "the old loyalist's story required more revision to render it fit for the public eye, than those of the series which have preceded it" (9:291). While professing great distance from those parts of the narrative that might incur the disfavor of readers, therefore, the narrator and his creator may simultaneously take credit for all parts that prove enjoyable.

The extradiegetic manipulations are probably demanded by this last tale's more tangential relation to documented history. William Howe *did* leave the Province-House when the colonial army proved victorious, and John Hancock *was* a successful Boston merchant as well as a leading participant in the American Revolution. Even so, these verified historical figures operate in the old loyalist's narrative more as symbols for conflicting political philosophies than as agents of historical forces, more as literary characters than as participants in historical events. Colacurcio explains in *The Province of Piety* that "at some level, *all* formal history is a fictive construct," and consequently "the story historians elect to tell is every bit as significant as the irreducible, but irrecoverable historical 'fact' itself" (391). In this sense, Hawthorne, his narrator, and the old loyalist are all "historians" to some degree, and thus, like other historians, they are creators of narratives—here a narrative drenched in Gothic mystification and indirection.

At times, "Old Esther Dudley" encourages readers to accept an event as entirely fabricated. For example, in his diegetic narrative the old loyalist plausibly conjectures that "Perhaps it was this invariable custom of walking her rounds in the hush of midnight, that caused the superstition of the times to invest the old woman with attributes of awe and mystery" (9:292–93). The whole series of disclaimers—*perhaps, superstition, awe, mystery*—encourages readers to dismiss the possibility of any actual preternatural agency. In the same way, after reading "Many and strange were the fables which the gossips whispered about [Esther], in all the chimney-corners of the town," we are encouraged to dismiss the historical likelihood of the following report both by the narrator's language and by the possibility that "Esther appears to have grown partially crazed" (9:298). The narrator passes along the rumor even so: Esther was able to conjure up "all the pageantry of gone days" in a "tall, antique mirror." Significantly, the narrator also describes these fantastic scenes, including "the Indian chiefs who had come up to the Province-House to hold council or swear allegiance, the grim Provincial warriors, the severe clergymen" (9:295). As is consistent with the uncertainty of the report, the scenes are not fully rendered in the old loyalist's diegetic narrative. Nevertheless, readers still encounter what Esther sees—or does not see. In the next paragraph, the old loyalist—or more probably Hawthorne's narrator—first labels what will follow as another fantastic "rumor" and then goes on to recount how Esther summoned a slave from within this mirror to invite spirits of dead loyalists to visit her in the mansion. Despite the clear implication that these events never actually occurred, this account is much more detailed than the story about the mirror, even presenting direct dialogue from the preternatural slave: "My mistress, old Esther Dudley, bids you to the Province-House at midnight" (9:296). In another sense, of course, the events *did* occur—just a few seconds ago as Hawthorne's readers were taking in the words he had written down days, or months, or years ago.

These fantastic episodes contribute significantly to our sense of what Hawthorne was trying to do as a writer in the late 1830s. Although the conventions of Gothic fiction compelled him to use various narrative subterfuges to discount the reappearance of historical figures in Esther Dudley's mirror—or perhaps merely her imagination—Hawthorne could still give John Hancock or Thomas Hutchinson the same sort of life he could give to Bela Tiffany or Lady Eleanore Rochcliffe. In this sense, Esther Dudley can stand as a displaced representative of the author, and her imaginative experiences, or fantasies, as representatives of Hawthorne's fiction. Especially in the paragraph immediately following the two devoted to "gossip" and "rumor," we can follow Esther's resemblance to Hawthorne as she entertains the children of Boston with historical anecdotes. After a day of gorging on gingerbread and listening to Esther's "stories of a dead world," the children go home to "talk of all the departed worthies of the Province, as far back as Governor Belcher, and the haughty dame of Sir William Phips." The children's experience of history was not purely cerebral, nor documentable, as is evident in their sense of having "toyed with the embroidery of [the dead figures'] rich waistcoats, or roguishly pulled the long curls of their flowing wigs." For this reason, if parents should object that "Governor Belcher has been dead this many year," and ask with great suspicion, "And did you really see him?" a child could honestly answer, "Oh, yes, dear mother! yes!" (9:297). Surely, this is the response Hawthorne would like his readers to give, if quizzed about their exposure to the "Legends."

These parallels suggest that Hawthorne's "Legends" are not simply about history, but about writing history—and by extension about writing narrative. The suggestion is hardly original here. Building on the earlier work of Jane Donahue Eberwein, Evan Carton has argued that these tales convey very discouraging lessons about the possible relations of fiction and history. In this view, the thematics of the tales require Hawthorne's narrator to abandon the rich historical past, Bela Tiffany, and the old loyalist in order to return to quotidian life in nineteenth-century America. As Carton writes in "Hawthorne and the Province of Romance": "It is always necessary for Hawthorne to recoil from creative power when it begins to seem too absolute, too self-authorized. Its threat at such times to swallow up all certainties, to efface all boundaries, is too great . . ." (347). A purely thematic reading supports such a claim, but readings of this sort seem to me overly restricted by the assumption that the narrator speaks for Hawthorne. But, as we have seen, these narrators are not necessarily thematic reflections of the author's deepest feelings; they are narratological conveniences by which Hawthorne may introduce material he considers useful to the story he wishes to tell and which he cannot devise any other way of introducing. Rather than dramatizing what narrative cannot do with history, then, the "Legends" show what narrative, at least as written by Hawthorne, can do. According to Hayden White, in "The Value of Narrativity in the Representation of Reality," "storytelling becomes a problem only after two orders of events dispose themselves before the storyteller as possible components of stories[,] and storytelling is compelled to exfoliate under the injunction to keep the two orders unmixed in discourse" (3). Contrary to the readings proposed by critics such as Eberwein and Carton, this "problem" finds its own solution by means of the narratological strategies that Hawthorne discovered in the process of telling these historical tales.

In writing the "Legends," Hawthorne demonstrated that the writer of fictional narrative can use actual and supposed events interchangeably as it suits him. He can turn to historical documents for verification when that is convenient, and he can invent impossibilities when such documentation is lacking. He can call up characters from the past and have them interact with real or imagined persons in the present. He can even invent dialogue for them. Despite some obvious shortcomings in terms of their sentimentality, patriotic excess, and Gothic claptrap, these four tales and their framing narrative served to teach Hawthorne many valuable narratological lessons. This is probably nowhere more evident than in *The House of the Seven Gables*, written over a decade later.

Most commentators on *The House of the Seven Gables*, including its author, have emphasized the operations of historical forces in the romance. In his preface, Hawthorne declares that his book exemplifies "the attempt to connect a by-gone time with the very Present that is flitting away from us" (2:2). Following Hawthorne's lead, critics as varied as James Russell Lowell (1851), F. O. Matthiessen (1941), Hyatt H. Waggoner (1955), Roy Harvey Pearce (1964), Michael Davitt Bell (1980), Susan Mizruchi (1988), and Emily Miller Budick (1989) have analyzed the nature and power of these forces. Waggoner, for example, proposes in *Hawthorne: A Critical Study* that Hawthorne's interests in the book center on "the tension . . . between the conservative and the liberal views of history" (181). Writing over thirty years later, Mizruchi argues, in *The Power of Historical Knowledge*, that *The Seven Gables* can best be understood as dramatizing the conflict between "different conceptions of history" (106). Hawthorne and his critics have agreed furthermore that the operations of history may be thematized as a key to the book's meaning. Again in his preface, Hawthorne fancifully proposes the theme of the romance to be "that the wrong-doing of one generation lives into the successive ones, and, divesting itself of every temporary advantage, becomes a pure and uncontrollable mischief" (2:2). More sophisticatedly—and more seriously—Mizruchi sees the book's meaning to lie in a new-historical tension between "a mythic view of time as a stilled realm of eternal and unchanging significance" and "experiences as part of an ongoing process of historical change" (106). While subscribing in general to this line of argument, I would like to propose a redirection of its emphasis from the thematic to the narratological. That is to say, *The House of the Seven Gables* certainly involves history, but these historical formulations are as significant in terms of what they allow Hawthorne to do with his narrative as of what they cause his characters to suffer or what they tell us about "life." I would argue that in this book history also interests Hawthorne as a means of solving narrative problems.

To begin with the most fundamental proposition, let us observe that Hawthorne's principal diegesis in the romance recounts, usually in the past tense, fictional events occurring in a fictional present. Thus, for example, the second chapter begins as follows: "It still lacked half-an-hour of sunrise, when Miss Hepzibah Pyncheon . . . arose from her solitary pillow, and began what it would be mockery to term the adornment of her person" (2:30). At times, in accord with Longinus's advice in *On the Sublime* XXV (Bate 71), the diegetic narrative shifts into the present tense to create a more dramatic effect. Thus, a few sentences further on, the narrator tells us, "There is a rustling of stiff silks; a tread of backward and forward footsteps, to-and-fro across the chamber" (2:31). By means of such familiar devices, Hawthorne recounts his characters' adventures in "the very Present that is flitting away from us."

Since the narrator requests in his preface that the reader grant the narrative "a certain latitude, both as to its fashion and material" (2:1), we might expect some elements of Hawthorne's tale to require a different narrative strategy from that revealed in the preceding examples. For example, after saying in the second paragraph of the narrative that he intends "to make short work with most of the traditionary lore" surrounding the house of Pyncheon, the narrator devotes twenty-two paragraphs (2:6–16) to recounting an event that occurred in the seventeenth century, the mysterious death of Colonel Pyncheon on the day his house was first shown to the Puritan community. In an instance of the fantastic that falls nicely between the marvelous and the uncanny, the narrator attributes this death alternatively to a curse leveled by the unjustly executed Matthew Maule (2:7) and to apoplexy (2:16). The peculiar narratological significance of the episode lies in Hawthorne's equally alternative use of documentary history and of "traditionary lore." Thus, the narrator says, "There were many rumors, some of which have vaguely drifted down to the present time," that violence was involved in the colonel's death, and that "It was averred, likewise," that an open window might have afforded escape to the murderer. However, he also adds that "it were folly to lay any stress on stories of this kind" (2:16). Since "stories of this kind" are unreliable, one might assume the greater historical authenticity of the sermon preached by the Reverend Mr. Higginson at the funeral, since the sermon is a document "which was printed and is still extant." However, because this sermon avers that the cruel and rapacious colonel died with "[h]is duties all performed" and "his race and future generations fixed on a stable basis" (2:17)—observations that the rest of the book discounts—Hawthorne effectively blocks such safe assumptions about history. The narrator further muddies the waters by observing in the same paragraph: "Tradition—which sometimes brings down truth that history has let slip, but is oftener the wild babble of the time, such as was formerly spoken at the fireside, and now congeals in newspapers—tradition is responsible for all contrary averments" (2:17). Readers seeking certainty—perhaps like the readers who will want to know nine years later whether Donatello actually had pointed ears—can't tell how much credence to place in historical testimony.

Throughout the book, Hawthorne uses similar narrative devices to subvert historical authority. The narrator says, for example, that all historical evidence for thirty years has testified to the disappearance of the Maule family: "[N]either town-record, nor grave-stone, nor the directory, nor the knowledge or memory of man, bore any trace of Matthew Maule's descendants" (2:25–26). At this early point in the narrative, the extinction of the Maules might be thematically justified as focusing the reader's attention more forcefully on how the Pyncheon past affects the Pyncheon present. In such a good cause, historical testimony might serve the narrator well. Experienced readers of romances might question the reliability of such historical evidence, however, and even translate an avowal of the family's absence as a harbinger of some later reappearance. If they did so, readers would grasp Hawthorne's intentions quite accurately. The last of the Maules, under the assumed name Holgrave, figures prominently in the narrative even though his actual identity is not revealed until the last chapter. Surely most readers have guessed Holgrave's connection to the Maules long before this revelation and have consequently also guessed that history may be an untrustworthy source of authority in this book. Another passage makes this point even more forcefully. The chapter entitled "The Pyncheon of Today" develops moral parallels between the title character, Judge Jaffrey, and the seventeenth-century colonel who may have brought a curse down on his descendants. About the latter, the narrator cites the records of "his tombstone" and "history, so far as he holds a place upon its page" concerning "the consistency and uprightness of his character." Having already detected the ironies contained in the printed version of the colonel's funeral sermon, readers might doubt the correctness of these historical records. Therefore, readers might be inclined also to discount the narrator's assurance about Judge Jaffrey that "neither clergyman, nor legal critic, nor inscriber of tombstones, nor historian of general or local politics, would venture a word against this eminent person's sincerity as a christian, or respectability as a man . . ." (2:121).

Perhaps it might be objected that Hawthorne's tone is so obviously ironic that nothing further need be said in analysis. On the other hand, it seems significant to me that, as an element of narrative strategy, these ironically discounted historical sources are immediately balanced with "traditions about the ancestor, and private diurnal gossip about the Judge, remarkably accordant in their testimony" as to both men's cruelty and corruption. The narrator clearly avows his reliance on "the woman's, the private and domestic view, of a public man" (2:121–22). The narrator might have added that this view is not only less biased by public rhetorical considerations, but is also more useful for introducing the Gothic fictional properties that contribute to perceptions of the book as a romance. An episode near the end of the book illustrates the advantages of this strategy. Until this point in the final chapter, most readers have probably assumed, on the basis of Hawthorne's sympathetic characterization, that Clifford Pyncheon did not murder his uncle and thus did not deserve to be imprisoned for thirty years. They have probably also suspected, on the basis of Hawthorne's unsympathetic characterization, that Judge Pyncheon was somehow involved in the murder. Because of Hawthorne's habitual narrative indirection, however, such suspicions have thus far been clouded with Gothic uncertainty.

Hawthorne is determined to tidy up all his loose narrative ends in this concluding chapter, however, and so he proceeds to resolve his readers' uncertainty on this score. First the narrator presents information in light of public opinion: "Whencesoever originating, there now arose a theory that undertook so to account for these circumstances as to exclude the idea of Clifford's agency [in his uncle's murder]." We may safely assume that this "theory" actually originated not with local gossip, but with Hawthorne—as did the original murder. For narratological reasons, another explanation must be offered: "Many persons affirmed, that the history and elucidation of the facts, long so mysterious, had been obtained by the Daguerreotypist [Holgrave] from one of those mesmerical seers, who, now-a-days, so strangely perplex the aspect of human affairs, and put everybody's natural vision to the blush, by the marvels which they see with their eyes shut" (2:310–11). Hawthorne's negative views on mesmerism have attracted considerable twentieth-century criticism—from Rita Gollin, for example. Even without such commentary, and even without the well-known letter (18 November 1841) in which Hawthorne warns his fiancee Sophia to keep clear of the practice (15:588–91), the heavy sarcasm of the quoted passage should alert attentive readers that mesmeric testimony is unreliable. Nevertheless, the narrator proceeds to recount what happened on the night of the uncle's murder as it was reported by Holgrave, most likely on the authority of a "mesmerical seer." At first, the testimony is hedged with narrative reservations such as the following: "Now, it is averred—but whether on authority available in a court of justice, we do not pretend to have investigated—

that the young man [Jaffrey] was tempted by the devil, one night, to search his uncle's private drawers . . ." (2:311). Soon, however, the narrator is recounting the scene with the same sort of confidence he earlier displayed when describing Hepzibah's early morning activities. Thus, we read: "With the cool hardihood, that always pertained to him, the young man continued his search of the drawers, and found a will of recent date . . ." (2:312). In such passages, Hawthorne gains "a certain latitude" to present information that suits his narrative purposes without subjecting his account to the test of a historical accuracy that he has elsewhere undermined.

By mooting the issue of historical authority in this way, Hawthorne frees himself to introduce any narrative materials he wishes into *The Seven Gables*. Sometimes fictional characters present what readers are clearly intended to regard as accurate information, as when Hepzibah says to her cousin Phoebe, "Your great, great, great, great grandmother had these cups, when she was married. . . . She was a Davenport, of a good family" (2:77). By the same token, Uncle Venner should be regarded as speaking the truth when he recalls a scene from Hepzibah's childhood: "It seems as if I saw you now; and your grandfather, with his red cloak, and his white wig, and his cocked hat, and his cane, coming out of the house, and stepping so grandly up the street!" (2:62–63). Readers are encouraged to accept that the ancestral lady *was* a Davenport, that she *was* as far removed from Phoebe historically as all the "greats" signify, and that when the ancestor came out of the house many years ago, he *was* dressed as Uncle Venner remembers. Diegetic characters are not the only sources of reliable testimony, however. At one point, the narrator authenticates his description of the miniature of Clifford painted by Malbone by writing, "It was once our good fortune to see this picture" (2:31). On another occasion, this narrator refuses to supply personal testimony concerning the uncanny cough that presages Judge Pyncheon's fantastic death, claiming that "the writer never did hear, and therefore cannot describe" (2:124) this physical symptom of a purely fictional character. A similarly qualified tone colors the narrator's presentation of the Pyncheon family's hereditary guilt over displacing the Maules: "For various reasons, however, and from impressions often too vaguely founded to be put on paper, the writer cherishes the belief that many, if not most, of the successive proprietors of this estate, were troubled with doubts as to their legal right to hold it" (2:20). In these passages, the narrator's personal authority is inflected in various ways. The final effect in all cases is approximately the same, however: the narrator succeeds in communicating fictional information to his readers as certainly as if it had "actually happened." Readers thus know what Malbone's miniature of Clifford looks like, they know that the judge may be destined for the same fate as the colonel, and they know that the Pyncheons have felt insecure in their right to the house of the seven gables, even though only the miniature is purportedly verifiable by means of historical evidence.

At other times, the narrator manipulates historical events even more aggressively, giving support to Roy Harvey Pearce's observation about this book: "History is the past in the present about to become the future" (241). As early as Chapter 10, for example, the narrator predicts what will eventually happen to Clifford: "Fate has no happiness in store for you; unless your quiet home in the old family residence, with the faithful Hepzibah, and your long summer-afternoons with Phoebe, and these Sabbath festivals with Uncle Venner and the Daguerreotypist, deserve to be called happiness!" (2:158). With the single substitution of Judge Pyncheon's beautiful country seat for the guilt-ridden house of the seven gables, this is exactly how events are developing at the end of the story. The same can be said about the narrator's predictions for Holgrave in Chapter 12: "[T]he haughty faith, with which he began life, would be well bartered for a far humbler one, at its close, in discerning that man's best-directed effort accomplishes a kind of dream, while God is the sole worker of realities" (2:180). This prophecy is also fulfilled in the concluding chapter, by which point Holgrave has given up his utopian politics as well as his vendetta against the Pyncheons in favor of a happily-ever-after marriage with Phoebe. In view of the narrator's overall plans for their futures, Clifford is never in any real danger of arrest following the judge's death, and Holgrave is never a real threat—as Mizruchi would surely agree—to the dominant economic forces of society. This narrator may prophesy so accurately because Hawthorne has placed him fully in charge of the narrative. By writing usually in the past tense, the narrator tacitly concedes that the events he is recounting have already taken place, and by entering the narrative directly, in the first person, he acknowledges that these events are controlled by him, not by the inexorable forces of history. Suspense about what is to come is therefore a mere function of the narrator's strategy, as is uncertainty about the accuracy of historical records. This is, after all, entirely a work of fiction, as the narrator freely admits in his preface.

The narrator manipulates historical testimony in particularly cavalier fashion toward the end of the book in the chapter entitled "Governor Pyncheon." This stylized piece of narrative was highly praised by Hawthorne's contemporaries, with Evert Duyckinck applauding it as exhibiting "dramatic effect of a remarkable character" (193) and Edwin Whipple calling it "a masterpiece of fantastic description" (200). For my purposes the most striking section occurs after the narrator has alluded to "stories," "tales," and a "ridiculous legend" that the ghosts of dead Pyncheons appear every midnight in the parlor where the judge sits motionless. The narrator then writes, "We are tempted to make a little sport with the idea" (2:278–79) and proceeds to describe this procession of the dead in the present tense. Since the judge marches in the procession, he assuredly is dead. So, apparently, is his only child, although this fact is not confirmed until the last chapter when "one of the Cunard steamers brought intelligence of the death, by cholera, of Judge Pyncheon's son" (2:313). After recounting the procession, the narrator writes, "The fantastic scene, just hinted at, must by no means be considered as forming an actual portion of our story" (2:281). But, of course, it does. Under the narrator's guidance, readers have not only relished the Gothic delights commended by Duyckinck and Whipple, but they have learned that the only two characters legally or realistically capable of obstructing a happy ending have been removed.

The crowning example of this narrator's play with historical authority is Chapter 13 of the romance. The premise for this section of the narrative is established at the end of Chapter 12, when Holgave tells Phoebe, "I have put an incident of the Pyncheon family-history, with which I happen to be acquainted, into the form of a legend, and mean to publish it in a magazine" (2:186). All of Chapter 13 is supposedly the "legend" that Holgrave then reads to Phoebe, printed without any surrounding quotation marks to identify it as Holgrave's dialogue, and thus carrying much the same authority as the sections proceeding directly from the narrator. Writing from a New-Critical thematic perspective in 1954, Clark Griffith condemned the chapter as "an awkward, obviously contrived flashback" (195). Writing from a narratological perspective, we can identify this section of the book as the sort of metadiegetic narrative to which Genette, in *Narrative Discourse*, attributes an "*explanatory* function" (232). Elaborating on Genette, we might say that Holgrave's fictionalized version of the "history" of Alice Pyncheon and Matthew Maule can help readers better understand the long-protracted enmity between the two families, especially how the Maules may have caused the disappearance of the Pyncheons' legal deed to a large part of Maine.

Throughout the chapter, Hawthorne creates various degrees of distance and engagement between the narrator's diegesis and Holgrave's metadiegetic narrative. In the opening chapters of *The Seven Gables*, for example, the narrator qualifies the charge of witchcraft brought against the original Matthew Maule by suggesting the superstitious character of the seventeenth-century Puritans and Colonel Pyncheon's designs on Maule's property. In his story, Holgrave writes affirmatively that Maule "had been a famous and terrible wizard, in his day" (2:188). It seems that at this distance from the principal narrative, readers can experience Gothic thrills with no more hedging from the narrator than an offset "in his day" within Holgrave's supposed text. Then Holgrave emphatically retells how Matthew Maule established his homestead in the woods and how Colonel Pyncheon legally stole it from him, even though Hawthorne's readers already know the story, having read it in the book's first chapter. Then Holgrave describes how the house has been decorated by the Pyncheon of his tale, Gervayse. The "elegant and costly style, principally from Paris" (2:193) serves to establish this Pyncheon's decadent aestheticism, a significant function of Holgrave's theme but not the narrator's.

Other details in the description serve to connect Holgrave's Pyncheon historically to his ancestor, the colonel, and his descendant, the judge, thereby furthering a thematic intention more important to the narrator than to Holgrave:

> There were two objects that appeared rather out of place in this very handsomely furnished room. One was a large map, or surveyor's plan of a tract of land, which looked as if it had been drawn a good many years ago, and was now dingy with smoke, and soiled, here and there, with the touch of fingers. The other was a portrait of a stern old man, in a Puritan garb, painted roughly, but with a bold effect, and a remarkably strong expression of character. (2:193)

These Pyncheon belongings must seem familiar to Hawthorne's readers since the narrator has described them twice already: in the first chapter, at the time of the colonel's death, and in the second, when Hepzibah first enters her kitchen. Since Holgrave's audience, Phoebe, has often seen both of these objects in Hepzibah's kitchen, she also needs little of this elaboration. How sly of the narrator, then, to have Holgrave refer to them remotely as *a* map and *a* portrait, an act of narrative distancing even more adventurous than the narrator's own in Chapter 2 when he describes *a* map but *the* portrait (2:33).

The passage suggests that even though he is a diegetic character, Holgrave shares a number of narrative practices with Hawthorne's narrator. Confirmatory evidence abounds. Just as the narrator earlier attests to the authenticity of Malbone's miniature of Clifford, so Holgrave avers that "[a] portrait of this young lady, painted by a Venetian artist and left by her father in England, is said to have fallen into the hands of the present Duke of Devonshire" (2:200–01). Unlike Hawthorne's narrator, Holgrave does not actually claim to have seen a fictional portrait, but the effect is the same as if he had. Earlier in the book, however, the narrator provides another sort of support for Holgrave's depiction of Alice when he says, on his own narrative authority, that a song composed by Alice and "written down by an amateur of music . . . was so exquisitely mournful that nobody, to this day, could bear to hear it played, unless when a great sorrow had made them know the still profounder sweetness of it" (2:84). Another bonding with Hawthorne's narrator surfaces when Holgrave relays a "wild, chimney-corner legend" (2:197) of the fantastic, and then undercuts his own narrative by agreeing that "such incredible incidents are merely to be mentioned aside" (2:198). As is the case with Hawthorne's narrative overall, it does not matter much rhetorically whether such matters are recounted "aside" or head-on: readers cannot help absorbing them. This is especially evident a few pages earlier in the metadiegetic narrative when Matthew Maule responds deviously to a request from Gervayse Pyncheon, "and it is said that a smile came over his face" (2:195). Since there were no witnesses to this encounter, the phrase "it is said" probably affords Holgrave the same sort of protection that Hawthorne's narrator seeks elsewhere when introducing similar hints of the Gothic. Holgrave attaches another disclaimer to Maule's next answer: "and again, it is said, there was a dark smile on his face" (2:195). When Maule speaks the next time, however, Holgrave apparently feels ready to forsake the protection afforded by Todorov's uncanny, because he affirms outright: "but still there was that dark smile, making a riddle of his countenance" (2:197). We may therefore assume that in Holgrave's narrative, as in Hawthorne's, the important goal is to communicate fictional material rather than to scruple over its veracity.

Holgrave's imbrication in Hawthorne's narrative strategy comes to a head in the book's concluding paragraphs. Having disclosed the deed hidden in the secret panel behind the Pyncheon portrait—which both his metadiegetic narrative and the narrator's diegesis have previously hinted at— Holgrave goes on to explain: "This is the very parchment, the attempt to recover which cost the beautiful Alice Pyncheon her happiness and life." That is to say, Holgrave's story about Matthew Maule and Alice Pyncheon is "true," all hypnotism and Gothic hocus-pocus notwithstanding. The narrator then goes on to absorb this Alice Pyncheon material into his own account with the following attribution: "said the artist, alluding to his legend" (2:316)—a "legend" actually attributable to the narrator.

A final illustration of the narrator's ventriloquial use of Holgrave can be drawn from the first paragraph of Chapter 14. Chapter 13, containing Holgrave's story of Alice Pyncheon, concludes with a paragraph on Alice's death. The next chapter begins with a sentence cast in the past tense, by which Hawthorne's narrative is returned to the fictionalized present. Then the narrator says Holgrave "now observed that a certain remarkable drowsiness (wholly unlike that with which the reader possibly feels himself affected) had been flung over the senses of his auditress" (2:211). Instead of taking advantage of this psychological vulnerability by mesmerizing Phoebe, Holgrave wakes her up. Critics intent on thematizing Hawthorne's fiction can cite this episode as evidence that Holgrave understands the proper relations of the heart and the head and thus proves himself deserving of a happy ending. In the words of Richard H. Millington, for example, "Holgrave's refusal to claim Phoebe as his erotic property or the object of his dominion . . . provokes an endorsement of his character that carries the full authority of [the] narrator . . ." (140). In terms of the argument I am pursuing, however, the passage is significant primarily for the metalepsis by which the narrator ironically establishes parallels between Phoebe's experience and that of Hawthorne's readers. Like postmodern, metafictional writers, Hawthorne displays great variety in the poses he gives his narrator throughout the book and even greater variety in the acts of authentication performed by the narrator and his diegetic characters. History, documentation, rumor, superstition, conjecture, repetition with difference, metadiegesis, and interventions by the narrator—all of these are directed toward the single end of getting Hawthorne's story told. These narratological pyrotechnics on Hawthorne's part are directed not to deconstructing his readers' epistemological relations to their everyday lives, as some ingenious critics have maintained, but to engaging their rhetorical participation in his act of imagination. Mepleptically recognizing his readers' place in this endeavor can thus be seen as merely facing the central facts of literary discourse.

Critical discussions ranging from Evert Duyckinck's 1851 review of *The Seven Gables* to Evan Carton's *The Rhetoric of American Romance* (1985) have approached Hawthorne's preface to this book primarily in terms of its distinction between the novel and the romance. This critical focus is understandable, since issues of genre drew Hawthorne's editorial commentary throughout his career. However, this preface may also be considered in terms of its contribution to the author's narrative strategy. When Hawthorne refers to some audience in the preface as "the Reader," he is establishing a mutual complicity that will continue throughout the following narrative. In this rhetorical compact, the writer's obligation is to get the story into the reader's imagination by any means possible. The reader's role, specified in relation to the tale's "legendary mist," is to believe the story as much as possible while it is being told. Thus, Hawthorne's entire narrative, whether designated as legendary mist, traditionary lore, dream, the vision of a mesmerical seer, metadiegetic narrative, or documented history, is presented so that the reader, "according to his pleasure, may either disregard, or allow it to float almost imperceptibly about the characters and events, for the sake of a picturesque effect" (2:2). The ultimate issue is thus not whether any event actually happened as Hawthorne reports it but rather whether readers are willing to grant the event credence while they are reading. In this light, the issue of whether any event in the book is historically documented or merely invented out of thin air may be seen from a narratological perspective to be finally—and surprisingly—irrelevant.

SIX

# Narrative Transformations of Romanticism

My argument in the previous chapter was that Hawthorne deliberately appropriated and transformed the elements of history—in which he had considerable interest and personal involvement—to create problematic fictional narratives available to repeated reevaluation and interpretation. In creating other fictional works, Hawthorne freely exploited more contemporary materials including the semiotics, ideology, and literary structures central to his own mid-nineteenth-century culture—once again despite whatever attraction these romantic properties exercised on Hawthorne the man. In this respect, larger thematic narrative elements including historical events and romantic ideology can be seen to function analogously with the smaller narratological elements of verb tenses and personal pronouns as forces useful for destabilizing reader responses. When confronting these larger elements of Hawthorne's narratives, our natural tendency as readers is to interpret organically, to select the more "correct" alternative. As George Haggerty wisely concludes, "It is the nature of Hawthorne's affective form . . . to create an indeterminacy that encourages closure in private and personal terms" (109). Even while recognizing this tendency, it is still possible simply to recognize the presence of two or more contending choices. Insofar as I am able, therefore, I will attempt to defer interpretive closure in favor of tracking some instances in which Hawthorne both solicits conventional romantic responses from his readers and problematizes them.

It is unsurprising that Hawthorne incorporated contemporary as well as historical materials into his narratives, since the first admonition given to apprentice writers of fiction is that they should write about what they know.

However, Hawthorne rejected absolute realism, the most obvious strategy for fulfilling this literary program, as he explains in the preface to his most patently contemporary longer work of fiction, *The Blithedale Romance*. Having conceded that "many readers will probably suspect a faint and not very faithful shadowing of BROOK FARM" in Hawthorne's depiction of the Blithedale commune, the preface continues:

> The Author does not wish to deny, that he had this Community in his mind, and that (having had the good fortune, for a time, to be personally connected with it) he has occasionally availed himself of his actual reminiscences, in the hope of giving a more lifelike tint to the fancy-sketch in the following pages. He begs it to be understood, however, that he has considered the Institution itself as not less fairly the subject of fictitious handling, than the imaginary personages whom he has introduced there. (3:1)

That is to say, Hawthorne will write directly and realistically about contemporary culture when this approach seems most useful, and he will transform these materials imaginatively when that strategy seems more immediately appropriate.

In a similarly mixed formula, Hawthorne explains in the preface to *The House of the Seven Gables* that, although "The Reader may perhaps choose to assign an actual locality to the imaginary events of this narrative," the author would prefer that "the book . . . be read strictly as a Romance, having a great deal more to do with the clouds overhead, than with any portion of the actual soil of the County of Essex" (2:3). Both prefaces insist that, despite any reader's desire for unmixed realistic depiction, realism will constitute only one element of Hawthorne's narratives. These narratological discussions in Hawthorne's prefaces furnish the materials upon which the generic critics cited in my first chapter develop their theories about Hawthorne's theory of romance. From my perspective, these discussions are also interesting in what they reveal about how Hawthorne approaches his readers' attitudes toward contemporary materials.

As was true of history, moreover, no matter how much or how little autobiographical significance some element of contemporary culture might represent, Hawthorne accords it authority in his fiction primarily as his immediate narrative strategy requires. Hawthorne was, in this sense, simultaneously a highly aware participant in the romantic culture of his time and an exploiter of its dearest beliefs in the service of narrative effect. In some fictional works, Hawthorne both dramatizes and undermines contemporary attitudes toward natural symbols. In other works, he exploits and challenges his contemporaries' confidence in the inevitability of progress. Elsewhere, he imitates through parody the popular narrative structure of the romantic quest. As was true of the more narrowly technical experiments considered in earlier chapters, Hawthorne's adoption of this complex approach creates thematic ambiguity. D. H. Lawrence speaks for many when he writes: "That blue-eyed darling Nathaniel knew disagreeable things in his inner soul. He was careful to send them out in disguise" (83). At the same time, these strategies also allowed Hawthorne to continue writing originally about subjects that might appear to have been exhausted by other writers.

A fundamental doctrine of many mid-nineteenth-century American writers was a belief in the symbolic authority of nature. In 1836 Ralph Waldo Emerson enunciated a theory of symbol in his first book, Nature, that retained its validity through much of the century: "Particular natural facts are symbols of particular spiritual facts" (31). In consequence, as he later explains, "To the wise . . . a fact is true poetry, and the most beautiful of fables" (55). In illustration of this doctrine, Emerson's poetry and prose during the 1830s and 1840s—the decades in which Hawthorne was writing his tales and sketches—are filled with particular natural facts directing attention onward and upward to the inspiring spiritual facts of truth, beauty, and unity. Gertrude Reif Hughes observes about this transcendental practice: "The relationship between affirmation and confirmation is subtle. . . . Temporally of course, affirmation comes first. Without affirmation there can exist no confirmation, for where nothing has been projected nothing can be verified" (xi). In the work of Hawthorne's contemporaries, optimistic assumptions so often authorized symbolic literary confirmations that readers might easily assume an inescapable causal relationship. Even today, we can hardly ignore the rhetorical force of this symbolic equation when reading these works.

In 1849 Emerson appended to Nature a verse epigraph that captures both the semiotics and the teleological metaphysic of contemporary romanticism. The poem concludes: "[S]triving to be man, the worm / Mounts through all the spires of form" (21). To the optimistic romantic imagination, this representation of the worm's successful efforts to evolve can stand as an emblem of the soul's quest for spiritual transcendence. Emerson's verse narrative of a worm's ascent therefore articulates an act of great romantic faith, even if symbolically displaced to what some might consider a trivial level of experience. Emerson reveals little discomfort with this possible discrepancy, however, as is clear in another passage from *Nature*: "In their primary sense these are trivial facts, but we repeat them for the value of their analogical import" (35); and what the worm analogically represents is spiritual progress.

Such literary appropriations of the natural world do not indicate merely a private inclination of Emerson's. Throughout *Walden*, Henry David Thoreau shows his agreement with this program by using imagery drawn from nature to validate romantic optimism. Thus in the chapter "The Bean-Field," Thoreau identifies his literary purpose in undertaking this physical exercise: "[S]ome must work in fields if only for the sake of tropes and expression" (142). Such natural tropes abound in *Walden*. In a brilliantly metaphorical explanation of metaphor, Thoreau writes about animals that "they are all beasts of burden, in a sense, made to carry some portion of our thoughts" (189). One such animal, reminiscent of Emerson's striving worm, is the grub, which functions successfully in two metaphorical capacities. First the grub serves as an illustration during Thoreau's lecture on etymological evolution: "Thus, also, you pass from the lumpish grub in the earth to the airy and fluttering butterfly. The very globe continually transcends and translates itself, and becomes winged in its orbit" (247). Physical transcendence is suggested as the tenor. Second and more significantly, the grub functions as the first stage in a process intended to symbolize the evolution of consciousness that Thoreau sees as the ultimate goal of all naturalistic study: "The perch swallows the grub-worm, the pickerel swallows the perch, and the fisherman swallows the pickerel; and so all the chinks in the scale of being are filled" (231). In one sense, the most striking facet of this literary exercise is Thoreau's refusal to develop the process logically into a completed circle. Shakespeare or Marvell could not resist concluding the anecdote with the fisherman's death and subsequent return to the earth and the grub-worm. The symbolic strategy of American romanticism is unlikely to turn in this ironic direction, however, as readers are well aware.

Hawthorne's narrators frequently problematize the rhetorical assumptions implicit in this symbolic system. In *The Scarlet Letter*, for example, the narrator ironically explains that "nothing was more common" among the American Puritans "than to interpret all meteoric appearances, and other natural phenomena, that occurred with less regularity than the rise and set of sun and moon, as so many revelations from a supernatural source" (1:154). Comments of this sort are, of course, valuable to critics investigating Hawthorne's attitudes toward Puritanism or toward the exceptionality of American democracy. At the same time, the narrator's reservations may also be aptly applied to the interpretive dispositions of Hawthorne's romantic contemporaries. At this point in *The Scarlet Letter*, the narrator raises the issue of Puritanical interpretation primarily to contextualize Arthur Dimmesdale's conviction that a meteor has just signified across the sky his concealed adultery. The narrator continues:

> We impute it, therefore, solely to the disease in his own eye and heart, that the minister, looking upward to the zenith, beheld there the appearance of an immense letter,—the letter A,—marked out in lines of dull red light. Not but the meteor may have shown itself at that point, burning duskily through a veil of cloud; but with no such shape as his guilty imagination gave it; or, at least, with so little definiteness, that another's guilt might have seen another symbol in it. (1:155)

This narrator insists that when fictional characters engage in interpretation, the results are highly subjective. The sexton therefore explains to Dimmesdale at the end of this chapter how the members of his congregation have otherwise deciphered the same natural fact: "[W]e interpret [the meteor] to stand for Angel. For, as our good Governor Winthrop was made an angel this past night, it was doubtless held fit that there should be some notice thereof" (1:158). These contradictory interpretations surely problematize Dimmesdale's private interpretation within Hawthorne's narrative. At the same time, the interpretive conflicts may suggest why later critics have discovered so many metaphorical tenors for the scarlet letter.

Hawthorne also exploits his contemporaries' fondness for symbolic interpretation in his seldom-discussed tale "The Great Stone Face." At first glance, this material seems particularly suited to a transcendental treatment since its plot as well as its title is derived from a sublime freak of nature whose spiritual significance depends entirely on human perception. According to the narrator, the Great Stone Face seemed, "when viewed at a proper distance, precisely to resemble the features of the human countenance" (11:27), thus affording an opportunity for the kind of symbolic interpretation practiced by Hawthorne's Concord neighbors. Hawthorne complicates the process, however, when the narrator adds: "True it is, that if the spectator approached too near, he lost the outline of the gigantic visage, and could discern only a heap of ponderous and gigantic rocks, piled in chaotic ruin one upon another." According to the narrator, any resemblance between a human being and these rocks is probably more coincidental than profoundly spiritual, since the formation is merely "a work of Nature in her mood of majestic playfulness" (11:27). As this explanation implies, the natural facts in this tale have been carefully preselected by the author to make the whole issue of interpretation problematic. If the rocks do represent a face, "It seemed as if an enormous giant, or a Titan, had sculptured his own likeness on the precipice." In other words, the natural sign would have been produced by another product of human imagination rather than by the tutelary genius of unmediated nature. Furthermore, the Great Stone Face may be seen to affect nature, rather than vice versa: "According to the belief of many people, the valley owed much of its fertility to this benign aspect that was continually beaming over it, illuminating the clouds, and infusing its tenderness into the sunshine" (11:27). Throughout the introductory paragraphs, Hawthorne's narrator insists on the effects of human consciousness. The implication is that the villagers see in natural facts what they expect to see, that their ideas precede their experiences of nature. As Larzer Ziff says in *Literary Democracy: The Declaration of Cultural Independence in America*, Hawthorne "treats the sky, forest, and river as impersonal carriers of messages projected by the beholder, not those sent down from a higher reality" (145).

The narrator's description of the tale's setting also stresses human intervention rather than primal nature:

> Embosomed amongst a family of lofty mountains, there was a valley so spacious that it contained many thousand inhabitants. Some of these good people dwelt in log huts, with the black forest all around them, on the steep and difficult hill-sides. Others had their homes in comfortable farm-

houses, and cultivated the rich soil on the gentle slopes or level surfaces of the valley. Others, again, were congregated into populous villages, where some wild, highland rivulet, tumbling down from its birth-place in the upper mountain region, had been caught and tamed by human cunning, and compelled to turn the machinery of cotton factories. (11:26).

These people do not live in an unspoiled natural environment charged with spiritual truth. Even apart from the agriculture and manufacturing, the narrator's description emphasizes human agency and creativity. These villagers probably do not live even in New England, but in a story book. The narrator's vocabulary—"good people," "gentle slopes," "highland rivulet"—clearly signals a chronotope of pastoralism rather than of realism.

Another element in the tale shows Hawthorne's transformation of another contemporary belief. The central character, aptly named Ernest, is one of nature's noblemen, somewhat like William Wordsworth's shepherd, Michael. Ernest spends his whole life in this pastoral valley, working conscientiously at simple agricultural tasks and meditating constantly on the primary natural fact in the story. Although "Ernest had had no teacher, save only that the Great Stone Face became one to him" (11:29), he nevertheless becomes wise and good. Eventually wise men flock to Ernest because "the report had gone abroad that this simple husbandman had ideas unlike those of other men, not gained from books, but of a higher tone—a tranquil and familiar majesty, as if he had been talking with the angels as his daily friends" (11:42). In this light, the tale seems compatible with contemporary romantic thinking about nature and natural imagery. Since Hawthorne is not Wordsworth—or Emerson or Thoreau—the experiences of his natural man often run contrary to expectations. At one point, after his great spiritual development has taken place, Ernest gazes at the source of his wisdom and "could hardly believe but that a smile beamed over the whole visage, with a radiance still brightening, although without motion of the lips." Since the object of Ernest's perception is a rock formation, the narrator is surely correct in noting that there is no movement of the lips, but even this qualification is insufficient. The narrator goes on to insist that, in any case, Ernest's perception should be understood as uncanny rather than marvelous: "It was probably the effect of the western sunshine, melting through the thinly diffused vapors that had swept between him and the object that he gazed at" (11:37). Thus, even while creating a character perfectly suited to interpret natural facts according to the prevailing romantic mode, Hawthorne cannot help problematizing the issue.

Since the tale is about interpreting natural facts, its very few incidents all hinge on the villagers' acceptance of the Great Stone Face as a sign that some great man will eventually come to their valley. The narrator questions this interpretation first of all by presenting the view of those who "had seen more of the world, had watched and waited till they were weary, and had beheld no man with such a face, nor any man that proved to be much greater or nobler than his neighbors." These people have come to the conclusion that the prophecy is "nothing but an idle tale" (11:28). Despite all their worldly experience, these folk may be mistaken, and yet the plot's unfolding tends to support rather than contradict their view. As the tale develops, the narrator satirizes the gullibility and foolish optimism of the less-traveled characters as they perceive the fulfillment of the prophecy in the successive arrivals of Mr. Gathergold, a rich merchant; General Blood-and-Thunder, a military hero; Old Stony Phiz, an eminent statesman; and a great poet. They are mistaken in each case, but unschooled by their errors, they continue to await the desired event as if practicing some form of Emersonian optimism.

The only hope that this tale might achieve romantic closure lies in Ernest's moral superiority to the other characters. In a negative sense, Ernest's great simplicity of heart enables him eventually to understand that none of the four claimants can be accepted as the long-awaited great man. In a positive sense, Ernest's mode of life eventually establishes an Emersonian connection among his deeds and words. As the narrator says, Ernest's "words had power, because they accorded with his thoughts, and his thoughts had reality and depth, because they harmonized with the life which he had always lived" (11:47). In the writings of most citizens of Concord, this passage would probably inspire a narrative in which Ernest correctly interprets for his neighbors the spiritual facts underlying the facts of their natural environment. Hawthorne rejects this plot development, however. Ernest believes in the prophecy of a great man's coming as devotedly as do his gullible neighbors: "Though more than once disappointed, as we have seen, he had such a hopeful and confiding nature, that he was always ready to believe in whatever seemed beautiful and good" (11:39).

Although he is never fooled for long, Ernest initially accepts the candidacy of each claimant and is bitterly disappointed each time. His spiritual growth has done little to replace his illusions or to guarantee the validity of his interpretations of natural facts.

Ironically enough, by the end of the tale, Ernest's virtues have transformed him into the great man. He has come to resemble the Great Stone Face himself. The narrator observes that, even if Ernest has become the Great Stone Face, Ernest cannot perceive the resemblance. The tale's last paragraph insists on this irony rather than on the Emersonian perfection of Ernest's preaching:

> Then all the people looked, and saw that what the deep-sighted poet said was true. The prophecy was fulfilled. But Ernest, having finished what he had to say, took the poet's arm, and walked slowly homeward, still hoping that some wiser and better man than himself would by-and-by appear, bearing a resemblance to the GREAT STONE FACE. (11:48)

The beauties of nature are emphasized in this tale, as they might be in conventional romantic writing. One of nature's noblemen is celebrated. The possibility of natural-supernatural correspondences is raised. In the end, though, it is uncertain whether the natural facts in this tale actually signify spiritual facts; if they do so signify, these spiritual facts are not very sunny.

As "The Great Stone Face" suggests, Hawthorne was willing to transform his contemporaries' fondest images and ideas into fictional materials. One idea usually unquestioned by these contemporaries was the inevitability of material or spiritual progress. In recognition of this belief, Hawthorne's fiction often represents romantic aspiration in terms compatible with the writing of Emerson and Thoreau. Hester Prynne maintains a "firm belief, that, at some brighter period, when the world should have grown ripe for it . . . a new truth would be revealed, in order to establish the whole relation between man and woman on a surer ground of mutual happiness" (1:263). Despite all his Prufrockian quibbles, Miles Coverdale can still affirm some sort of optimism: "Yet, after all, let us acknowledge it wiser, if not more sagacious, to follow out one's day-dream to its natural consummation . . ." (3:10). Perhaps most impressively, in *The House of the Seven Gables*, the narrator applauds Holgrave's conviction that "we are not doomed to creep on forever in the old, bad way, but that, this very now, there are harbingers abroad of a golden era, to be accomplished in his own lifetime" (2:179). When Hawthorne's narrators provide romantic affirmations of this sort, however, they nearly always qualify them by offering the reader a statement of conservative skepticism. Hester realizes that she will not live to see the hoped-for day on which sexual inequality disappears. Similarly, Coverdale reflects: ". . . although, if the vision have been worth the having, it is certain never to be consummated otherwise than by a failure" (3:10–11). Holgrave moves to the country to found a rural dynasty. Through the tension between these two forces, Hawthorne consistently destabilizes the belief in inevitable progress central to contemporary romanticism, leaving the issue open to further literary investigation—and also to later critical argument.

Hawthorne's complex strategy may be seen in a series of passages that carefully balance affirmations and qualifications. In the first chapter of *The Scarlet Letter*, the narrator explains: "The founders of a new colony, whatever Utopia of human virtue and happiness they might originally project, have invariably recognized it among their earliest practical necessities to allot a portion of the virgin soil as a cemetery, and another portion as the site of a prison" (1:47). The sentence epitomizes Hawthorne's practice of juxtaposing the idealistic and the pragmatic: "Utopia" and "practical necessities." An equally illuminating example is the passage in which Coverdale explains the unlikelihood of establishing "Paradise" in "our bleak little world of New England": "Nor, with such materials as were at hand, could the most skilful architect have constructed any better imitation of Eve's bower, than might be seen in the snow-hut of an Esquimaux" (3:9–10).

"The New Adam and Eve," first published in 1843 and then included in *Mosses from an Old Manse*, provides an extended treatment of this ideological tension. This tale provides two characters a chance to act out the fantasies of romantic reformers: to begin all over, this time in keeping with man's "true" nature rather than under the influence of "the old, bad way"—those social institutions that reformers held responsible for the defects of modern life. In this tale there are no jaded world travelers, no cynics, no merchants, politicians, or generals to spoil the experiment by reminding the pair of age-old practices or historic unhappiness. In the opening paragraphs, human potential seems so great that Adam and Eve expect apotheosis. Hawthorne's narrator is less optimistic:

In the energy of new life, it appears no such impracticable feat to climb
into the sky! But they have already received a woful lesson, which may
finally go far towards reducing them to the level of the departed race, when
they acknowledge the necessity of keeping the beaten track of earth.
(10:250)

Many critics—from Chester E. Eisinger in 1954 to Milton R. Stern in
1991—have argued that the beaten track is Hawthorne's recommended
path through life. This thematic approach to Hawthorne has always seemed
sensible to me, striking a middle course between idealism and conservatism. As I have been arguing previously, however, I believe that it is also
useful to watch how Hawthorne lays down this track, especially how he
qualifies contemporary romantic thinking in the process.

Like many modern Utopian and dystopian fantasies, Hawthorne's specu-
lative tale is set just following the near-extinction of the world. The sketch
has as its premise not a war or a natural disaster, but the prophecy of Father
William Miller that the world would end in 1843. Here is a wonderful
chance to convert both the Millerites, who professed an imminent end to
time, and contemporary optimists, who professed an endlessly expanding
future, into narrative materials. The first sentence establishes the tale's thesis: "We, who are born into the world's artificial system, can never adequately know how little in our present state and circumstances is natural,
and how much is merely the interpolation of the perverted mind and heart
of man" (10:247). "We," in company with Hawthorne's narrator, are therefore free to investigate the romantic distinction between what ought to be
and what exists merely as a result of social expediency. Adam and Eve
quickly discover for us that social pressures cannot be easily ignored, even
in Utopia. Their first step down the beaten track requires them to recognize
and accept the external world. At the beginning, they are "content with an
inner sphere which they inhabit together." Soon, though, "they feel the
invincible necessity of this earthly life, and begin to make acquaintance
with the objects and circumstances that surround them" (10:248–49). If
even Adam and Eve, alone in the universe, cannot exist within their own
sphere, it is highly problematic whether a citizen of Concord might hope
to fulfill Emerson's injunction in the stirring conclusion to *Nature*:

Build therefore your own world. As fast as you conform your life to the
pure idea in your mind, that will unfold its great proportions. A correspon-

dent revolution in things will attend the influx of the spirit. So fast will disagreeable appearances, swine, spiders, snakes, pests, mad-houses, prisons, enemies, vanish; they are temporary and shall be no more seen. (56)

By taking seriously Emerson's question "Why should not we also enjoy an original relation to the universe?" (21), "The New Adam and Eve" both dramatizes and undermines such romantic optimism.

One impediment confronting Hawthorne's fictional pair is the powerful force of gender roles. In an uninhabited mansion, the only woman in the world soon experiences very conventional feelings:

> Eve ransacks a work-basket, and instinctively thrusts the rosy tip of her finger into a thimble. She takes up a piece of embroidery, glowing with mimic flowers, in one of which a fair damsel of the departed race has left her needle. . . . Eve feels almost conscious of the skill to finish it. . . . Passing through a dark entry, they find a broom behind a door; and Eve, who comprises the whole nature of womanhood, has a dim idea that it is an instrument proper for her hand. (10:257–58)

Later Adam intuits his true "maleness" in the abandoned library at Harvard. Just as Eve is instinctively attracted to her broom, so Adam's masculine intellectual curiosity is naturally roused by a book: "He stands poring over the regular columns of mystic characters, seemingly in studious mood; for the unintelligible thought upon the page has a mysterious relation to his mind, and makes itself felt, as if it were a burthen flung upon him" (10:264). Eve does not begin to sew and sweep, and she manages to drag Adam out of the library before he learns to read. The tale suggests, however, that contemporary social practices are not the only forces postponing the arrival of Utopia.

It is crucial at this point to distinguish the narrative strategies of tale writing from the imperatives of social responsibility. In *The Art of Authorial Presence*, G. R. Thompson warns against "the purely formal naivete of certain critical assertions about the univocal narrators of Hawthorne's fictions and the congruence or identity of Hawthorne's early narrators with Hawthorne" (37). The warning might also be appropriately raised here. "The New Adam and Eve" forces its characters into familiar gender roles. It does not necessarily follow, however, that the author of "The New Adam and Eve" believed only these roles appropriate to all men and women. Hawthorne's characters Hester Prynne, Miriam Schaefer, and Zenobia do not hold such restricted views of gender roles. Hawthorne's wife, Sophia, and her sister Elizabeth thought of gender in broader terms, as did their friend Margaret Fuller. We might assume that there was sufficient stimulus in Hawthorne's environment for him to write tales showing women happily fulfilling other roles—if not to illustrate his deepest convictions, at least to accommodate an important element of contemporary ideology. On the other hand, there was probably also sufficient stimulus for him to resist the influence of advanced thinkers and to side with the conservatives—again, if not to illustrate his deepest convictions, at least to write against the current grain. In any event, the issue under consideration is not what Hawthorne believed but how he manipulated the narrative materials available to him.

One form of manipulation involves the equation of narrative inevitability with social determinism. Hawthorne's strategy is clear when the narrator considers what might have happened if Eve had not been able to lure Adam away from his study:

> Happy influence of woman! Had he lingered there long enough to obtain a clue to its treasures,—as was not impossible, his intellect being of human structure, indeed, but with an untransmitted vigor and acuteness,—had he then and there become a student, the annalist of our poor world would soon have recorded the downfall of a second Adam. (10:265)

The implication is that Adam would have systematically gone about reestablishing the institutions of contemporary society simply because his studies would inevitably lead him to projective reasoning and social organization. Adam does not get a chance to re-create these social evils in the tale. Even so, this nonevent seriously challenges the romantic optimism of Hawthorne's contemporaries—whether or not Hawthorne actually believed in progress. In such cases, whether the subject is a Utopian project or an individual quest for fulfillment, Hawthorne's fiction often challenges contemporary orthodoxy by presenting a disjunction between desire and experience, as in "The New Adam and Eve," rather than a romantic unity of the two. His narrators draw their wit from an affectation of surprise that after so many centuries of human history, people still attempt to ignore this discrepancy.

"The Lily's Quest," a simple tale first published in 1839 and then added to the second edition of *Twice-told Tales*, provides a direct illustration. The plot sends an allegorically named young couple, Adam Forrester and Lily Fay, in search of the perfect piece of land on which to build their dream house. Natural facts signal their initial anticipations of success: "[T]here all pure delights were to cluster like roses among the pillars of the edifice, and blossom ever new and spontaneously" (9:442). Throughout the tale, however, the narrator views this youthful optimism with an amused tolerance that forces readers to suspect a dichotomy between desire and possibility. After the young lovers have been forced to abandon three promising sites because each has been emotionally polluted by earlier human sufferings, the narrator observes: "They set forth again, young Pilgrims on that quest which millions—which every child of Earth—has tried in turn." Establishing the pattern that will be thoroughly examined by R. W. B. Lewis in *The American Adam* a century later, the narrator then questions whether this lovely and loving couple can transcend the limits of earlier generations: "And were the Lily and her lover to be more fortunate than all those millions?" (9:446). Are they—in Lewis's words—"to be acknowledged in [their] complete emancipation from the history of mankind" (41)? Unhappily, they are not. The spot they finally select conceals, unbeknownst to them, an ancient cemetery. Lily dies there as so many have before, and her dream house becomes her tomb. To soften this bitter conclusion, Hawthorne's narrator brings the grieving Adam to accept mortality and to express a faith in immortality. Adam's final speech affirms that transcendence will be achieved: "On a Grave be the site of our Temple; and now our happiness is for Eternity!" (9:450). Contrary to most readers' desires, however, this triumph will take place only in another world, after death. Hawthorne's narrator affirms that Adam and Lily pursue the highest goals with the highest hearts for the highest motives, but he frustrates them even so. As is often the case in Hawthorne's fiction, furthermore, natural facts serve as both signs and agents of the gap between optimistic projection and achievement.

Dualistic tales of this sort contributed greatly to Herman Melville's judgment of Hawthorne, expressed in a letter written in 1851:

> There is the grand truth about Nathaniel Hawthorne. He says NO! in thunder; but the Devil himself cannot make him say *yes*. For all men who say

*yes*, lie; and all men who say *no*,—why, they are in the happy condition of judicious, unencumbered travellers in Europe; they cross the frontiers into Eternity with nothing but a carpet-bag,—that is to say, the Ego. Whereas those *yes*-gentry, they travel with heaps of baggage, and, damn them! they will never get through the Custom House. (125)

Today, most critics of nineteenth-century American literature would probably endorse Melville's view, because anyone alternately reading the works of Hawthorne and Emerson—for example—cannot help but recognize two very different literary sensibilities at work on two very different thematic projects. I wish to reassert that the differences are not only thematic: they can be traced through Hawthorne's narrative strategies as well as through the patterns of thought created by these strategies.

Hawthorne's plot structures often make this clear. As the plot of "The Lily's Quest" suggests, Hawthorne sometimes uses simple quest narratives to reinflect contemporary romantic thinking. M. H. Abrams's *Natural Supernaturalism* supplies a helpful context for Hawthorne's experiments by exhaustively analyzing quests for spiritual significance in the works of many European romantic writers. According to Abrams, the basic narrative pattern adopted by both literary and philosophical writers of the time may be represented as follows:

> [T]he most apt and available vehicle was the traditional one of the history of mankind as a circuitous journey back home. So represented, the protagonist is the collective mind or consciousness of men, and the story is that of its painful pilgrimage through difficulties, sufferings, and recurrent disasters in quest of a goal which, unwittingly, is the place it had left behind when it first set out and which, when reachieved, turns out to be even better than it had been at the beginning. (191)

Abrams easily supplies illustrations of this psychomachia from the writings of G. W. F. Hegel, F. W. J. von Schelling, S. T. Coleridge, and Thomas Carlyle. Since, according to Abrams, "The chief antecedent of this narrative form is the Christian allegory of the journey of life" (193), we might also assume Hawthorne's candidacy for the list, in light of his pronounced fondness for the works of Edmund Spenser and John Bunyan. In fact, Hawthorne's fiction shows both his involvement in this world-historical imaginative project and his transformations of its elements to suit his own narrative purposes.

Typical of Hawthorne's approach is the narrator's ironic description, in "Passages from a Relinquished Work," of how he initiated his own quest: "Never was Childe Harold's sentiment adopted in a spirit more unlike his own." Another typically parodic note is struck when this narrator continues: "Naturally enough, I thought of Don Quixote" (10:410). Usually, Hawthorne's romantic questers attain much less distance from their own enterprises than this highly fictionalized narrator exhibits, and so it falls to the undifferentiated narrator to ridicule the quest and its hero for unreasonable assumptions about the malleability of existence. The plot that appeals most strongly to Hawthorne is not, then, the romantic quest that terminates in the hero's psychic unity, but the ironic quest that terminates in making the hero, as Northrop Frye says in "The Archetypes of Literature," "a prey to [the] frustration and weakness" that blight everyday existence (18). I suspect that the principal appeal of this structure for Hawthorne probably lay in the tonal and emotional variety that it provided narratives such as "The Threefold Destiny," "Wakefield," and "Ethan Brand."

In "The Threefold Destiny," Hawthorne presents an ironic quest schematically, without the displacement required in his more realistic tales. According to the narrator—perhaps the Ashley Allen Royce identified as the author when the tale first appeared in *American Monthly Magazine* in 1838—the tale is actually "a Faery Legend":

> Rather than a story of events claiming to be real, it may be considered as an allegory, such as the writers of the last century would have expressed in the shape of an eastern tale, but to which I have endeavored to give a more life-like warmth than could be infused into those fanciful productions. (9:472).

As Luther Luedtke explains (128–32), Hawthorne's mention of the eastern tale serves to justify the introduction of all sorts of romantic exoticism: Hindostan, Spain, Arabia, Turkey, the Arctic. The reader suspects that "The Threefold Destiny" is intended primarily as a literary exercise. Therefore, as Frye proposes in "Myth, Fiction, and Displacement" (27–29), structure may take prominence—here, the forthright structure of a circle.

The hero of this quest, Ralph Cranfield, left his native New England village many years ago to search throughout the world for a treasure, a position of "extensive influence and sway over his fellow-creatures" (9:474), and a beautiful woman. As the tale opens, he returns to the village frustrated, soon to discover the treasure to be his boyhood home, the position of influence to be master of the village school, and the beautiful woman to be his childhood sweetheart, Faith Egerton. In a sense, this tale has a happy ending because Cranfield does find his destiny in life, and—more significantly in light of the issues discussed in Chapter 7—he has hope of domestic salvation. Even so, the ironies of the tale are striking. Since everything Cranfield sought was available to him in the same form before his departure, his "long and remote travel" (9:472) has been a futile quest. This moral is stated explicitly in the narrator's concluding remarks:

> Would all, who cherish such wild wishes, but look around them, they would oftenest find their sphere of duty, of prosperity, and happiness, within those precincts and in that station where Providence itself has cast their lot. Happy they who read the riddle without a weary world-search, or a lifetime spent in vain! (9:482)

Cranfield is spared the more devastating consequences of his "wild wishes" in that his whole "lifetime" has not been "spent in vain," merely the years of his young manhood in which he pursued his "weary world-search." Throughout the tale, though, Hawthorne uses devices that might be redirected to scathing ridicule by the slightest change of emphasis.

The narrator presents the inspiration for Cranfield's quest in terms that subtly discount its wisdom in advance. He says first that "Ralph Cranfield, from his youth upward, had felt himself marked out for a high destiny." Readers may accept this information univocally if they choose, because the stress on "felt himself" is so slight. The next sentence forecloses a univocal reading, however, and invites readers to share the narrator's amused scorn of Cranfield's design:

> He had imbibed the idea—we say not whether it were revealed to him by witchcraft, or in a dream of prophecy, or that his brooding fancy had palmed its own dictates upon him as the oracles of a Sybil—but he had imbibed the idea, and held it firmest among his articles of faith, that three marvellous events of his life were to be confirmed to him by three signs. (9:473)

The discrepancy here between the "high destiny" of the previous sentence and the judgmental terms "imbibed" and "palmed . . . upon him" creates an ironic context that shadows the narrator's subsequent treatment of Cranfield's "destiny." Because of this context, the narrator is able to dispense with the quest itself in three sentences of deflation:

> With this proud fate before him, in the flush of his imaginative youth, Ralph Cranfield had set forth to seek the maid, the treasure, and the venerable sage, with his gift of extended empire. And had he found them? Alas! it was not with the aspect of a triumphant man, who had achieved a nobler destiny than all his fellows, but rather with the gloom of one struggling against peculiar and continual adversity, that he now passed homeward to his mother's cottage. (9:475)

The commonplace terminus of this quest—"his mother's cottage"—epitomizes the disproportion of Cranfield's world-wide search for significance. A few sentences later the narrator underscores this point by stressing the inconsequence of these efforts: "There had been few changes in the village . . ." (9:475). That is to say, Cranfield's effect on the world, great and small, has been nil, and his adventure has been circular rather than an evolutionary movement toward a "higher good."

About midpoint in the tale, Cranfield begins to think about his life in more down-to-earth terms. As he is preparing to enter his mother's cottage after so many years' absence, he sees on a tree in the front yard something resembling the sign that was to have marked the treasure he has sought. He reflects, "Now a credulous man . . . might suppose that the treasure which I have sought round the world, lies buried, after all, at the very door of my mother's dwelling. That would be a jest indeed!" (9:476). That would be, in fact, the jest that Hawthorne intends here, a joke he often used to undermine the pretensions of the romantic quest. In this case, the severity of the joke is benignly muted. Although Cranfield is exposed as an egotistical fool, he is not humiliated by the narrator as many of Hawthorne's protagonists are.

Cranfield's conversion to domesticity is appropriately depicted in terms of his interpretive activities. When the squire and two selectmen of the village come to offer Cranfield the position of schoolmaster, he begins by "enveloping their homely figures in the misty romance that pervaded his mental world" (9:478). This misinterpretation is soon corrected, however, when "At every effort of his memory he recognized some trait of the dreamy

Messenger of Destiny, in this pompous, bustling, self-important, little great man of the village" (9:480). Once Cranfield can see the squire without the distortion produced by "misty romance," he is on the road to domestic happiness. He may thus be spared the narrator's more severe judgments. This changed position is evident when the squire takes on the role of pompous victim and absorbs the sort of ridicule that the narrator earlier directed toward Cranfield. Cranfield's salvation is confirmed when he is overwhelmed by sudden affection for the village children. As soon as "a flow of natural feeling gushed like a well-spring in his heart" (9:480), Cranfield is free of his delusion and safe from the more severe exactions of Hawthorne's narrator. Elsewhere, Hawthorne rearranges the constituents of Cranfield's quest to produce a bitter and biting condemnation.

In "Wakefield" Hawthorne uses the same plot to organize a more vigorous critique. As we have seen in Chapter 2, the protagonist of this tale leaves home in order to discover "how the little sphere of creatures and circumstances, in which he was a central object, will be affected by his removal" (9:134). Like Cranfield's, Wakefield's quest is ironically fulfilled. Returning home after twenty years, he discovers his absence to have been of little consequence to anyone. The principal difference between Cranfield's fate and Wakefield's lies in the fact that the former is destined for domestic salvation and the latter is destined, by the newspaper account from which the tale originates, to enact "as remarkable a freak as may be found in the whole list of human oddities" (9:130). Because Wakefield is intended to fulfill this absurd role, the narrator feels free to abuse him throughout the narrative.

After summarizing the newspaper account of Wakefield's quest, the narrator affects a pose of objectivity: "The fact, thus abstractly stated, is not very uncommon, nor—without a proper distinction of circumstances—to be condemned either as naughty or nonsensical" (9:130). Immediately, the narrator shows that he will not be treating the matter "abstractly." Having raised the question "What sort of a man was Wakefield?", the narrator explains that "We are free to shape out our own idea, and call it by his name." "We" may—if the narrator wishes—create a Wakefield capable of experiencing Cranfield's deep rush of love or Adam Forrester's supernatural reassurance. The narrator says instead that Wakefield "was intellectual, but not actively so; his mind occupied itself in long and lazy musings, that tended to no purpose. . . ." More ominous is the judgment that Wakefield had "a cold, but not depraved nor wandering heart" (9:131). Most damaging is the opinion of Wakefield's wife. She was "partly aware of a quiet selfishness, that had rusted into his inactive mind—of a peculiar sort of vanity, the most uneasy attribute about him—of a disposition to craft, which had seldom produced more positive effects than the keeping of petty secrets, hardly worth revealing . . ." (9:132). Having attributed intellectual abstraction, emotional coldness, egotism, and pointless craftiness to Wakefield, the narrator goes on to criticize these qualities throughout the tale, finally reaching the condemnation that he originally affects to withhold.

One sign of the narrator's attitude is his use of the mock-heroic when discussing Wakefield's quest. As Wakefield prepares to depart, he is described in terms that effectively discount the quest through ironic echoes of chivalric trappings: "His equipment is a drab great-coat, a hat covered with an oil-cloth, top-boots, an umbrella in one hand and a small portmanteau in the other" (9:132). Here the distance between these pedestrian details and their romantic antecedents is insistent: an umbrella in place of a sword, for example. Elsewhere the effect is even more obvious, as when the narrator describes Wakefield's recovery after almost entering his home inadvertently: "Will not the whole household . . . raise a hue-and-cry, through London Streets, in pursuit of their fugitive lord and master? Wonderful escape!" (9:135). The disproportionate chivalric term "lord and master" so impugns Wakefield's imagined importance that the concluding exclamation—"Wonderful escape!"—can function with ironic appropriateness. The most damaging of these mock-heroic deflations goes right to the heart of the quest itself. After Wakefield leaves home to discover his importance in the world, he settles down for twenty years in the next street. The narrator dispatches this physical quest in one sentence: "He is in the next street to his own, and at his journey's end" (9:133). Describing Wakefield's activity with the elevated term "journey" mocks his enterprise even in relation to Ralph Cranfield's foolish quest.

As a result of such ridicule, the narrator can easily descend from satire to lampoon, as when he calls Wakefield a "crafty nincompoop" and his quest a "long whim-wham" (9:135). This low abuse prevents any positive movement comparable to Cranfield's developing self-knowledge. A higher unity is out of the question for Wakefield because the narrator insists throughout the tale that—contrary to the prevailing ideology—Wakefield's consciousness does not evolve. The natural symbol for this fixity of character is Wakefield's smile, the outer sign of his "craftiness." After he has taken leave of his wife, Wakefield opens the door for a last look, and his wife sees a strange smile on his face. As his absence lengthens, she often thinks of this smile:

> In her many musings, she surrounds the original smile with a multitude of fantasies, which make it strange and awful; as, for instance, if she imagines him in a coffin, that parting look is frozen on his pale features; or, if she dreams of him in Heaven, still his blessed spirit wears a quiet and crafty smile. (9:132–33)

When Wakefield enters the same house again after twenty years, the narrator observes: "As he passes in, we have a parting glimpse of his visage, and recognize the crafty smile, which was the precursor of the little joke, that he has ever since been playing off at his wife's expense" (9:139–40). The Wakefield invented by this narrator is more like a "humour" character from an English stage comedy than like a romantic protagonist.

Wakefield's story thus sheds a very unflattering light on the romantic quests for spiritual knowledge popular with Hawthorne's contemporaries. Like Ralph Cranfield, Wakefield completes a circular quest and returns home, but, because there has been no growth in his perception of his place in the world, Wakefield's quest has resulted in ironic frustration. He has "los[t] his place forever." The narrator is thus appropriately severe: "Stay, Wakefield! Would you go to the sole home that is left you? Then step into your grave!" (9:139). "Wakefield" suggests a picture of Hawthorne sitting at his writing desk with the grid of a romantic quest for higher knowledge laid out before him and a conversion chart by which every positive element can be represented negatively, every negative element, positively.

Hawthorne problematizes the romantic quest most profoundly in "Ethan Brand." In this highly esteemed tale, the title character devotes eighteen years to a quest far nobler than Wakefield's or Cranfield's, but eventually he also comes full circle—back to the lime kiln from which he set forth. Then, as if following the advice offered by the narrator to Wakefield, Brand jumps to his fiery death. The narrator diminishes Brand's quest by insisting that his absence, like Cranfield's and Wakefield's, has had very little effect

on the world he left behind. In this tale, the unbroken continuity of ordinary life is represented by the experience of "three or four individuals who
had drunk flip beside the bar-room fire, through all the winters, and
smoked their pipes beneath the stoop, through all the summers, since
Ethan Brand's departure" (11:90). While Brand has roamed the world pursuing spiritual truth, the world has gone on just fine without him. Additional evidence appears when these townsfolk are joined by "A number of
the youth of the village, young men and girls, [who] had hurried up the
hill-side, impelled by curiosity to see Ethan Brand, the hero of so many a
legend familiar to their childhood." They are quickly disappointed: "Find-
ing nothing, however, very remarkable in his aspect—nothing but a sun-
burnt wayfarer, in plain garb and dusty shoes . . . these young people speed-
ily grew tired of observing him" (11:94). By opposing the chivalric
vocabulary of "hero" and "legend" to details like Brand's "dusty shoes," the
narrator undercuts the character, his quest, and his motives.

The narrator's attitude is surprising since, unlike Cranfield and Wakefield, Ethan Brand is motivated by an admirable, even noble, intention.
Eighteen years ago, Brand was "a simple and loving man" whose concern
for his fellow creatures led him to meditate on the doctrine of the Unpardonable Sin, the cause of much human fear and anguish. Looking back
from the present of the tale, Brand "remembered with what tenderness,
with what love and sympathy for mankind, and what pity for human guilt
and wo, he had first begun to contemplate those ideas which afterwards
became the inspiration of his life  . . ." (11:98). If he were to discover this
sin, Brand could show others that they were innocent of it and that they
could therefore anticipate divine forgiveness. What nobler motive could
one have?

The tale's moral complexity has led generations of critics to devote their
energies to mapping the theological implications of Brand's search and the
moral implications of his methods. In 1955, James E. Miller, Jr., writes that
Brand "takes upon himself the heavy knowledge which man was not meant
to have, the unbearable knowledge of the supreme evil which only God can
determine" (103). In 1965, Ely Stock quotes Martin Buber to explain that
the tale "tells how human knowledge of good and evil works out in post-
Paridisial time—'not as "original sin," but as the specific sin, only possible
in relation to God, which alone makes possible general sin against the fel-

low-man and hence, of course, once more against God as his guardian' "
(133). In 1985, Agnes McNeill Donohue argues that Brand "blasphemes
against the Holy Spirit by violating the soul of another human being and
studying it out of cold curiosity. This violation is blasphemous because the
investigator has cooly and defiantly assumed the role of the deity" (214–
15). These readings embody great wisdom but, when all is said and done,
the structure of Brand's quest is narratologically just as circular as Cranfield's or Wakefield's.

Brand discovers that while seeking the Unforgivable Sin, he has committed it himself. Like Cranfield, Brand suspects that he has been the victim of
a joke: "And then, without mirth in his countenance, but as if moved by an
involuntary recognition of the infinite absurdity of seeking throughout the
world for what was the closest of all things to himself, and looking into
every heart, save his own, for what was hidden in no other breast, [Brand]
broke into a laugh of scorn" (11:87). As in Hawthorne's other quest narratives, laughs, smiles, and some form of mental disequilibrium appear together. The narrator goes on to explain helpfully:

> Laughter, when out of place, mistimed, or bursting forth from a disordered
> state of feeling, may be the most terrible modulation of the human voice.
> The laughter of one asleep, even if it be a little child—the madman's
> laugh—the wild, screaming laugh of a born idiot, are sounds that we
> sometimes tremble to hear, and would always willingly forget. Poets have
> imagined no utterance of fiends or hobgoblins so fearfully appropriate as
> a laugh. (11:87)

We should assume that writers of fiction—of tales like "Ethan Brand," for
example—have made the same discovery about uncanny laughter. The
cause of Brand's madness, or whatever his maniacal laughs signifies, is not
far to seek: "The whole question on which he had exhausted life, and more
than life, looked like a delusion" (11:93).

This discovery is practically an affront to Hawthorne's transcendental
contemporaries—and to most readers today. Surely, none of us would have
developed the story this way, none of us would have had Brand throw himself into the lime kiln, none of us would have written that "The whole
question on which he had exhausted life, and more than life, looked like a
delusion." But none of us is Hawthorne. Even Hawthorne's narrator seems

somewhat unsatisfied when Brand makes this discovery—not because the conclusion Brand draws is too bleak, however, but because it is expressed baldly, in a direct statement. Even a spiritual fact unwelcome to the transcendental mind should be presented through an appropriate natural fact. Thus, the narrator soon represents Brand's circular quest through one of Hawthorne's finest symbols, an old dog chasing his own tail. The passage is lengthy but worth quoting in its entirety:

> But, now, all of a sudden, this grave and venerable quadruped, of his own mere notion, and without the slightest suggestion from anybody else, began to run round after his tail, which, to heighten the absurdity of the proceeding, was a great deal shorter than it should have been. Never was seen such headlong eagerness in pursuit of an object that could not possibly be attained; never was heard such a tremendous outbreak of growling, snarling, barking, and snapping—as if one end of the ridiculous brute's body were at deadly and most unforgivable enmity with the other. Faster and faster, roundabout went the cur; and faster and still faster fled the unapproachable brevity of his tail; and louder and fiercer grew his yells of rage and animosity; until, utterly exhausted, and as far from the goal as ever, the foolish old dog ceased his performance as suddenly as he had begun it. (11:96)

As Cyril A. Reilly has shown, Hawthorne's reworking of a journal entry into this richly symbolic passage clearly evidences the seriousness of his intentions. Thematically, as many critics have demonstrated, the tale is very complex. Structurally, it is very simple. Like this old dog, Brand has returned to his point of origin. Brand's circle is completed, and it is definitely a circle, not an Emersonian spiral.

In "Ethan Brand," Hawthorne uses the literary elements of plot and imagery created by his contemporaries to produce narrative effects that none of them—with the possible exception of Melville—would endorse. To the romantic imagination, the circle, a sign potentially signifying the static and finite, easily converts into a spiral, a "natural fact" signifying the inevitability of material and spiritual progress. Emerson, for example, writes in his essay "Circles": "The life of man is a self-evolving circle, which, from a ring imperceptibly small, rushes on all sides outwards to new and larger circles, and that without end" (2:304). Abrams says about Hegel:

> The self-moving circle . . . rotates along a third, a vertical dimension, to
> close where it had begun, but on a higher plane of value. It thus fuses the
> idea of the circular return with the idea of linear progress, to describe a
> distinctive figure of Romantic thought and imagination—the ascending
> circle, or spiral. (184)

In contrast, Brian Way accurately describes Ethan Brand's quest as follows:
"He had thought he was engaged in a vast cosmic journey through time and
space, whereas in fact he was travelling along the circumference of a circle—a movement which gives the illusion of constant progress, although it
is in reality constricted, always returning upon itself" (21). Even as the plot
of such tales opens the way to an organically appropriate happy ending,
Hawthorne's handling of the plot complicates the tale's progress, problematizes the hero's actions, and frustrates the reader's more optimistic inclina-
tions.

Hawthorne was as familiar with romantic modes of symbolic interpretation as his readers were. Therefore his character Ethan Brand can easily
construe the significance of a dog's chasing his own tail: "Meanwhile, Ethan
Brand had resumed his seat upon the log; and moved, it might be, by a
perception of some remote analogy between his own case and that of the
self-pursuing cur, he broke into the awful laugh, which, more than any
other token, expressed the condition of his inward being" (11:97). Hawthorne was also familiar with the dominant contemporary theories of progress, and yet Ralph Cranfield comes to realize that if "the treasure which I
have sought round the world, lies buried, after all, at the very door of my
mother's dwelling . . . [t]hat would be a jest indeed!" (9:476). Hawthorne
was surrounded by romantic ideology. In "Chiefly About War Matters" he
consequently wrote the following about a figure highly esteemed by most
romantic thinkers, the abolitionist John Brown: "Any common-sensible
man, looking at the matter unsentimentally, must have felt a certain intellectual satisfaction in seeing him hanged, if it were only in requital of his
preposterous miscalculation of possibilities" (328). Whether Hawthorne set
out to project some "Utopia of human virtue and happiness" or—more usually—to "acknowledge the necessity of keeping the beaten track of earth,"
he constructed his narratives out of the materials available to him in his
own contemporary culture, ingeniously transforming these narrative mate-

rials by writing against the grain of his readers' expectations. Hawthorne freely appropriated elements of contemporary romanticism, as he appropriated elements from the history of New England, not only to fulfill his own narrative strategies, but to keep readers reading attentively, to prevent their easy acquiescence in what goes without saying, to problematize even the simplest of matters, to make subsequent readings possible and productive. These are the usual effects today upon readers who long ago repudiated—eagerly or with reluctance—the romantic values of Hawthorne's contemporaries.

# SEVEN

# Narrative Transformations of Domesticity

The forces of adventure and domesticity contending in the typical romantic quest narrative are William C. Spengemann's subject in *The Adventurous Muse: The Poetics of American Fiction, 1789–1900*. While discussing St. Augustine, Spengemann advances a proposition relevant to my purposes in this chapter:

> Augustine calls heaven "home"; the Domestic Romance calls home "heaven." In both cases, home represents the unconditioned ground of man's being; the eternal unchanging place from which he has fallen into the world of time and change; the native land to which the exiled pilgrim longs to return so that he may be blessed. (70–71)

Spengemann's explanation provides a convenient opportunity for me to switch my focus from Hawthorne's fictional appropriations of contemporary romanticism to a consideration of how he used the ideology of domesticity popular among his contemporaries to create problematic fiction.

Unusually widespread agreement exists among critics that Americans in the middle third of the nineteenth century were deeply committed to the values represented by what Aileen S. Kraditor identified as "the cult of domesticity" (11) in *Up From the Pedestal: Selected Writings in the History of American Feminism*. Daniel Walker Howe explains in his essay "Victorian Culture in America" that "the most important locus for cultural transmission was the home, and Victorians acknowledged this with their cult of domesticity" (25). According to Nina Baym, in *Woman's Fiction*, this cult of domesticity:

assumes that men as well as women find greatest happiness and fulfillment in domestic relations, by which are meant not simply spouse and parent, but the whole network of human attachments based on love, support, and mutual responsibility. Domesticity is set forth as a value scheme for ordering all of life, in competition with the ethos of money and exploitation that is perceived to prevail in American society. (27)

Baym's emphasis on the reformist aspects of the cult of domesticity is echoed in Gillian Brown's feminist reading "Getting in the Kitchen with Dinah: Domestic Politics in *Uncle Tom's Cabin*." Brown writes that "Exponents of domesticity defined the home as a peaceful order in contrast to the disorder and fluctuations occasioned by competitive economic activity in the marketplace" (505). This line of political argument surely provides insight into the views of public and private economic activities shared by many of Hawthorne's contemporaries. As with Hawthorne's transformations of romanticism, however, his adaptations of contemporary domesticity can also be approached narratologically. Again, imagery provides a useful point of departure.

The terms in which domesticity was usually represented can be illustrated by a passage written by a contemporary author whose work Hawthorne, surprisingly, admired. Fanny Fern's introduction to her novel *Rose Clark* (1856) is quoted by Baym in *Woman's Fiction* to demonstrate that "literary women conceptualized authorship as a profession rather than a calling, as work and not art." For my purposes here, the passage from Fern's introduction might also serve as testimony concerning the cult of domesticity:

> When the frost curtains the windows, when the wind whistles fiercely at the key-hole, when the bright fire glows, and the tea-tray is removed, and father in his slippered feet lolls in his arm-chair; and mother with her nimble needle "makes auld claes look amaist as weel as new," and grand-mamma draws closer to the chimney-corner, and Tommy with his plate of chestnuts nestles contentedly at her feet; then let my unpretending story be read. For such an hour, for such an audience, was it written. (Baym 32)

Surely Hawthorne would eschew the Scots allusion; probably he would use somewhat different syntax, and he might introduce a cat into the family setting; but his basic images for domestic peace and security would be very similar to those employed by Fanny Fern.

Milton Stern agrees in *Contexts for Hawthorne*: "The snug, settled, fireside quality that was such a deep need of Hawthorne's personality is a quality of establishment, of closure, and is expressed in calm thoughtfulness rather than interjection" (140). A passage from *The English Notebooks*, written toward the end of 1854, illustrates the applicability of Stern's remark to the biographical Hawthorne: "I think I have been happier, this Christmas, than ever before,—by our own fireside, and with my wife and children about me. More content to enjoy what I had; less anxious for anything beyond it, in this life" (98). Despite his sincere personal attraction to certain elements of the contemporary cult of domesticity, however, Hawthorne the artist refused to endorse these values univocally in his fiction. A significant difference between Hawthorne and most of his contemporaries is that domestic scenes typically appear in Hawthorne's fiction as fantasies, dim recollections of bygone times, pictures that characters look longingly in on from the snowy outdoors, rather than as paradise regained in an actual present.

What Hawthorne refused to do may be illustrated by a representative passage from Harriet Beecher Stowe's *Uncle Tom's Cabin*—published in the same year as *The Blithedale Romance*—describing the home of Senator and Mrs. Bird:

> The light of the cheerful fire shone on the rug and carpet of a cosy parlor, and glittered on the sides of the tea-cups and well-brightened teapot, as Senator Bird was drawing off his boots, preparatory to inserting his feet in a pair of new handsome slippers, which his wife had been working for him while away on his senatorial tour. Mrs. Bird, looking the very picture of delight, was superintending the arrangements of the table, ever and anon mingling admonitory remarks to a number of frolicsome juveniles, who were effervescing in all those modes of untold gambol and mischief that have astonished mothers ever since the flood. (75)

We might observe some stylistic similarity between Stowe's description and the passage from *Rose Clark*, and yet considerable stylistic variety is compatible with the use of domestic imagery. Stowe's writing here does not sound very much like Susan Warner's or Henry Wadsworth Longfellow's or Frederick Goddard Tuckerman's, and yet their shared imagery shows how all these authors directly represented the domestic values of their era.

Representations of domestic bliss attained abound in the imagery used by Hawthorne's contemporaries. In "The Children's Hour" (1859), one of the most popular poems by one of the most popular writers of the age, Henry Wadsworth Longfellow shows his speaker genially roughhousing with his three daughters in the evening (64–65). Evidence of Longfellow's commitment to domesticity appears not only in the poem's subject matter—an imposing figure's willingness to unbend and play with his children within the usually sacred precincts of his study—but also in the imagery of cozy domestic enclosure. Outside, the "night is beginning to lower," but indoors everything is comfortably safe and secure. The action of the poem takes place within a space defined by "the lamplight," the girls sneak up on the speaker by climbing "O'er the arms and back of my chair," and soon "They almost devour me with kisses, / Their arms about me entwine." Although Longfellow hyperbolically describes the incident in the vocabulary of military siege—"turret . . . banditti . . . fortress . . . dungeon"—the hyperbole issues from the cult of domesticity as much as from the little girls' romantic imaginations. This warm, well-lighted study protects the speaker and his children from the harshness of the outside world as surely as steep castle walls and a moat.

The period was so thoroughly imbued with this sort of imagery that it appears even in contexts in which the writer's intentions are far less reassuring than Longfellow's. In Frederick Goddard Tuckerman's sonnet "And Change with Hurried Hand Has Swept these Scenes," for example, the theme involves the speaker's sadness because the wilderness is disappearing: "The woods have fallen, across the meadow-lot / The hunter's trail and trap-path is forgot." When the speaker contrasts the lost vigor of wild nature and the tameness of his contemporary world, however, he turns instinctively to the imagery popularized by the cult of domesticity:

> Here, but a lifetime back, where falls tonight
> Behind the curtained pane a sheltered light
> On buds of rose or vase of violet
> Aloft upon the marble mantel set,
> Here in the forest-heart, hung blackening
> The wolfbait on the bush beside the spring. (27)

Longfellow's speaker and his daughters might easily be envisioned in this room—if not living there, then at least visiting the owners. The possibility of a literary crossover is suggested by the scene's comparable atmosphere of warmth, subdued lighting, comfortable furnishings, and security from the outside world—here brilliantly symbolized by the blackening wolfbait.

Another contemporary source useful in contextualizing Hawthorne's fictional strategy is Susan Warner's novel *The Wide, Wide World*, published in the same year as *The Scarlet Letter* but far more successful in terms of sales. According to the afterword written by Jane Tompkins for the Feminist Press's paperback reprinting of Warner's book: "No novel written in the United States had ever sold so well. It went through fourteen editions in two years and became one of the best-selling novels of the nineteenth century both in this country and in England" (584). The reasons for this phenomenal success are easily apprehended. Both Tompkins and Baym, in *Woman's Fiction*, emphasize Warner's depiction of Ellen Montgomery's behavior as exemplary of contemporary stereotypes of correctness. I would like to stress, in addition, Warner's depiction of domesticity, especially through what Tompkins calls in one place "the homely sacraments (often the taking of food and tea)" (600).

Domestic happiness is illustrated in the very first chapter of *The Wide, Wide World*, where we find Ellen as a small child, alone with her seriously ill mother in a comfortable, warm room. For much of the chapter, Ellen's mother naps while the little girl looks out the window, watching the busy city street turn from afternoon to evening. The principal action in the chapter is slight enough: Ellen's "regular business" of making tea and toast for her mother, an even tamer evening activity than frolicking in a parent's study. The symbolic value of Ellen's domestic activity is confirmed in the next chapter, however, when Ellen and her mother contentedly sit holding hands "for two or three hours, without speaking," even though "Mrs. Montgomery was part of the time slumbering" (18). It is clear that, despite the mother's illness and the likelihood that they will soon be parted, probably forever, these two have achieved peace and happiness by sharing domestic isolation from the world.

None of Hawthorne's characters would be allowed to enjoy this domestic security in the present time of his fiction. Nor could Hawthorne's characters share in the ceremony exhaustively described in Chapter 26 in which Ellen and Alice Humphreys, with the assistance of Margery the maid and Parry the cat, lovingly prepare hot chocolate for Alice's father, who has gone out on a bitter, snowy evening to bring spiritual comfort to a dying child. When Mr. Humphreys's return is delayed, the two young women get to share this "homely sacrament" with Alice's brother John, another minister, who has arrived home unexpectedly. Warner's internalized point of view in this chapter also invites her readers to share in the ceremony of drinking home-made hot chocolate before the fire in this snug living room with Parry purring in the corner. Domestic community is clearly the author's rhetorical intention. Therefore, although nearly three hundred pages will pass before Ellen marries John, we might predict their happy marriage from this domestic scene at the novel's midpoint.

This marriage was not depicted in the phenomenally successful original publication of the novel by Putnam. However, a proposed final chapter by Warner was discovered in the Huntington Library by Mabel Baker and is included in Tompkins's paperback edition. In this chapter, the newly married Ellen and John return from Scotland to "a house in one of our pleasantest, though not one of our largest cities" (571), where John's father, Margery, and Parry are already installed. Ellen is of course delighted to be surrounded by loved ones, but in her eyes the greatest advantage of her new estate is a chamber on the second storey: "How delightfully private this room is—having no entrance but through other rooms where no one can intrude" (577). Surely this room is a purely imaginary setting, a place where we can have life as we would wish rather than as it is. In seeing this sort of absolute domestic happiness as imaginary, Warner is in agreement with Hawthorne. In depicting domestic happiness in the present time of her novel, as a state achieved by her characters, Warner follows a narrative strategy that is fundamentally different from his.

Hawthorne exploits elements of the cult of domesticity frequently, and he does so to achieve a wide variety of narrative effects. Occasionally, he creates happily-ever-after domestic resolutions like Warner's suppressed conclusion. "The Threefold Destiny" ends with Ralph Cranfield and Faith Egerton finally on the path to domestic fulfillment: "[T]heir kindred souls were destined to form a union here below, which all eternity should only bind more closely" (9:474). At the end of "The Great Carbuncle," Hannah and Matthew make the following life plan: "We will kindle the cheerful glow of our hearth, at eventide, and be happy in its light. But never again will we desire more light than all the world may share with us" (9:163). In both cases, narratives focused on excessive behavior and misguided searches for happiness achieve abrupt closure through the establishment of hearth, home, and domestic peace. Significantly, Hawthorne postpones these characters' domestic happiness until after his tale concludes. Unlike Longfellow and Warner, he is reluctant actually to write the scenes in which Ralph and Faith or Hannah and Matthew experience their salvation. His preferred strategy is to depict domestic fulfillment only as a condition deferred, wished for, or viewed from without.

"Roger Malvin's Burial" is an interesting example of Hawthorne's usual practice. Frequently anthologized, the tale has been extensively analyzed by Spengemann and declared characteristic of Hawthorne's work by John Updike in his review of Miller's *Salem Is My Dwelling Place* and by Richard E. Millington in his *Practicing Romance*. This recent popularity is understandable since both the plotting and thematics of the tale involve challenging questions. Having left the surely dying Roger Malvin unburied in the forest to save his own seriously threatened life, Reuben Bourne marries Malvin's daughter Dorcas and eventually fathers a dearly beloved son, Cyrus. Racked with guilt because he has concealed his abandonment of Malvin, Reuben fails at farming, alienates his neighbors, and resolves to start over on the frontier. During this migration, Reuben compulsively leads his family back to the spot where he left Malvin unburied and accidentally kills Cyrus there. The narrator concludes: "His sin was expiated, the curse was gone from him; and, in the hour, when he had shed blood dearer to him than his own, a prayer, the first for years, went up to Heaven from the lips of Reuben Bourne" (10:360). Millington plausibly observes that "An interpretation of this tale that is not repellent on humane grounds . . . depends upon our refusal to acquiesce in the potential tyranny of the story's forceful final paragraph." He sadly adds that "Hawthorne criticism will supply examples of such compliant reading" (20–21). From a thematic standpoint, then, the story is morally problematic and thus of great potential interest to critics.

"Roger Malvin's Burial" is interesting also in terms of how Hawthorne exploits domestic imagery. Toward the end of the tale, the family make camp in the wilderness one night during their migration. After Reuben and Cyrus go off to hunt for meat, Dorcas happily begins preparations for their evening meal. As she works, she sings a "rude melody . . . descriptive of a winter evening in a frontier-cottage, when, secured from savage inroad by the high-piled snow-drifts, the family rejoiced by their own fireside." As in the conclusion of "The Great Carbuncle," the ingredients of hearth, security from the outside world, and family solidarity combine to represent the values dear to the cult of domesticity. According to the narrator, the anonymous author of this song "instilled [into the lyrics] the very essence of domestic love and household happiness, and they were poetry and picture joined in one." This poetic depiction of domesticity powerfully moves Dorcas, so that "she no longer saw the gloomy pines, nor heard the wind" in the hostile environment that actually surrounds her. Instead her domestic imagination takes over, and "the walls of her forsaken home seemed to encircle her" (10:357–58).

Despite the similar imagery in the two tales, Dorcas and Reuben should not be expected to live happily ever after like the couple in "The Great Carbuncle." Soon Dorcas will discover that Reuben has accidentally shot their only child in ironic atonement for his failure to provide Christian burial for her father. Another significant difference lies in the fact that domestic happiness for Dorcas is presented through her memories and her experience of someone else's poetic vision rather than through her expectations for the future. These differences suggest the ingenuity with which Hawthorne adapts conventional domestic materials to suit his own narrative strategies. We may say that "The Great Carbuncle" is "about" obsessions and that "Roger Malvin's Burial" is "about" guilt. In addition to this thematic contrast, the two scenes of domestic happiness fulfill different narrative functions. One brings comic resolution to a satiric quest, and the other ironically provides a happy contrast to an imminent fatality. Significantly, neither narrative purpose entails representing domestic happiness in the present time of the plot.

Hawthorne transforms domestic imagery to serve still another narrative intention in "My Kinsman, Major Molineux." In their textbook *Literature: The Human Experience*, Richard Abcarian and Marvin Klotz write the following about this tale:

> The story opens with Robin crossing a river into an unnamed town after dark. If one takes a psychoanalytic stance, the mysterious opening nicely symbolizes a sort of spiritual journey into mysterious realms. More spe-

cifically, the opening suggests an inward journey into the dark recesses of the human spirit. (1212)

In other words, Robin Molineux's fictional experiences resemble the romantic quests discussed in Chapter 6. At times, the narrator stresses Robin's sense of adventure, as when "He then walked forward into the town, with as light a step, as if his day's journey had not already exceeded thirty miles, and with as eager an eye, as if he were entering London city, instead of the little metropolis of a New England colony" (11:210–11). At other times, the narrator emphasizes Robin's loneliness and isolation: "But the streets were empty, the shops were closed, and lights were visible only in the second storeys of a few dwelling-houses" (11:211–12). Robin is hungry, lost, confused, and humiliated. His quest clearly challenges some of the romantic conventions enumerated by M. H. Abrams. Hawthorne's use of domestic imagery is equally challenging.

After Robin has been laughed at, threatened, and nearly seduced while searching for his kinsman, he is told by a man with his face painted red and black, "Watch here an hour, and Major Molineux will pass by" (11:220). Dutifully, Robin settles down to wait and passes the time by thinking about this strange man, looking up and down the street, and inspecting a nearby church. Unnerved by the church cemetery, Robin tries to think happier thoughts by imagining how his family back in the country might have spent this "evening of ambiguity and weariness." Probably everyone back home would have assembled outdoors at sunset for "domestic worship." The narrator continues:

> Robin distinguished the seat of every individual of the little audience; he saw the good man in the midst, holding the Scriptures in the golden light that shone from the western clouds; he beheld him close the book, and rise up to pray. He heard the old thanksgivings for daily mercies, the old supplications for their continuance, to which he had so often listened in weariness, but which were now among his dear remembrances. He perceived the slight inequality of his father's voice when he came to speak of the Absent One; he noted how his mother turned her face to the broad and knotted trunk; how his elder brother scorned, because the beard was rough upon his upper lip, to permit his features to be moved; how his younger sister drew down a low hanging branch before her eyes; and how the little one of all, whose sports had hitherto broken the decorum of the

scene, understood the prayer for her playmate, and burst into clamorous grief. (11:223)

The passage up to this point provides an effective tonal contrast to the previous scenes of urban alienation, hostility, and immorality. It might almost appear in a handbook showing how to develop domestic scenes in sentimental fiction.

The passage continues with a sentence highly characteristic of Hawthorne's adaptable narrative strategies, however: "Then he saw them go in at the door; and when Robin would have entered also, the latch tinkled into its place, and he was excluded from his home" (11:223). The last clause especially shows Hawthorne's ingenuity. Any sensitive reader will respond to Robin's domestic fantasy, even if protesting all the while that the scene is too idealized to be true. Hawthorne's narrator seems to agree and snatches the scene away: "the latch tinkled into its place, and he was excluded from his home." We must ask, do we feel better after the scene has been exposed as fantasy? Are we pleased that we are—like Robin—too "shrewd" to be fooled by such sentimental depictions? Whatever our reactions, we have encountered, and probably responded positively to, a domestic scene for which the narrator refuses to take responsibility—just as other Hawthornean narrators refuse to take responsibility for Gothic marvels.

Hawthorne uses a similar strategy in "Night Sketches." As we may recall from the discussion in Chapter 3, the narrator of this sketch goes out walking alone on a cold and rainy evening. Along the way, he glimpses through a lighted window "a family circle" which represents "the golden mean": "the grandmother, the parents, and the children,—all flickering, shadow-like, in the glow of a wood-fire." The narrator sounds like a spokesman for the cult of domesticity as he declaims: "Bluster, fierce blast, and beat, thou wintry rain, against the window-panes! Ye cannot damp the enjoyment of that fireside." When the lonely narrator adds, "Surely my fate is hard, that I should be wandering homeless here, taking to my bosom night, and storm, and solitude, instead of wife and children" (9:431), he sounds less like an advocate of conventional domesticity than like the hungry and lonely Robin Molineux. As many commentators have plausibly argued, "Night Sketches" thematically epitomizes Hawthorne's characterizations of emotional isolatoes. As few have noticed, the sketch does so by ironically appropriating imagery popularized by the cult of domesticity.

A less popular piece entitled "The Village Uncle" shows Hawthorne handling domestic motifs with another interesting form of indirection. Lea Newman sensibly concludes that the "story brings little satisfaction to today's readers, except perhaps as a revelation of what the young man, Hawthorne, may have thought of as the options open to him—domestic happiness or the life of a writer" (306). This investigation of domestic ideology sufficiently repays our attention even so. The tale begins with Hawthorne's first-person narrator calling for "another log on the hearth" even though "our little parlor is comfortable." When the narrator explains that the increase in the fire is intended for symbolic rather than practical ends, he reveals his agreement with the values espoused by the cult of domesticity: "Higher yet, and clearer be the blaze, till our cottage windows glow the ruddiest in the village, and the light of our household mirth flash far across the bay to Nahant" (9:310). The scene might almost be taken as a depiction of the domestic life predicted for Hannah and Matthew, but there are several important differences between the two couples. Unlike Hannah and Matthew, the Village Uncle and his wife Susan apparently did not pursue a chimerical quest before settling down. Another difference emerges when this narrator says that Susan "kindled a domestic fire within my heart, and took up her dwelling there, even in that chill and lonesome cavern, hung round with glittering icicles of fancy" (9:316). Despite the positive imagery of the "domestic fire," the Village Uncle admits that he was lonely and isolated at some earlier point in his life. Whereas we encounter Matthew and Hannah only after their marriage, the Village Uncle can remember when he was "a hermit in the depths of my own mind; . . . a man who had wandered out of the real world and got into its shadow, where his troubles, joys, and vicissitudes were of such slight stuff, that he hardly knew whether he lived, or only dreamed of living" (9:311).

The contrasting emotional states are crucial because this narrator's account of domestic bliss turns out to be merely an imaginative projection. Actually, he is still a young, isolated artist, cut off from the enjoyments of Susan, children, and the "domestic fire." Hawthorne's use of domestic imagery is thus even more significant. The fact that this narrator does not himself enjoy these blessings operates to increase their attractiveness. Therefore, the narrator may plausibly choose to reaffirm domestic values as the moral of his tale: "In chaste and warm affections, humble wishes, and honest toil for some useful end, there is health for the mind, and quiet for the heart, the prospect for a happy life, and the fairest hope of Heaven" (9:323). No matter how strongly affirmed as ultimate goals, however, it is crucial to recall that these values are not represented in the present time of Hawthorne's narrative.

This narrator's separation from a domestic situation that he can understand but not enjoy may be taken as typical in Hawthorne's fiction. Habituated by writers like Longfellow, Fern, and Warner to fictional accounts of domestic bliss enjoyed in the present, Hawthorne's contemporary readers encountered domestic security in his work primarily through negatives, through his characters' separation from the desired estate, rather than through their blissful possession of its satisfactions. Hawthorne could probably create a character to look longingly in on the family scene depicted by Longfellow, or he might send one of his characters out into a dark evening to walk by Ellen Montgomery's window, or he might send a stage coach rattling past the humble cottage described by Fanny Fern so that some lonely character could catch a brief glimpse of the happiness of others. Hawthorne will not provide what his contemporaries expect, however— pictures of domestic bliss enjoyed in the here-and-now.

Domestic values are used to create just the opposite effect in "The Ambitious Guest." The thematic irony of this tale lies in the frustration of the title character, who expends his youth in an obsessive quest for fame, only to be excluded from the notoriety attained by the family whose death in an avalanche provides the tale's plot. In terms of the issues under discussion here, it is equally significant that this young man's ambitions have excluded him from the domestic pleasures enjoyed by the members of idealized families like the one depicted in this tale. The story opens with a picture of cozy domesticity:

> One September night, a family had gathered round their hearth, and piled it high with the drift-wood of mountain-streams, the dry cones of the pine, and the splintered ruins of great trees, that had come crashing down the precipice. Up the chimney roared the fire, and brightened the room with its broad blaze. The faces of the father and mother had a sober gladness; the children laughed; the eldest daughter was the image of Happiness at seventeen; and the aged grandmother, who sat knitting in the warmest place, was the image of Happiness grown old. They had found the "herb, heart's ease," in the bleakest spot of all New-England. (9:324)

This passage of description is noteworthy not only because it effectively establishes the tale's setting, but also because it recalls so many other domestic scenes in Hawthorne's fiction and in the work of his contemporaries, as, for example, the passages quoted above from *Rose Clark* and *Uncle Tom's Cabin*.

As we might expect, Hawthorne transposes domestic imagery to suit his own purposes. For this one evening, "a prophetic sympathy impelled the refined and educated youth to pour out his heart before the simple mountaineers" so that he is able to participate in the "unity among themselves, and separation from the world at large, which, in every domestic circle, should keep a holy place, where no stranger may intrude" (9:327). But, of course, this domestic unity lasts for only a few hours. Love never ripens between the ambitious guest and the daughter of the family. As B. Bernard Cohen and Kenneth Walter Cameron have shown in their analyses of the tale's sources, this last detail is especially ironic since Hawthorne added five years to the daughter's actual age, in order, as Cameron says, to "make her attractive to the guest" (27). Therefore, the young man never builds a cabin for himself and his bride, even an imaginary one like the Village Uncle's. Instead, the ambitious guest dies, unmourned, unremembered, and unfulfilled, having failed to participate completely in the cult of domesticity. In a typically Hawthornean stroke, the young man becomes fully aware of the happiness he could derive from domesticity only as he is deprived of that happiness.

Perhaps the most peculiar adaptation of domestic motifs in Hawthorne's shorter fiction appears in "The Artist of the Beautiful," a tale that has attracted a wealth of analysis for reasons that the title should make clear. Hawthorne's narrator encourages this critical activity by explaining that the tale's protagonist, a watchmaker named Owen Warland, had "the love of the Beautiful, such as might have made him a poet, a painter, or a sculptor, and which was as completely refined from all utilitarian coarseness, as it could have been in either of the fine arts" (10:450). This aesthetic genius leads Warland to create a fabulous mechanical butterfly about which, the narrator says, "It is impossible to express by words the glory, the splendor, the delicate gorgeousness, which were softened into the beauty of this object" (10:470). In the tale's last paragraph, the sturdy baby of Warland's childhood friends, Robert Danforth and Annie Hovendon, accidentally crushes this butterfly, and the narrator concludes, "When the artist rose high enough to achieve the Beautiful, the symbol by which he made it perceptible to mortal senses became of little value in his eyes, while his spirit possessed itself in the enjoyment of the Reality" (10:475). When an artist writes about an artist in this way, interpretive critics naturally take note.

Even an uninterpretive critic may note how the actual artist uses domestic imagery in connection with his fictional artist. Like the ambitious guest and the narrator of "Night Sketches," Warland has no lover, although he occasionally thinks of Annie as his potential mate: "And then the thought stole into his mind, that this young girl possessed the gift to comprehend him, better than all the world beside. And what a help and strength would it be to him, in his lonely toil, if he could gain the sympathy of the only being whom he loved!" (10:459). Many of Hawthorne's contemporaries might have written these sentences, but probably none of them would have written Warland's reflection a few paragraphs later: "I have deceived myself, and must suffer for it. I yearned for sympathy—and thought—and fancied—and dreamed—that you might give it me. But you lack the talisman, Annie, that should admit you into my secrets" (10:460). Warland must remain alone, but the narrator has rendered this isolation more affecting by raising and then rejecting the possibility of true love. The narrator therefore exclaims: "Poor Owen Warland! He had indeed erred, yet pardonably; for if any human spirit could have sufficiently reverenced the process so sacred in his eyes, it must have been a woman's" (10:460). Warland encounters no such spirit in the tale, however, and so domestic happiness is denied him.

Warland gets a peculiar glimpse of what he has missed when he brings his mechanical butterfly to Annie as a belated wedding gift. In this scene, Hawthorne's narrator clearly establishes his own presence to prepare the way for some very interesting editorializing:

> Pass we over a long space of intense thought, yearning effort, minute toil, and wasting anxiety, succeeded by an instant of solitary triumph; let all this be imagined; and then behold the artist, on a winter evening, seeking admittance to Robert Danforth's fireside circle. There he found the Man of Iron, with his massive substance thoroughly warmed and attempered by domestic influences. And there was Annie, too, now transformed into a matron, with much of her husband's plain and sturdy nature, but imbued, as Owen Warland still believed, with a finer grace that might enable her to be the interpreter between Strength and Beauty. (10:468)

The passage resonates with conventional domestic terms: *winter evening, fireside circle, thoroughly warmed, domestic influences, matron.* Even so, the narrator's attitude is ambiguous. Warland "still believed" that Annie was "imbued . . . with a finer grace." The narrator refuses to confirm this belief and thus refuses to say whether Owen is excluded from the only situation that can bring him domestic fulfillment or only from this "plain and sturdy" group.

The narrator claims, as Longfellow might, that the Danforths' baby is "a little personage who had come mysteriously out of the infinite." Unlike any univocal adherent of the cult of domesticity, the narrator adds that the baby has "something so sturdy and real in his composition that he seemed moulded out of the densest substance which earth could supply" (10:468–69). The narrator later observes that "The infant on the floor, followed its course with his sagacious little eyes" as the butterfly soars about the family circle (10:471). This sturdy, sagacious baby does not belong to the cult of domesticity. It is no surprise, therefore, that he squashes Warland's butterfly. Hawthorne's narrator greatly complicates our responses to domestic values through his editorializing. Just before the baby crushes the butterfly, for example, Danforth observes, "How wise the little monkey looks!" The following sentence typifies Hawthorne's indirection in this tale: " 'I never saw such a look on a child's face,' answered Annie, admiring her own infant, and with good reason, far more than the artistic butterfly" (10:474). Even if we dismiss the term *monkey*, the passage is problematic. From a realistic standpoint, Annie's doting attitude toward her baby is plausible, but what about the narrator's attitude? "[W]ith good reason" is the narrator's judgment here, but this opinion conflicts with his valorization of art and his criticism of the pedestrian elsewhere in the tale. "The Artist of the Beautiful" shows Hawthorne inflecting domestic motifs positively and negatively in order to complicate and enrich our responses as readers, just as Hawthorne's other narrators manipulate technical devices. If we cannot therefore stipulate some ultimate interpretation of this tale "done up neatly, and condensed into the final sentence," as the narrator says in "Wakefield" (9:131), this failure should come as no surprise.

Hawthorne also exploits domestic motifs with great ingenuity in his longer works. At the end of *The Scarlet Letter,* for example, the narrator proposes a "brighter period" in which "the whole relation between man and woman [is established] on a surer ground of mutual happiness" (1:263), but he locates this time in the future of Hester Prynne's imagination rather than in the present of Hester's New England. When Hester thinks of bygone days, furthermore, she remembers "the look of heedful and anxious love which [her mother's face] always wore" (1:158) rather than idyllic evenings of toast and tea. In the present time of the plot, Hester experiences no sunny breakfasts or afternoon teas, only systematic exclusion from all scenes of domestic felicity.

In "Hester at Her Needle," the chapter devoted to accounting for Hester's behavior in the years immediately following her condemnation, the narrator says in summary that "In all her intercourse with society . . . there was nothing that made her feel as if she belonged to it." He continues metaphorically:

> She stood apart from mortal interests, yet close beside them, like a ghost that revisits the familiar fireside, and can no longer make itself seen or felt; no more smile with the household joy, nor mourn with the kindred sorrow; or, should it succeed in manifesting its forbidden sympathy, awakening only terror and horrible repugnance. (1:84)

The Gothic possibilities implicit in a ghost's efforts to communicate with the living might elsewhere have engaged Hawthorne's imaginative energies. Even here the image is metaphorically appropriate to describe Hester's incomplete participation in the Puritan community. For my purposes, however, the interesting fact is Hawthorne's characteristic association of the "familiar fireside," "household joy," and a sense of domestic security. Equally characteristic is the narrator's insistence that his principal character can experience these conditions only negatively, by means of exclusion, rather than positively, by means of participation.

This point is reenforced in "Another View of Hester" when the narrator again typifies Hester's behavior during the course of several years. By selflessly "giv[ing] of her little substance to every demand of poverty" and fearlessly nursing the stricken "when pestilence stalked through the town," Hester has forced many people to reinterpret the scarlet letter to mean "Able; so strong was Hester Prynne, with a woman's strength" (1:161). The narrator explains that Hester "came, not as a guest, but as a rightful inmate, into the household that was darkened by trouble" (1:161). Readers might therefore anticipate a more satisfactory domestic life for Hester. Even though the circumstances are unfortunate, some sort of alternative community might be projected from the narrator's terms *guest* and *household*. Any such expectations are dashed by the narrator's concluding remarks:

> It was only the darkened house that could contain her. When sunshine came again, she was not there. Her shadow had faded across the threshold. The helpful inmate had departed, without one backward glance to gather up the meed of gratitude, if any were in the hearts of those whom she had served so zealously. (1:161–62)

This passage probably throws some light on the narrator's speculations about whether Hester is motivated by "pride" or "humility." Another idea is also suggested. No matter how "Able" Hester may be in serving the other citizens of Boston, and whether these abilities arise from her pride or her humility, Hester may participate in the Puritans' domestic circles only temporarily. Once the crisis has passed, Hester must depart. She cannot share in any family's breakfasts. She cannot share toast and tea before the fire on a cozy evening. Hester's usual domestic situation is on the outside, looking through the window at the happy households of others.

Hester's exclusion from domestic fulfillment is also reflected in the situation of her lover. During the period in which Hester is going about doing good for her fellow man, Arthur Dimmesdale is securely installed in the best rooms in the house of "a pious widow, of good social rank": "a front apartment, with a sunny exposure, and heavy window-curtains to create a noontide shadow, when desirable." With biblical tapestries on the walls and an ample library of "parchment-bound folios of the Fathers, and the lore of Rabbis, and monkish erudition," Dimmesdale might seem to be very suitably housed. In terms of Hawthorne's plot, however, Dimmesdale's apparently enviable domestic situation is ironically compromised by the presence of his unrecognized nemesis, Roger Chillingworth, in the same house. With two unacknowledged adversaries "familiarly passing from one apartment to the other, and bestowing a mutual and not incurious inspection into one another's business" (1:126), Dimmesdale's living conditions are more suited to Gothic than domestic fiction.

In terms of the cult of domesticity, Dimmesdale's situation is undesirable in still another way. No matter how luxurious his accommodations might

be, Dimmesdale still lives a bachelor's—in domestic terms, an incomplete—
life. The narrator introduces this issue ironically while stressing the "pater-
nal and reverential love for the young pastor" evidenced by his direst en-
emy, "this sagacious, experienced, benevolent, old physician." Floating
above this irony is the narrator's examination of Dimmesdale's apparent
choice of a celibate life in which he is "Doomed by his own choice . . . to
eat his unsavory morsel always at another's board, and endure the life-long
chill which must be his lot who seeks to warm himself only at another's
fireside" (1:125). The more desirable, married, clerical state is suggested by
a passage from the sketch "Fire-Worship," in which Hawthorne's narrator
imagines the life of an earlier inhabitant of the Old Manse: "At eventide,
probably, the study was peopled with the clergyman's wife and family; and
children tumbled themselves upon the hearth-rug, and grave Puss sat with
her back to the fire, or gazed, with a semblance of human meditation, into
its fervid depths" (10:143). Even without the machinations of Chillingworth, then, Dimmesdale's life seems woefully incomplete when contrasted
to this domestic fantasy.

Within the terms of Hawthorne's plot, optimistic readers might still be
able to conceive of some happy domestic situation for Dimmesdale and
Hester. Perhaps the two might find a way to live together among the citizens
of Boston, disgraced but sustained by love. With a pathetically false optimism, Hester promises Pearl something along these lines after meeting with
Dimmesdale in the forest: "[I]n days to come he will walk hand in hand
with us. We will have a home and fireside of our own; and thou shalt sit
upon his knee; and he will teach thee many things, and love thee dearly"
(1:212). If the intolerance of the Puritans cannot be overcome, the little
family might thrive, as Hester says, "among the wisest and the most renowned of the cultivated world" (1:198). Some sort of better domestic life is
conceivable for them in any case. Hawthorne allows none of these domestic
resolutions to develop, however. Hester and Dimmesdale will be connected
not only through their adultery and their daughter, but also through their
mutual exclusion from domestic happiness. In this respect, the two characters typify the inverse fashion in which Hawthorne often appropriates domestic motifs.

The House of the Seven Gables affords Hawthorne ample opportunity to
affirm domestic values directly. First of all, the principal action of the narra-

tive is set in the same mid-nineteenth-century America inhabited by Henry Wadsworth Longfellow and Susan Warner rather than in the historically remote seventeenth century of the Puritan settlements. Second, the plot attains closure with a marriage rather than with the separation of two lovers by death. Furthermore, as Susan VanZanten Gallagher plausibly argues in her essay "A Domestic Reading of *The House of the Seven Gables*," Hawthorne's heroine, Phoebe Pyncheon, closely resembles the heroines in contemporary domestic novels like *The Wide, Wide World*. Recognizing the presence of these conventional elements surely helps to create a much-needed domestic context for *The Seven Gables*, but—as is usually true when dealing with Hawthorne—we should assume that he adapts this context to his own purposes.

Gallagher helpfully observes that "The detailed descriptions of the [Pyncheon] house echo those of the domestic novel." She continues:

> Hawthorne's particulars, however, work in an ironic fashion. The cool parlors and cosy kitchens of the typical domestic novel become the dark, gloomy house, full of spiders and rats, furnished with straight and stiff chairs, and plagued by a mysterious, cold draft. (6)

Gallagher develops this imagery toward an interpretation of the book in terms of the popular plot in which a woman deprived of conventional familial support successfully makes her own way in the world, a view shared by Nina Baym in *Woman's Fiction*. *The House of the Seven Gables* certainly supports the interpretations advanced by Gallagher and Baym, as well as other interpretations focused on history, art, sex, and guilt. At the same time, the book also shows how Hawthorne can absorb the imagery familiar to his readers into a strategy devoted to showing the absence rather than the presence of household warmth and security.

When Hepzibah Pyncheon first comes downstairs in the second chapter, she is clearly unsuited to the role of Angel in the House. First of all, Hepzibah enters "a low-studded room, with a beam across the ceiling, panelled with dark wood, and having a large chimney-piece . . . closed by an iron fire-board, through which ran the funnel of a modern stove" (2:32). No nurturing hearth burns here. The furniture in this room, as Gallagher points out, is equally uninviting. No one would be tempted to make tea and toast for her mother in this setting or to frolic with his three daughters.

Although the room is uncomfortable, dark, and dreary, Hepzibah does not light a lamp, open curtains, or start a fire in the stove. Instead, she stares at the portrait of her ancestor for awhile before screwing up her courage to enter her cent shop. Through this description, the narrator inverts the terms by which warmth, security, and protection from the outside world were defined by the cult of domesticity. In fact, by opening the shop, Hepzibah allows the world to invade her home. Hepzibah is still domestically ineffectual in Chapter 15, and as a result, "The house itself shivered, from every attic of its seven gables, down to the great kitchen-fireplace, which served all the better as an emblem of the mansion's heart, because, though built for warmth, it was now so comfortless and empty" (2:224). Hepzibah's sadness is the result of what is happening in the plot, especially threats by her cousin Judge Pyncheon against her brother Clifford. Characteristically, the narrator represents her sadness through images denoting the absence of domestic security rather than presence of threats. The narrator even employs Hawthorne's preferred term *emblem* to identify this strategy.

Another proximate cause of Hepzibah's unhappiness is the departure of her young cousin Phoebe to visit her family in the country. Throughout the book, in fact, these two characters are related not only through the plot but also through domestic imagery. In "Clifford and Phoebe," for example, the narrator develops an elaborate contrast between the two female characters. First he explains Clifford's attraction to the young girl: "to him, this little figure of the cheeriest household-life was just what he required, to bring him back into the breathing world" (2:140). Phoebe's embodiment of domestic values is clearly established through this vocabulary, as it is later when the narrator says Clifford regarded Phoebe as "a verse of household poetry" (2:142). Hepzibah's efforts to create some sort of domestic security for Clifford are, in contrast, unavailing: "How patiently did she endeavor to wrap Clifford up in her great, warm love, and make it all the world to him, so that he should retain no torturing sense of the coldness and dreariness, without!" (2:134). Hawthorne's plot makes Hepzibah incapable of providing domestic security either for Clifford or for herself even while depicting such happiness as the solution to all their problems.

A final example must suffice to illustrate Hawthorne's use of domestic imagery in relation to these two female characters. In Chapter 5, on her first morning in the house of the seven gables, Phoebe quickly transforms her new bedroom into a home, in striking contrast to Hepzibah's domestic inaction in the second chapter. The narrator first confesses, "What was precisely Phoebe's process, we find it impossible to say," but he acknowledges that Phoebe "had fully succeeded in throwing a kindly and hospitable smile over the apartment." The success of these domestic improvements is then expressed metaphorically: "No longer ago than the night before, it had resembled nothing so much as the old maid's heart; for there was neither sunshine nor household-fire in one nor the other" (2:72). Assuredly the passage demonstrates, as many readers have argued, the superiority of Phoebe's outgoing personality to Hepzibah's emotional repression. Phoebe is also a success in the terms popularized by women's fiction like *The Wide, Wide World*, while Hepzibah is a failure. At the same time, the imagery may be considered outside its restricted application to these two characters, as evidence of Hawthorne's adaptation of imagery derived from the cult of domesticity.

Perhaps the clearest evidence lies in the images that Hawthorne uses almost in passing throughout the book—not necessarily to support his ongoing plot or to reenforce characterization, but simply to refer to what everyone knows to be true. For example, when the narrator wishes to illustrate how Clifford's mind occasionally grows more focused, he uses the following metaphor: "It betokened that his spiritual part had returned, and was doing its best to kindle the heart's household-fire, and light up intellectual lamps in the dark and ruinous mansion, where it was doomed to be a forlorn inhabitant" (2:105). A reader sufficiently committed to critical organicism could probably establish a thematic relationship between these images and the story's setting or demonstrate their proleptical relation to Judge Pyncheon's death. For my purposes, it is significant that Hawthorne uses these domestic images so casually as vehicles for the tenors spirit, life, and human sympathy. Shortly after Phoebe has been compared to "a verse of household poetry," the narrator justifies his use of this imagery by explaining: "But we strive in vain to put the idea into words. No adequate expression of the beauty and profound pathos, with which it impresses us, is attainable" (2:142). In other words, the narrator claims along with T. S. Eliot's character J. Alfred Prufrock that "It is impossible to say just what I mean!" but he also adopts Prufrock's method of metaphorical indirection: "But as if. . . ." Of especial relevance are the narrator's assumptions about his readers and their stock of ready responses. We may thus assume that the image "household poetry" is primarily intended to connote positive values, values that need not—perhaps cannot—be stated.

The same might be said about a very peculiar detail contained in the narrator's account of the first meal prepared under Phoebe's influence: "The half-starved rats . . . stole visibly out of their hiding-places, and sat on their hind-legs, snuffing the fumy atmosphere, and wistfully awaiting an opportunity to nibble" (2:99). Whereas rats might, in most other contexts, engender Poe-esque associations of horror, here they are subsumed into a picture of domestic comfort suitable for a children's book. The narrator is adopting a symbolic shorthand of domestic imagery that he seems confident his readers will recognize and endorse. The primary difference between this breakfast and other domestic scenes scattered throughout Hawthorne's works is that here he attempts to depict this happiness directly, in the manner of Stowe and Warner, rather than through his usual method of denial. Perhaps because the potential for sentimentality seems so strong in direct affirmations of domestic values, the narrator suggests that it might be better not to attempt this sort of treatment after all since "No adequate expression . . . is attainable." Whatever the reason, such passages are rare in Hawthorne's work.

More typical are Hawthorne's transformations of domestic motifs in *The Blithedale Romance*. Modern hotels and boarding houses, the idealistic commune that gives the romance its title, even a cottage for two that might elsewhere provide the setting for a happily-ever-after resolution—all are converted here into images of absence rather than presence. The most consistent exemplar of domestic exclusion is Hawthorne's fictionalized narrator, Miles Coverdale, whom we find at the beginning of the story lodged in a snug apartment "in one of the midmost houses of a brick-block." Here Coverdale has surrounded himself with all the material comforts: "my cosey pair of bachelor-rooms—with a good fire burning in the grate, and a closet right at hand, where there was still a bottle or two in the champagne-basket, and a residuum of claret in a box, and somewhat of proof in the concavity of a big demijohn" (3:10). Like a nineteenth-century Dimmesdale, Coverdale has constructed a celibate parody of the sort of home revered in the cult of domesticity.

This inversion of domestic values is emphasized when Coverdale achieves a comparable degree of happiness in a "dingy room in the bustling hotel" (3:146) to which he has fled to escape the complexities of communal life. In this hotel Coverdale contentedly spends two days "in the laziest manner possible, in a rocking-chair, inhaling the fragrance of a series of cigars, with my legs and slippered feet horizontally disposed, and in my hand a novel, purchased of a railroad bibliopolist" (3:147). Perhaps fearing that Coverdale's situation here might seem too attractive to readers tired of, or insufficiently committed to, the cult of domesticity, Hawthorne quickly has his narrator point out the inadequacies of this arrangement. Life in a paradise of bachelors can soon grow tedious: "At intervals . . . when its effects grew a little too soporific—not for my patience, but for the possibility of keeping my eyes open—I bestirred myself, started from the rocking-chair, and looked out of the window" (3:147). What Coverdale sees while watching the inhabitants of a "row of fashionable dwellings" opposite his hotel (3:149) serves even more effectively than his boredom to demonstrate the inadequacy of his domestic situation.

In terms of Hawthorne's plot, Coverdale's most important discovery is that Zenobia has rented the lower floor of the opposite house. Thus, Coverdale can speculate on the relations among Zenobia, Priscilla, and Westervelt while spying on them from a safe distance. Less significant in terms of plot but more revealing of Coverdale's domestic state are his perceptions of the young bachelor who occupies the top floor of the opposite house: "I saw a young man in a dressing-gown, standing before the glass and brushing his hair, for a quarter-of-an-hour together." In addition to vanity, unproductive leisure is also suggested by this grooming, as it is by the observation that the young man "spent an equal space of time in the elaborate arrangement of his cravat" (3:150). We might ask, who but a young bachelor is so free of obligations as to devote this much care and time to his appearance? The answer, of course, is: an aging bachelor—the same aging bachelor who has devoted such attention to his own comfort throughout the book. When Coverdale remarks, therefore, that he is getting to be "a frosty bachelor, with another white hair, every week or so, in my moustache" (3:9), we might inquire how much more productive his life has been than that of the young man with the carefully combed hair and carefully knotted tie.

In this respect, as Barton Levi St. Armand suggests, in "The Love Song of Miles Coverdale," J. Alfred Prufrock slouches toward Boston to be born.

Prufrock's vanity, his distorted perceptions of reality, and his timidity are all anticipated by Coverdale's. The two characters share also a reluctance to make any sort of real commitment to another human being. Thus they both exchange domestic security experienced from the inside for a voyeuristic isolation. The most instructive discovery Coverdale makes while snooping on his neighbors clearly fits Hawthorne's familiar pattern of domestic exclusion:

> At a window of the next story below, two children, prettily dressed, were looking out. By-and-by, a middle-aged gentleman came softly behind them, kissed the little girl, and playfully pulled the little boy's ear. It was a papa, no doubt, just come in from his counting-room or office; and anon appeared mamma, stealing as softly behind papa, as he had stolen behind the children, and laying her hand on his shoulder to surprise him. Then followed a kiss between papa and mamma, but a noiseless one; for the children did not turn their heads. (3:150–51)

The scene contrasts forcefully not only with Coverdale's bachelor condition but also with the other incomplete domestic units throughout the romance. Coverdale says, "I bless God for these good folks" (3:151), but he is incapable of any action directed toward making his own situation more nearly approach theirs.

In this sense, Coverdale resembles not only Prufrock but another character cut off from domestic happiness. In Zenobia's metadiegetic narrative, "The Silvery Veil," Hawthorne develops Theodore as another emotionally distant bachelor, too egocentric and careful to make any real emotional commitment. For these reasons, Theodore cannot pledge himself totally and unquestioningly to the Veiled Lady even though "all the felicity of earth and of the future world" might be his reward (3:113). Like Coverdale's Prufrockian indecisiveness, Theodore's second thoughts render him incapable of fulfilling the role of a romantic hero. His punishment is also similar to Coverdale's—perpetual exclusion from domestic happiness: "His retribution was, to pine, forever and ever, for another sight of that dim, mournful face—which might have been his life-long, household, fireside joy—to desire and waste life in a feverish quest, and never meet it more!" (3:114). While the romantic tradition supplies the pining and questing, the "life-long, household, fireside joy" clearly derives from the cult of domesticity.

Theodore is emotionally barred from the former, and he participates in the latter only in a negative, Hawthornean manner.

Another reversal of the cult of domesticity may be seen in Chapter 4 of *Blithedale*, in which the community seems most nearly to approach the condition of a true family. Even twelve years after that evening, Coverdale recalls the picture with unusual feeling: "The blaze from an armful of substantial sticks, rendered more combustible by brush-wood and pine, flickered powerfully on the smoke-blackened walls, and so cheered our spirits that we cared not what inclemency might rage and roar, on the other side of our illuminated windows" (3:23). Unusual too are Coverdale's easy use of the pronouns *our* and *we* and his description of the scene from within the "illuminated windows" instead of from the outside looking in. Here we seem to see the emotional as well as the physical dimensions of domesticity, the cheer as well as the blazing fire. Readers might recall *The Wide, Wide World*. And yet Hawthorne's intentions are much different from Warner's, as his narrative strategy makes clear. Undercutting Coverdale's idyllic description of this evening is his ironic reassessment of the communards' self-righteous professions of solidarity with their rural servants. Coverdale says in summary, "If ever I have deserved . . . to be soundly cuffed by a fellow-mortal, for secretly putting weight upon some imaginary social advantage, it must have been while I was striving to prove myself ostentatiously his equal, and no more" (3:24–25). That is to say, this supposedly realistic picture of domesticity is essentially false. The people sitting around this fire and later around the supper table are not truly members of the same family, socially or emotionally, and that is why their experiment in communal living is doomed to failure. Simon Foster's realistic observation therefore becomes symbolically predictive: "The blaze of that brush-wood will only last a minute or two longer" (3:25). It would appear that the domestic bliss of the Blithedale family may be more accurately considered in terms of its absence than of its presence.

Hawthorne uses a similar technique elsewhere in the book to depict the domestic situations of other characters. During the period of her childhood, for example, Priscilla is depicted with her father, Old Moodie/Fauntleroy, in these surroundings: "Tattered hangings, a marble hearth, traversed with many cracks and fissures, a richly-carved oaken mantel-piece, partly hacked-away for kindling-stuff, a stuccoed ceiling, defaced with great, unsightly patches of the naked laths" (3:184). A conventional adherent of the cult of domesticity might easily have transvalued these images of physical poverty into symbols of those familial affections that are worth more than gold. Hawthorne's narrator implies on the other hand that the domestic feelings of this incomplete family are as impoverished as their circumstances. Fauntleroy lives in the past, and Priscilla, bereft of her mother and deprived of her father's attentions, lives in fantasies woven around her unknown sister. Hawthorne's grim picture of this tattered family seems a twisted parody of domestic bliss: "For Fauntleroy, as they sat by their cheerless fireside—which was no fireside, in truth, but only a rusty stove—had often talked to the little girl about his former wealth, the noble loveliness of his first wife, and the beautiful child whom she had given him" (3:186). Apparently the obvious and appropriate subjects for domestic discourse— the little girl in front of him and what might be done to better her current or future life—were of no interest to this man whose fatherly affections seem to have been exhausted in self-pity. The "rusty stove" in this dysfunctional home is thus metonymic, representing the lamentable situation, predicted in "Fire-Worship," in which the domestic values long associated with the family hearth have been exterminated by the proliferation of Franklin stoves.

Even the two characters who attain something resembling domestic fulfillment achieve only a highly restricted form of happiness. Unlike much of Hawthorne's fiction, *The Blithedale Romance* attains domestic closure, but not the kind of closure dictated by the practices of Hawthorne's contemporaries or by the desires of his readers. In the penultimate chapter, Hollingsworth and Priscilla have married and settled down in "a small cottage" (3:242). Any work of domestic fiction would suitably idealize the happiness of a couple so situated, but Hawthorne is not writing domestic fiction. When Coverdale pays a visit to inspect the pair, he notes that Priscilla displays "a deep submissive, unquestioning reverence, and also a veiled happiness in her fair and quiet countenance" as she walks along a forest path with her husband. Readers might think of Warner's Ellen and John Humphreys or Hawthorne's own Hannah and Matthew. However, Hawthorne's narrative challenges these familiar patterns. When Coverdale asks "whether [Hollingsworth] were a happy man or no" in this apparently regained paradise, he discovers that Hollingsworth now wears "a depressed and melancholy look, that seemed habitual; the powerfully built man showed a self-distrustful weakness, and a childlike, or childish, tendency to press close, and closer still, to the side of the slender woman whose arm was within his" (3:242). Under these circumstances, Coverdale says, "[T]he tears gushed to my eyes, and I forgave him" (3:243). If this is how things have worked out for Hollingsworth, even Coverdale need not be too envious. As so often in his work, Hawthorne uses familiar forms of domestic imagery to propose domestic security for his characters only to deny it to them.

This continues to be the case in Hawthorne's last completed romance. In "Miriam's Studio," Chapter 5 of *The Marble Faun*, Donatello, the naive young Count of Monte Beni, visits Miriam Schaefer in her artist's studio located in a three-hundred-year-old Roman palace. The purpose of this visit is not altogether clear in terms of Hawthorne's plot. In fact, Miriam asks Donatello, "But why do you come into this shadowy room of mine?" (4:41). Perhaps Donatello is worried about Miriam after her disturbing encounter with her mysterious model in the catacombs described in the previous chapter. Perhaps he has come to take the model's place. The latter seems plausible when Miriam tells Donatello to "amuse" himself by looking at some of her pen-and-ink sketches until "by and by I shall be in the mood to begin the portrait we were talking about" (4:41). Considering Hawthorne's customary exploitation of the cult of domesticity, Donatello's visit most likely is intended to provide the narrator with an opportunity to contrast the two sides of Miriam's artistic sensibility represented by her unfinished sketches.

The first group of sketches consists of biblical scenes depicting "the idea of woman, acting the part of a revengeful mischief towards man" (4:44). Specifically, Miriam has drawn Jael driving a nail through the brain of Sisera, Judith gazing at the severed head of Holofernes, and Herodias contemplating the head of John the Baptist on a charger. Even Donatello, whom Miriam has earlier characterized as "a simpleton" (4:15), cannot help but be disconcerted by such drawings: "He gave a shudder; his face assumed a look of trouble, fear, and disgust; he snatched up one sketch after another, as if about to tear it in pieces" (4:44). Like the village doctor in "The Minister's Black Veil," Donatello seems to suspect that something must be "amiss with [Miriam's] intellects." As it turns out, these drawings were not inspired by incipient insanity but by Miriam's perceptions of the restricted roles available to women in her time. Earlier in the scene Miriam says about her female manikin that "the true end of her being" is "to wear rich shawls and other garments in a becoming fashion" and that "[f]or most purposes, she has the advantage of the sisterhood" (4:41–42). Echoes of Zenobia's feminism ring through this analysis, as does a note of Zenobia's self-deprecating humor: "Upon my word, I am satirical unawares" (4:41). As many readers, including Philip Rahv (1941) and Luther Luedtke (1989), have observed, Miriam resembles Zenobia not only in her exotic sexuality but also in the strength of her intelligence. As Donatello's horrified reaction here portends, Miriam will also resemble Zenobia in her failure to attain domestic happiness.

Miriam's second set of drawings induce a more favorable response from Donatello and thus might seem a more promising artistic avenue. These are sketches of "domestic and common scenes, so finely and subtly idealized that they seemed such as we may see at any moment, and everywhere; while still there was the indefinable something added, or taken away, which makes all the difference between sordid life and an earthly paradise" (4:45). The specific scenes are as representative of idealized domesticity as the first were of feminist vengeance:

> There was the scene, that comes once in every life, of the lover winning the soft and pure avowal of bashful affection from the maiden, whose slender form half leans towards his arm, half shrinks from it, we know not which. There was wedded affection in its successive stages, represented in a series of delicately conceived designs, touched with a holy fire, that burned from youth to age in those two hearts, and gave one identical beauty to the faces, throughout all the changes of feature.
>
> There was a drawing of an infant's shoe, half-worn out, with the airy print of the blessed foot within; a thing that would make a mother smile or weep out of the very depths of her heart; and yet an actual mother would not have been likely to appreciate the poetry of the little shoe, until Miriam revealed it to her. (4:45)

One might assume at first that Miriam is illustrating the same kinds of idealized domestic scenes that Susan Warner and Henry Wadsworth Longfellow proposed as models of practically attainable happiness.

The assumption would be erroneous, however. The narrator first explains that as "the productions of a beautiful imagination," the drawings represent "a truer and lovelier picture of the life that belongs to woman, than an actual acquaintance with some of its hard and dusty facts could have inspired" (4:46). "Sordid life" is real life, in other words, and any "lovelier picture" is merely an imaginative artistic projection. This distinction by the narrator is reenforced symbolically by a motif peculiar to Miriam's domestic drawings:

> In all those sketches of common life, and the affections that spiritualize it, a figure was pourtrayed apart; now, it peeped between the branches of a shrubbery, amid which two lovers sat; now, it was looking through a frosted window, from the outside, while a young wedded pair sat at their new fireside, within; and, once, it leaned from a chariot, which six horses were whirling onward in pomp and pride, and gazed at a scene of humble enjoyment by a cottage-door. Always, it was the same figure, and always depicted with an expression of deep sadness; and in every instance, slightly as they were brought out, the face and form had the traits of Miriam's own. (4:46)

Unlike the fantasies of "earthly paradise" that proved imaginatively satisfactory to Hawthorne's contemporaries, Miriam's domestic visions lapse into Hawthorne's usual pattern: airy projections of complete peace and love from which the dreamer is consistently excluded. Miriam's artistic intuitions prove accurate in terms of the plot. In the epilog we learn that she has not been imprisoned for her model's murder. Since Donatello has been locked in a deep dungeon, however, Miriam is perpetually cut off from love and domestic fulfillment. Instead of a domestic future of shared joys and sorrows such as Edith and Edgar expect in "The May-Pole of Merry Mount," these two lovers are condemned to live separately ever after.

If domestic salvation comes to anyone in The Marble Faun, the beneficiaries are Kenyon the sculptor and Hilda the copyist, whose romance shadows that of Miriam and Donatello throughout the book. In "The Virgin's Shrine," the chapter immediately following "Miriam's Studio," the narrator describes Hilda's living quarters at the top of a tower. Then he characterizes Hilda's artistic talent as follows: "She was endowed with a deep and sensitive faculty of appreciation; she had the gift of discerning and worshipping excellence, in a most unusual measure" (4:56). Therefore, instead of creating original renderings of feminist vengeance or of contemporary domestic bliss, Hilda imitates the work of the great artists of the past. According to the narrator, this is just as well: "Would it have been worth Hilda's while to relinquish this office, for the sake of giving the world a picture or two which it would call original; pretty fancies of snow and moonlight; the counterpart, in picture, of so many feminine achievements in literature!" (4:61). Perhaps because, unlike Hester and Miriam, Hilda does not create her own visions of domestic perfection, she need not be excluded from them. Instead, Hilda epitomizes the domestic fantasies of another character, Kenyon.

Kenyon's version of domestic paradise is first articulated when he looks worshipfully up at Hilda in her tower, surrounded by doves, as she trims the devotional lamp before the shrine of the Virgin Mary. While the setting sun casts "a golden glory on Hilda's hair," Kenyon thinks:

> How like a spirit she looks, aloft there, with the evening glory round her head, and those winged creatures claiming her as akin to them! . . . How far above me! How unattainable! Ah, if I could lift myself to her region! Or—if it be not a sin to wish it—would that I might draw her down to an earthly fireside! (4:372)

Kenyon's visions are as predictive as Miriam's. In the penultimate chapter, which Hawthorne had originally intended to serve as his last word on the subject, we learn with little surprise that "Hilda was coming down from her old tower, to be herself enshrined and worshipped as a household Saint, in the light of her husband's fireside" (4:461). It is significant that Hawthorne does not depict this happy domestic scene in the present time of the plot's action, either in this chapter or when he returns to the material in the "Postscript." Hilda and Kenyon may be entering into what Kenyon anticipates to be "earthly paradise," but the author refuses to depict this realized happiness for us.

As in the case of Hilda's unpainted original works, however, perhaps this is just as well. Probably few readers can fully accept the evidence given of this couple's ideal compatibility. Soon after Kenyon first aspires to bring Hilda down to his fireside, the two young Americans discover themselves to be virtually alone in Rome, and this proximity quickly ripens into love. Kenyon then discovers that his work is taking a different direction: "Kenyon's genius, unconsciously wrought upon by Hilda's influence, took a more delicate character than heretofore. He modeled, among other things, a beautiful little statue of Maidenhood, gathering a Snow-drop." Putting aside the question of whether this subject can be considered an advance over Kenyon's earlier statue of Cleopatra, the practical consequences do not seem encouraging: "It was never put into marble, however; because the sculptor soon recognized it as one of those fragile creations which are true only to the moment that produces them, and are wronged, if we try to imprison their airy excellence in a permanent material" (4:374–75). This does not bode well for Kenyon's future as an artist. Love has a similar effect on Hilda's career: "It is questionable whether she was ever so perfect a copyist thenceforth" (4:375). Perhaps Kenyon and Hilda will live happily ever after, but on the basis of these early developments, readers may find it difficult to visualize the couple's life in their "earthly paradise."

As Edwin Haviland Miller suggests in *Salem Is My Dwelling Place* (461–80), it was probably just as difficult for the author, who had been married to his dove Sophia for nearly twenty years, to envision such a condition. As in the cases of Hester's and Miriam's visions of domestic perfection, the combination of Hawthorne's personal skepticism and his artistic conscience would not permit him to represent the state of domestic bliss, however desirable, as a realized condition. Unlike Susan Warner, Hawthorne could not write a concluding chapter showing the newly married Kenyons inspecting the perfectly satisfactory furnishings of their new home or entertaining the narrator with toast and tea before their cozy fireside. Hawthorne's dissenting narrative strategy, as in his earlier works, was to transform domestic imagery, as he transformed contemporary romanticism. As a result, *The Marble Faun* challenged his readers' expectations and assumptions as his earlier works had done, and as they continue to challenge ours today.

# EIGHT

# Conclusion

Whether Hilda and Kenyon will live happily ever after—or whether they deserve to—is only one of the many issues confronting readers at the end of *The Marble Faun*. The book also encourages us to wonder, as Miriam and Kenyon do, whether Donatello's fall into sin was ironically fortunate after all. These questions—and others concerning the moral value of art, the psychological effects of guilt, the influences of history, the lure of Europe to Americans, the nature of human consciousness—have been asked, and variously answered, by generations of critics. In light of this thematic complexity, Hawthorne's last completed work of fiction can be seen to resemble closely his earlier works and thus to provide a convenient opportunity to restate my argument.

Nina Baym observes in *The Shape of Hawthorne's Career* (1976), "*The Marble Faun* is by far the most complex and ambitious of Hawthorne's mature romances" (229). As we might expect, therefore, the book has elicited a dazzling variety of interpretation. In *Hawthorne's Contemporaneous Reputation*, Bertha Faust summarizes an allegorical interpretation, first published in 1861, as follows: "Miriam is Soul; Hilda is Conscience; Kenyon is Reason; and Donatello is Nature. The monk is Temptation. In these terms the narrative can be worked out very neatly, and it is even possible to explain the much criticized conclusion" (130). Hubert H. Hoeltje offers an equally "neat" reading in *Inward Sky: The Mind and Heart of Nathaniel Hawthorne* (1962): "Stated quite simply . . . there is in *The Marble Faun* a joining of the Christian faith in immortality with the Socratic conviction that in wisdom lies the salvation of man" (515). While these tidy interpretations, developed a century apart, seem to share common ground, neither can be easily reconciled with the view expressed by F. O. Matthiessen during the interim (1941): "[T]he unintended impression of self-righteousness and priggishness that exudes from these characters [Hilda and Kenyon] brings to the fore some extreme limitations of the standards that Hawthorne took for granted" (356–57). Thematic reconciliation becomes even more elusive when the list is extended.

Baym, for example, goes on to explain that *The Marble Faun* "records the distorting effect of repressive institutions on human life" and that "It attempts to discover the origins of reverence for the authoritarian within the psyche" (229). Jonathan Auerbach interprets the book in 1980 as "a self-interpreting confession that compels the reader to participate in the fiction" (103). In 1985, Evan Carton is equally decisive in *The Rhetoric of American Romance*: "Art takes up a history that is comprised of other works of art, a history whose origins are imaged and obscured in a welter of models" (259). In 1988, John Michael writes that, "especially" in *The Marble Faun*, Hawthorne "undermines the simplistic epistemological and moral assumptions on which the practice of nineteenth-century history depends" (150). In the same year, Edgar A. Dryden writes with equal assurance: "Indeed, the entire novel is dominated by the difficulties of representing and interpreting the problems of writing and reading . . ." (34). The list could be greatly expanded and the basic point would remain: nearly everyone who writes about *The Marble Faun* has a good idea of what the book "means," and nearly everyone disagrees about what this meaning is.

Some of the more recent disagreements extend far beyond conflicts in interpretation, touching upon the most fundamental critical issues. Returning to the book in *The Marble Faun: Hawthorne's Transformations* (1992), Evan Carton writes that "the longest, loosest, and murkiest of Hawthorne's four completed novels . . . poses a challenge to the very idea of a literary 'masterwork' by forcing us to define what qualifies or disqualifies a work for that status and to examine the values that contribute to and the consequences that follow from our definition" (13). Milton Stern meets this challenge, in *Contexts for Hawthorne: The Marble Faun and the Politics of Openness and Closure in American Literature* (1991), by developing aesthetic definitions that lead to rather negative conclusions:

In the conflicting representations of his utopian conservatism (Miriam, Donatello) and his ideological conservatism (Hilda, Kenyon), Hawthorne was faced with mutual annihilations. He ended his story before its ultimate conclusion. Nevertheless, because his utopian and ideological conservatisms tend to annihilate each other, Hawthorne produced not a fascinating, rich, ironical book, but a fascinating, rich, botched one. (112)

Stern would prefer that *The Marble Faun* proceed toward "its ultimate conclusion," legitimating some interpretation that could be specifically articulated even if the statement required great subtlety.

Stern also writes that "It would be silly to insist that Hawthorne should have written different fictions" (153). Kenneth Marc Harris agrees, writing in *Hypocrisy and Self-Deception in Hawthorne's Fiction* (1988), "Admittedly, it would be unfair to fault Hawthorne for not having written *Crime and Punishment*" instead of *The Marble Faun*. Even so, Harris concludes: "Having assembled the makings for what might have been his most serious novel, Hawthorne scarcely begins to write it" (143). In *The Office of The Scarlet Letter* (1991), Sacvan Bercovitch goes further than Harris in suggesting what Hawthorne should have done:

But we should also keep in mind the hurricanes of the actual which a decade earlier had not disturbed Hawthorne's fantasies: Southern slavery; Native American genocide; the Mexican War (through which General Pierce became a national hero); expansionist demands of men like Pierce for war against Cuba and Latin America; pervasive ethnic and religious discrimination; child labor in Northern mill towns; the grievances listed in the Seneca Falls Convention; and the manifold abuses documented in the petitions circulated by New England's abolitionist sewing circles. (106)

If Hawthorne had been suitably alert to these issues while writing *The Marble Faun*, Bercovitch feels that it would have been a better book.

The variety of these interpretations—and of the interpretive strategies behind them—could be used to illustrate a history of critical opinion in America. This great variety also provides strong support for the thesis I have been pursuing in this book. The profundity of its themes is not the only reason why Hawthorne's last completed romance has demanded continual reinterpretation. In this challenging book, as in his earliest works, Hawthorne practices highly varied narrative strategies calculated to unsettle readers even while keeping them reading. As in his earlier narratives, Hawthorne manipulates verb tenses, personal pronouns, narrative voices, and diegetic levels in *The Marble Faun*. He does so, moreover, within a narrative that incorporates his own notebook entries, history, literature, several of the plastic arts, and ideas transformed from the cult of domesticity and from contemporary romantic attitudes toward progress, love, art, and human nature. In consequence, it is impossible to read the book without choosing repeatedly among the narrative alternatives it proposes, and it is equally impossible to choose so as to absolutely foreclose other plausible interpretations.

Instead of another extended chapter of illustration, two examples relating to Miriam will perhaps suffice to demonstrate that Hawthorne uses the same techniques in his last work as in his first. In the chapter aptly entitled "Fragmentary Sentences," the narrator claims to treat a conversation between Miriam and her model realistically. Unsurprisingly, this realistic treatment is problematized with strategic indirection:

> Many words of deep significance—many entire sentences, and those possibly the most important ones—have flown too far, on the winged breeze, to be recovered. If we insert our own conjectural amendments, we perhaps give a purport utterly at variance with the true one. Yet, unless we attempt something in this way, there must remain an unsightly gap, and a lack of continuousness and dependence in our narrative; so that it would arrive at certain inevitable catastrophes without due warning of their imminence. (4:92–93)

We may recall Hawthorne's similar handling of a conversation between Zenobia and Westervelt in the woods at Blithedale. The effect is similar in the two cases: readers equipped with insufficient information will probably imagine the worst, but this is a worst for which the narrator—owing to his incomplete access to the original events—will take only very limited responsibility. If readers assume on the basis of the incomplete testimony provided that Miriam is guilty of murder, incest, or even some worse Gothic outrage, the narrator bears little responsibility for such assumptions.

The narrator handles the apparently simple issue of Miriam's family background with equal ingenuity. In Chapter 47 Miriam explains her ancestry as "springing from English parentage, on the mother's side, but with a vein, likewise, of Jewish blood, yet connected, through her father, with one of those few princely families of southern Italy, which still retain a great wealth and influence" (4:429–30). In terms of conventional Gothicism, Miriam's descent could hardly be improved upon. The general hints of exoticism take on added force when Miriam "revealed a name, at which [Kenyon] started, and grew pale; for it was one, that, only a few years before, had been familiar to the world, in connection with a mysterious and terrible event." Readers may at this point fill in the scandalous blanks with any real or imaginary villainy of their choice, but the narrator also allows for a specific identification when he adds metaleptically, "The reader—if he think it worth while to recall some of the strange incidents which have been talked of, and forgotten, within no long time past—will remember Miriam's name" (4:430). Even today, unacquainted with the long-dead scandals of the time, readers cannot avoid the assumption that Miriam is based on some actual, historical villainess.

Claude M. Simpson's probable identification of the original as a French governess named Henriette Deluzy-Desportes does little to confirm or dispute this assumption, because, as Simpson explains in his introduction to the *Centenary Edition*, "This is a commonplace fictional gambit, for which one need not expect to find a counterpart in actuality" (4:xlii). The proof lies in the fact that, while we quickly forget Mlle. Deluzy's name, we cannot help remembering that Miriam was once involved in something so shocking that it became a public scandal. The narrator's unreliable memory provides little guidance. On the book's penultimate page, during his final interview with Kenyon and Hilda, the narrator asks, "[W]hat were Miriam's real name and rank, and precisely the nature of the trouble that led to all these direful consequences?" (4:466). Probably the only thing we can be sure of is that Miriam's name, if not actually Schaefer, was not originally Deluzy. Beyond that, everything is—as the narrator says—"clear as a London Fog" (4:465). Either the information provided about Miriam's lineage a few pages back is incorrect, or the narrator has forgotten it, or it was more useful then than now to make specific Gothic allusions to her ancestry. Readers cannot help deciding something about Miriam's background in any case, and whatever they decide will influence their interpretations of Miriam's character and thus of *The Marble Faun*.

Just as we cannot avoid making hermeneutic choices while reading, so we can hardly avoid believing that our choices capture the essence of Hawthorne's book more nearly than the choices made by other readers. This personal conviction might demonstrate to us the power of Hawthorne's fiction. The enormous body of criticism focused on *The Marble Faun*—which I have merely hinted at in this chapter—provides an even more compelling demonstration. All of the critics mentioned must have read Hawthorne's book all the way through, making hermeneutic choices along the way. This is true of critics like Hoeltje and Carton who apparently felt that they were reading a masterwork. Even critics like Matthiessen and Stern who felt that they were reading a botched book must have read through to the last page in order to reach this conclusion. Critics who were so stimulated by *The Marble Faun* that they felt compelled to imagine their own (superior) versions of the book—as Harris and Bercovitch were—perhaps provide the strongest testimony to Hawthorne's success. Studying how Hawthorne keeps all of us reading to the end, rather than uncovering what he tells us about life, therefore seems to me the most productive way of explaining the continuing appeal not only of *The Marble Faun*, but of all Hawthorne's fiction.

Tracing the operations of Hawthorne's narrative strategies provides a useful perspective on narrative discourse in general and also a sense of what Baym has called "the shape of Hawthorne's career." Creating varying degrees of narrative authority by simulating a wide variety of voices on the page occupied much of Hawthorne's attention in his tales, and the question is still a factor in his last work. Experimenting with authority in sombre, symbolic tales as well as in the lighter sketches popular with his contemporaries also taught Hawthorne lessons crucial to the production of longer narratives like *The House of the Seven Gables* and *The Marble Faun*. By raising questions about what fiction could be made out of and by appropriating history and the material provided by his own culture, Hawthorne learned another lesson, not unlike the one taught by the high modernists: that fiction can be made out of anything. Hawthorne also learned a lesson more popular with the successors of the high modernists: that fiction is fiction and not life. Perhaps for this reason, Hawthorne's narratives remain open to reinterpretation even today, permitting us to turn and return to the text for subtly or vastly different reading experiences. Each time we probably come away convinced that we have mastered the text, that Hawthorne has finally yielded up his secrets to us. When we return to the text with an open mind, however, we find that this is, alas, not quite the case. Hawthorne remains Hawthorne, and so we can only say with certainty that his narratives will remain problematic, frustrating, and fascinating.

# Works Cited

Abcarian, Richard, and Marvin Klotz, eds. *Literature: The Human Experience*. 3rd ed. New York: St. Martin's, 1982.

Abrams, M. H. *Natural Supernaturalism: Tradition and Revolution in Romantic Literature*. New York: Norton, 1971.

Adkins, Nelson F. "The Early Projected Works of Nathaniel Hawthorne." *Papers of the Bibliographical Society of America* 39 (1945): 39–57.

Allen, Margaret V. "Imagination and History in Hawthorne's 'Legends of the Province House.'" *American Literature* 43 (1971): 432–37.

Aristotle. *Poetics*. In Bate, 19–39.

Auerbach, Jonathan. "Executing the Model: Painting, Sculpture, and Romance-Writing in Hawthorne's *The Marble Faun*." *ELH* 47 (1980): 103–20.

Bakhtin, M. M. *The Dialogic Imagination: Four Essays*. Ed. Michael Holquist. Trans. Caryl Emerson and Michael Holquist. Austin: University of Texas Press, 1981.

Barth, John. "Lost in the Funhouse." 1967. Reprinted in *Lost in the Funhouse: Fiction for Print, Tape, Live Voice*, 72–97. Garden City, New York: Doubleday, 1968.

Barthes, Roland. "Introduction to the Structural Analysis of Narratives." In *Image—Music—Text*, 79–124. Trans. Stephen Heath. New York: Hill and Wang, 1977.

Bate, Walter Jackson, ed. *Criticism: The Major Texts*. Enlarged ed. New York: Harcourt, 1970.

Baym, Nina. *Novels, Readers, and Reviewers: Responses to Fiction in Antebellum America*. Ithaca: Cornell University Press, 1984.

———. *The Shape of Hawthorne's Career*. Ithaca: Cornell University Press, 1976.

———. *Woman's Fiction: A Guide to Novels by and about Women in America, 1820–1870*. Ithaca: Cornell University Press, 1978.

Bell, Michael Davitt. *The Development of American Romance: The Sacrifice of Relation*. 1980. Reprint, Chicago: University of Chicago Press, 1983.

———. *Hawthorne and the Historical Romance of New England*. Princeton: Princeton University Press, 1971.

Bensick, Carol Marie. *La Nouvelle Beatrice: Renaissance and Romance in "Rappaccini's Daughter"*. New Brunswick: Rutgers University Press, 1985.

Benveniste, Emile. *Problems in General Linguistics*. Trans. Mary Elizabeth Mack. Coral Gables, FL: University of Miami Press, 1971.

Bercovitch, Sacvan. *The Office of The Scarlet Letter.* Baltimore: The Johns Hopkins University Press, 1991.

Berlant, Lauren. *The Anatomy of National Fantasy: Hawthorne, Utopia, and Everyday Life*. Chicago: University of Chicago Press, 1991.

Booth, Wayne C. "Rhetorical Critics Old and New: the Case of Gerard Genette." In *Reconstructing Literature*, 123–41. Ed. Laurence Lerner. Totowa, NJ: Barnes & Noble, 1983.

———. *The Rhetoric of Fiction*. 2nd ed. Chicago: University of Chicago Press, 1983.

Brodhead, Richard H. *The School of Hawthorne*. New York: Oxford, 1986.

Brooks, Cleanth, Jr., and Robert Penn Warren, eds. *Understanding Fiction*. 2nd ed. New York: Appleton, 1959.

Brown, Gillian. "Getting in the Kitchen with Dinah: Domestic Politics in *Uncle Tom's Cabin*." *American Quarterly* 36 (1984): 503–23.

Budick, E. Miller. *Fiction and Historical Consciousness: The American Romance Tradition*. New Haven: Yale University Press, 1989.

———. "Sacvan Bercovitch, Stanley Cavell, and the Romance Theory of American Fiction." *PMLA* 107 (1992): 78–91.

Byers, John R., Jr., and James J. Owen. *A Concordance to the Five Novels of Nathaniel Hawthorne*. 2 vols. New York: Garland, 1979.

Cameron, Kenneth Walter. *Genesis of Hawthorne's "The Ambitious Guest"*. Hartford, CT: Transcendental Books, 1955.

Carpenter, Frederick I. "Puritans Preferred Blondes: The Heroines of Melville and Hawthorne." *NEQ* 9 (1936): 253–72.

Carton, Evan. "Hawthorne and the Province of Romance." *ELH* 47 (1980): 331–54.

———. *The Marble Faun: Hawthorne's Transformations*. New York: Twayne, 1992.

———. *The Rhetoric of American Romance: Dialectic and Identity in Emerson, Dickinson, Poe, and Hawthorne*. Baltimore: The Johns Hopkins University Press, 1985.

Chase, Richard. *The American Novel and Its Tradition*. 1957. Reprint, Baltimore: The Johns Hopkins University Press, 1980.

Coffey, Dennis G. "Hawthorne's 'Alice Doane's Appeal': The Artist Absolved." *ESQ* 21 (1975): 230–40.

Cohen, B. Bernard. "The Sources of Hawthorne's 'The Ambitious Guest.'" *Boston Public Library Quarterly* 4 (1952): 221–24.

Colacurcio, Michael J. "Idealism and Independence." In Elliott, 207–26.

———. Introduction to *Nathaniel Hawthorne: Selected Tales and Sketches*. New York: Penguin, 1987. vii–xxxv.

———. *The Province of Piety: Moral History in Hawthorne's Early Tales*. Cambridge: Harvard University Press, 1984.

Coover, Robert. "The Babysitter." In *Pricksongs & Descants: Fictions*, 206–39. New York: Dutton, 1969.

Crane, R.S. "Questions and Answers in the Teaching of Literary Texts." 1953. Reprinted in *The Idea of the Humanities and Other Essays Critical and Historical*, 2: 176–93. 2 vols. Chicago: University of Chicago Press, 1967.

Crews, Frederick C. *The Sins of the Fathers: Hawthorne's Psychological Themes*. New York: Oxford University Press, 1966.

Crowley, J. Donald. "The Unity of Hawthorne's *Twice-Told Tales*." *Studies in American Fiction* 1 (1973): 35–61.

———, ed. *Hawthorne: The Critical Heritage*. New York: Barnes & Noble, 1970.

———, ed. *Mosses from an Old Manse*. Vol. 10 of *The Centenary Edition of the Works of Nathaniel Hawthorne*.

———, ed. *Twice-told Tales*. Vol. 9 of *The Centenary Edition of the Works of Nathaniel Hawthorne*.

Dekker, George. "Once More: Hawthorne and the Genealogy of American Romanticism." *ESQ* 35 (1989): 69–83.

Donohue, Agnes McNeill. *Hawthorne: Calvin's Ironic Stepchild*. Kent, OH: Kent State University Press, 1985.

Doubleday, Neal Frank. *Hawthorne's Early Tales: A Critical Study*. Durham: Duke University Press, 1972.

Dryden, Edgar A. *The Form of American Romance*. Baltimore: The Johns Hopkins University Press, 1988.

Duyckynck, Evert Augustus. Review of *The House of the Seven Gables*, by Nathaniel Hawthorne. *The Literary World* (26 April 1851): 334–35. Reprinted in Crowley, *The Critical Heritage*, 192–94.

Eberwein, Jane Donahue. "Temporal Perspective in 'The Legends of the Province House.'" *American Transcendental Quarterly* 14 (1972): 41–45.

Eisinger, Chester E. "Hawthorne as Champion of the Middle Way." *NEQ* 28 (1954): 27–52.

Eliot, T. S. *The Complete Poems and Plays, 1909–1950*. New York: Harcourt, 1952.

Elliott, Emory, et al., eds. *Columbia Literary History of the United States*. New York: Columbia University Press, 1988.

Emerson, Ralph Waldo. *Selections from Ralph Waldo Emerson*. Ed. Stephen E. Whicher. Boston: Houghton Mifflin, 1960.

Erlich, Gloria C. *Family Themes and Hawthorne's Fiction: The Tenaceous Web*. New Brunswick, NJ: Rutgers University Press, 1984.

Faust, Bertha. *Hawthorne's Contemporaneous Reputation: A Study of Literary Opinion in America and England 1828–1864*. 1939. Reprint, New York: Octagon, 1968.

Federman, Raymond. "Self-Reflexive Fiction." In Elliott, 1142–57.

Feidelson, Charles, Jr. *Symbolism and American Literature*. Chicago: University of Chicago Press, 1953.

Felperin, Howard. *Beyond Deconstruction: The Uses and Abuses of Literary Theory*. 1985. Oxford: Clarendon Press, 1987.

Foerster, Norman, ed. *American Poetry and Prose*. 4th ed. Boston: Houghton Mifflin, 1957.

Fogle, Richard Harter. *Hawthorne's Fiction: The Light and the Dark*. Norman: University of Oklahoma Press, 1964.

———, ed. *The Romantic Movement in American Writing*. New York: Odyssey, 1966.

Fossum, Robert H. "Time and the Artist in 'Legends of the Province House.'" *NCF* 21 (1967): 337–48.

Frye, Northrop. *Fables of Identity: Studies in Poetic Mythology*. New York: Harcourt, 1963.

Gallagher, Susan Van Zanten. "A Domestic Reading of *The House of the Seven Gables*." *Studies in the Novel* 21 (1989): 1–13.

Genette, Gerard. *Figures of Literary Discourse*. Trans. Alan Sheridan. Oxford: Basil Blackwell, 1982.

———. *Narrative Discourse: An Essay in Method*. Trans. Jane E. Lewin. Ithaca: Cornell University Press, 1980.

———. *Narrative Discourse Revisited*. Trans. Jane E. Lewin. Ithaca: Cornell University Press, 1988.

Gollin, Rita K. *Nathaniel Hawthorne and the Truth of Dreams*. Baton Rouge: Louisiana State University Press, 1979.

Griffith, Clark. "Substance and Shadow: Language and Meaning in *The House of the Seven Gables*." *MP* 51 (1954): 187–95.

Haggerty, George. *Gothic Fiction/Gothic Form*. University Park: Pennsylvania State University Press, 1989.

Harris, Kenneth Marc. *Hypocrisy and Self-Deception in Hawthorne's Fiction*. Charlottesville: University Press of Virginia, 1988.

Hawthorne, Nathaniel. *The Centenary Edition of the Works of Nathaniel Hawthorne*. 20 vols. Ed. William Charvat, et al. Columbus: Ohio State University Press, 1962–.

———. "Chiefly About War Matters." In *Tales, Sketches, and Other Papers*. Vol. 12 of *The Complete Works of Nathaniel Hawthorne*, 299–345. Ed. George Parsons Lathrop. Cambridge, MA: Riverside Press, 1885.

———. *The English Notebooks*. Ed. Randall Stewart. 1941. Reprint, New York: Russell & Russell, 1991.

Hoeltje, Hubert H. *Inward Sky: The Mind and Heart of Nathaniel Hawthorne*. Durham, NC: Duke University Press, 1962.

Howe, Daniel Walker. "Victorian Culture in America." In *Victorian America*, 3–28. Ed. Howe. Philadelphia: University of Pennsylvania Press, 1976.

Hughes, Gertrude Reif. *Emerson's Demanding Optimism*. Baton Rouge: Louisiana State University Press, 1984.

Iser, Wolfgang. *The Implied Reader: Patterns of Communication in Prose Fiction from Bunyan to Beckett*. Baltimore: The Johns Hopkins University Press, 1974.

———. "Representation: A Performative Act." In *Prospecting: From Reader Response to Literary Anthropology*, 236–48. Baltimore: The Johns Hopkins University Press, 1989.

James, Henry. "The Art of Fiction." 1884. Reprinted in *The House of Fiction*, 23–45. Ed. Leon Edel. 1957. Westport, CT: Greenwood, 1973.

———. *Hawthorne*. 1887. New York: AMS, 1968.

Johnson, Samuel. "Preface to Shakespeare." In Bate, 207–17.

Kent, Thomas. *Interpretation and Genre: The Role of Generic Perception in the Study of Narrative Texts*. Lewisburg, PA: Bucknell University Press, 1986.

Kirby, John T. "Toward a Rhetoric of Poetics: Rhetor as Author and Narrator." *The Journal of Narrative Technique* 21.1 (1992): 1–22.

Kraditor, Aileen S. Introduction to *Up From the Pedestal: Selected Writings in the History of American Feminism.* Chicago: Quadrangle, 1968. 3–24.

Lawrence, D. H. *Studies in Classic American Literature.* 1923. Reprint, New York: Viking, 1964.

Leavis, Q. D. "Hawthorne as Poet." 1951. In *Collected Essays,* 2: 30–76. 2 vols. Ed. G. Singh. Cambridge: Cambridge University Press, 1985.

Levin, David. *In Defense of Historical Literature.* New York: Hill and Wang, 1967.

Lewis, R. W. B. *The American Adam: Innocence, Tragedy, and Tradition in the Nineteenth Century.* Chicago: University of Chicago Press, 1955.

Longfellow, Henry Wadsworth. *The Poetical Works of Henry Wadsworth Longfellow in Six Volumes.* Vol. 3. New York: AMS, 1966.

Longinus. *On the Sublime.* In Bate, 62–75.

Lowell, James Russell. "To Nathaniel Hawthorne." 24 April 1851. In *Nathaniel Hawthorne and his Wife: A Biography,* by Julian Hawthorne, 1: 390–92. 2 vols. 1884. Reprint, [Hamden, CT]: Archon Books, 1968.

Luedtke, Luther S. *Nathaniel Hawthorne and the Romance of the Orient.* Bloomington: Indiana University Press, 1989.

Lundblad, Jane. *Nathaniel Hawthorne and the European Literary Tradition.* New York: Russell & Russell, 1965.

Male, Roy R. *Hawthorne's Tragic Vision.* Austin: University of Texas Press, 1957.

Marks, Alfred H. "German Romantic Irony in Hawthorne's Tales." *Symposium* 7 (1953): 274–305.

Martin, Terence. *Nathaniel Hawthorne.* New York: Twayne, 1965.

Martin, Wallace. *Recent Theories of Narrative.* Ithaca: Cornell University Press, 1986.

Matthiessen, F. O. *American Renaissance: Art and Expression in the Age of Emerson and Whitman.* 1941. Reprint, New York: Oxford University Press, 1968.

McWilliams, John P., Jr. " 'Thorough-going Democrat' and 'Modern Tory': Hawthorne and the Puritan Revolution of 1776." *Studies in Romanticism* 15 (1976): 549–71.

Melville, Herman. "To Nathaniel Hawthorne." 16? April? 1851. In *The Letters of Herman Melville,* 123–25. Ed. Merrell R. Davis and William H. Gilman. New York: Yale University Press, 1960.

Michael, John. "History and Romance, Sympathy and Uncertainty: The Moral of the Stones in Hawthorne's *Marble Faun.*" *PMLA* 103 (1988): 150–61.

Miller, Edwin Haviland. *Salem Is My Dwelling Place: A Life of Nathaniel Hawthorne.* Iowa City: University of Iowa Press, 1991.

Miller, James E., Jr. "Hawthorne and Melville: The Unpardonable Sin." *PMLA* 70.1 (1955): 91–114.

Millington, Richard H. *Practicing Romance: Narrative Form and Cultural Engagement in Hawthorne's Fiction.* Princeton: Princeton University Press, 1992.

Mizruchi, Susan L. *The Power of Historical Knowledge: Narrating the Past in Haw-thorne, James, and Dreiser*. Princeton: Princeton University Press, 1988.

Newberry, Frederick. *Hawthorne's Divided Loyalties: England and America in His Works*. Rutherford, NJ: Associated University Presses, 1987.

Newman, Lea Bertani Vozar. *A Reader's Guide to the Short Stories of Nathaniel Haw-thorne*. Boston: G. K. Hall, 1979.

Ong, Walter J., S. J. "The Writer's Audience is Always a Fiction." *PMLA* 90 (1975): 9–21.

Orians, G. Harrison. "The Angel of Hadley in Fiction: A Study of the Sources of Hawthorne's 'The Grey Champion.'" *AL* 4 (1932): 257–69.

Pauly, Thomas H. "The Literary Sketch in Nineteenth-Century America." *Texas Studies in Literature and Language* 17 (1975): 489–503.

Pearce, Roy Harvey. "Romance and the Study of History." In Pearce, 221–44.

———, ed. *Hawthorne Centenary Essays*. Columbus: Ohio State University Press, 1964.

Poe, Edgar Allan. "The Balloon-Hoax." In *Tales*. Ed. James A. Harrison. Vol. 4 of *The Complete Works of Edgar Allan Poe*, 224–40. 17 vols. 1902. Reprint, New York: AMS, 1965.

Ponder, Melinda M. *Hawthorne's Early Narrative Art*. Lewiston, NY: Edwin Mellen, 1990.

Prince, Gerald. *A Dictionary of Narratology*. Lincoln: University of Nebraska Press, 1987.

———. "Introduction to the Study of the Narratee." Trans. Francis Mariner. In *Reader-Response Criticism: From Formalism to Post-Structuralism*, 7–25. Ed. Jane P. Tompkins. Baltimore: The Johns Hopkins University Press, 1980.

Rahv, Philip. "The Dark Lady of Salem." *Partisan Review* 8 (1941): 362–81.

Reed, P. L. "The Telling Frame of Hawthorne's 'Legends of the Province-House.'" *Studies in American Fiction* 4 (1976): 105–11.

Reilly, Cyril A. "On the Dog's Chasing His Own Tail in 'Ethan Brand.'" *PMLA* 68 (1953): 975–81.

Reynolds, David S. *Beneath the American Renaissance: The Subversive Imagination in the Age of Emerson and Melville*. New York: Knopf, 1988.

Richards, Jeffrey H. "Hawthorne's Posturing Observer: The Case of 'Sights from a Steeple.'" *ATQ* 59 (March 1986): 35–41.

Ricoeur, Paul. "The Model of the Text: Meaningful Action Considered as a Text." *New Literary History* 5 (1973): 91–117.

Scholes, Robert, and Robert Kellogg. *The Nature of Narrative*. New York: Oxford, 1966.

Schorer, Mark. "Technique as Discovery." *The Hudson Review* 1 (1948): 67–87.

Simpson, Claude M., ed. *The Marble Faun*. Vol. 4 of *The Centenary Edition of the Works of Nathaniel Hawthorne*.

Smith, Julian. "Hawthorne's 'Legends of the Province-House.'" *NCF* 24 (1969): 31–44.

Spengemann, William C. *The Adventurous Muse: The Poetics of American Fiction, 1789–1900.* New Haven: Yale University Press, 1977.

St. Armand, Barton L. "The Love Song of Miles Coverdale: Intimations of Eliot's 'Prufrock' in Hawthorne's *Blithedale Romance.*" *ATQ* 2.2 (1988): 97–100.

Stern, Milton. *Contexts for Hawthorne: The Marble Faun and the Politics of Openness and Closure in American Literature.* Urbana: University of Illinois Press, 1991.

Stock, Ely. "The Biblical Context of 'Ethan Brand.' " *AL* 37 (1965): 115–34.

Stowe, Harriet Beecher. *Uncle Tom's Cabin.* 1852. Reprint, New York: Bantam, 1981.

Stubbs, John Caldwell. *The Pursuit of Form: A Study of Hawthorne and the Romance.* Urbana: University of Illinois Press, 1970.

Swann, C. S. B. "The Practice and Theory of Storytelling: Nathaniel Hawthorne and Walter Benjamin." *Journal of American Studies* 12 (1978): 185–202.

Thompson, G. R. *The Art of Authorial Presence: Hawthorne's Provincial Tales.* Durham: Duke University Press, 1993.

Thoreau, Henry David. *The Variorum Walden.* Ed. Walter Harding. New York: Twayne, 1962.

Thorpe, T. B. "The Big Bear of Arkansas." In *The Hive of "The Bee-Hunter": A Repository of Sketches,* 72–93. New York: D. Appleton, 1854.

Todorov, Tzvetan. *The Fantastic: A Structural Approach to a Literary Genre.* Trans. Richard Howard. Cleveland: Case Western Reserve University Press, 1973.

———. "The Limits of Edgar Allan Poe." In *Genres in Discourse,* 93–102. 1978. Trans. Catherine Porter. Reprint, Cambridge: Cambridge University Press, 1990.

———. *The Poetics of Prose.* Trans. Richard Howard. Ithaca: Cornell University Press, 1977.

Tompkins, Jane. Afterword to *The Wide, Wide World,* by Susan Warner, 584–608. New York: Feminist Press, 1987.

———. *Sensational Designs: The Cultural Work of American Fiction, 1790–1860.* New York: Oxford University Press, 1985.

Tuckerman, Frederick Goddard. *The Complete Poems of Frederick Goddard Tuckerman.* Ed. N. Scott Momaday. New York: Oxford University Press, 1965.

Turner, Arlin. *Nathaniel Hawthorne: An Introduction and Interpretation.* New York: Barnes & Noble, 1961.

Updike, John. "Man of Secrets." Review of *Salem Is My Dwelling Place: A Life of Nathaniel Hawthorne,* by Edwin Haviland Miller. *The New Yorker* 28 September 1992, 114–19.

Van Tassel, Mary M. "Hawthorne, His Narrator, and His Readers in 'Little Annie's Ramble.' " *ESQ* 33 (1987): 168–79.

Wagenknecht, Edward. *Nathaniel Hawthorne: The Man, His Tales and Romances.* New York: Ungar, 1989.

Waggoner, Hyatt H. "Art and Belief." In Pearce, 167–95.

———. *Hawthorne: A Critical Study.* 1955. Cambridge: Harvard University Press, 1963.

Walsh, Thomas F., Jr. "'Wakefield' and Hawthorne's Illustrated Ideas: A Study in Form." *Emerson Society Quarterly* 25 (1961): 29–35.

Warhol, Robyn R. "Toward a Theory of the Engaging Narrator: Earnest Interventions in Gaskell, Stowe, and Eliot." *PMLA* 101 (1986): 811–18.

Warner, Susan. *The Wide, Wide World.* 1850. Reprint, New York: Feminist Press, 1987.

Way, Brian. "Art and the Spirit of Anarchy: A Reading of Hawthorne's Short Stories." In *Nathaniel Hawthorne: New Critical Essays*, 11–30. Ed. A. Robert Lee. Totowa, NJ: Barnes & Noble, 1982.

Webster, Grant. *The Republic of Letters: A History of Postwar American Literary Opinion.* Baltimore: The Johns Hopkins University Press, 1979.

Whipple, E. P. Review of *The House of the Seven Gables*, by Nathaniel Hawthorne. *Graham's Magazine*, May 1851, 467–68. Reprinted in Crowley, *The Critical Heritage*, 197–201.

White, Hayden. "The Value of Narrativity in the Representation of Reality." *Critical Inquiry* 7 (Autumn 1980): 5–28. Reprinted in *The Content of the Form: Narrative Discourse and Historical Representation*, 1–25. Baltimore: The Johns Hopkins University Press, 1987.

Winters, Yvor. "Maule's Curse, or Hawthorne and the Problem of Allegory." 1938. In *In Defense of Reason*, 157–75. 3rd ed. Reprint, Chicago: Swallow, 1947.

Ziff, Larzer. *Literary Democracy: The Declaration of Cultural Independence in America.* New York: Viking, 1981.

# Index

Abcarian, Richard, and Marvin Klotz, 162
Abrams, M. H., 143, 152, 163
Adam and Eve, biblical, 74
Adkins, Nelson F., 23, 78
"Alice Doane's Appeal," 20, 78–86
Allen, Margaret V., 104, 144
"Artist of the Beautiful, The," 91, 167–69
Aristotle, 65, 87, 91, 111
Auerbach, Jonathan, 187

Bakhtin, Mikhail, 18, 30–31, 35, 73–75, 99–
    100, 135
Barth, John, 70, 71
Barthelme, Donald, 70
Barthes, Roland, 15, 17
Baym, Nina, 14, 23, 47, 49, 54, 63, 104,
    155–56, 159, 173, 186, 187, 191
Bell, Michael Davitt, 12, 101, 103, 117
Bensick, Carol Marie, 76
Benveniste, Emile, 15, 56, 57
Bercovitch, Sacvan, 11, 12, 13, 19, 87, 188,
    191
Berlant, Lauren, 11, 12, 19, 87
"Birthmark, The," 7
*Blithedale Romance, The,* 6, 8, 9, 20, 45, 74,
    75, 87–96, 130, 137–38, 141, 157,
    176–81, 182, 189
Booth, Wayne C., 17, 83
Brodhead, Richard, 3, 4, 11
Brooks, Cleanth, and Robert Penn Warren, 7,
    49, 59
Brown, Gillian, 156
Browne, Sir Thomas, 75, 76, 78
Budick, Emily Miller, 10, 12, 13, 104, 118

Cameron, Kenneth Walter, 167
Carpenter, Frederick I., 74
Carton, Evan, 3, 12, 13, 104, 116–17, 128,
    187, 191
Cellini, Benvenuto, 75, 97, 98, 100

Chase, Richard, 12
"Chippings with a Chisel," 48
Cohen, B. Bernard, 167
Colacurcio, Michael, 10, 16, 19, 24, 64, 80,
    101, 103, 104, 106, 107, 115
Coover, Robert, 70, 71
Crane, R. S., 49
Crews, Frederick C., 8–9, 78
Crowley, J. Donald, 23, 34, 43, 48, 49, 54,
    63, 64, 72

Dante Alighieri, 73
"David Swan," 36–38, 45
Deictic, 57, 84
Dekker, George, 10
Diegesis, 20–21, 59, 65–69, 71, 73, 75,
    78–89, 92, 95–100, 106–09, 112, 114,
    115, 118, 125–28, 189
Domesticity, Cult of, 21, 63, 64, 145, 146,
    147, 155–85, 189
Donohue, Agnes McNeill, 151
Doubleday, Neal Frank, 19, 23, 43, 47, 49,
    54, 193
"Dr. Heidegger's Experiment," 32–34, 39,
    40, 42
Dryden, Edgar, 12, 13, 187
Duyckinck, Evert, 55, 124, 128

Eberwein, Jane Donahue, 116, 117
"Edward Randolph's Portrait," 104, 107–11,
    112, 113
Eisinger, Chester E., 139
Emerson, Ralph Waldo, 14, 131–32, 135,
    136, 137, 139, 140, 143, 152
"Endicott and the Red Cross," 47
*English Notebooks, The,* 157
Erlich, Gloria C., 8
"Ethan Brand," 94, 144, 149–53
Extradiegetic, 66, 67, 71, 73, 77, 78, 84, 106,
    108, 113, 114

"Fancy's Show Box," 38–39, 43, 104, 108
Fantastic, 27, 30–33, 41, 109, 115, 116, 119, 122
Faust, Bertha, 186
Federman, Raymond, 70
Feidelson, Charles, 7
Felperin, Howard, 17
Fern, Fanny, 156, 157, 166, 167
"Fire-Worship," 172, 180
Foerster, Norman, 72
Fogle, Richard Harter, 7–8, 18, 72, 74
Fossum, Robert H., 104
Frost, Robert, 68
Frye, Northrop, 144

Gallagher, Susan VanZanten, 173
Genette, Gerard, 15, 16, 17, 20, 23, 36, 42, 50, 51, 55, 56, 59, 67, 71, 124–25
"Gentle Boy, The," 26, 28–29
Gnomic present (W. Martin), 37, 44, 59
Gollin, Rita, 121
Gothicism, 6, 20, 25, 27, 32, 48, 62, 73, 80–83, 85–86, 87, 88, 90, 91, 93, 96, 100, 106–07, 108–10, 112, 115–17, 121, 124–27, 164, 170, 171, 189–90
"Gray Champion, The," 26, 30–31
"Great Carbuncle, The," 40–42, 160, 161, 162, 165, 180
"Great Stone Face, The," 133–37
Griffith, Clark, 124

Haggerty, George, 6, 129
Harris, Kenneth Marc, 188
"Haunted Mind, The," 59–64, 80
History, Hawthorne and, 9–12, 15, 19, 20–21, 26–31, 78, 80, 84–85, 101–28, 130, 188
Hoeltje, Hubert H., 186, 191
"Hollow of the Three Hills, The," 30, 31–32, 40, 48
House of the Seven Gables, The, 9, 13, 20, 87, 88, 92, 117–28, 130, 137, 172–76, 191
"Howe's Masquerade," 104, 105–07, 112, 114, 155
Howe, Daniel Walker, 155
Hughes, Gertrude Reif, 131

Interpretation of texts, 6–8, 16, 19, 21, 49–50, 64, 67, 68–69, 77, 84, 100, 105,

116–18, 124–25, 129, 133, 139, 140–41, 143, 161, 162, 166, 168, 172–73, 175, 186–89
Irving, Washington, 86
Iser, Wolfgang, 4–5, 6, 18, 20, 32, 85, 96

James, Henry, 46, 49–50, 56, 64, 66, 68, 70, 88, 90, 94, 99, 104
Johnson, Samuel, 113

Kent, Thomas, 50
Kirby, John T., 61
Kraditor, Aileen S., 155

"Lady Eleanore's Mantle," 47, 54, 104, 111–13, 116
Lawrence, D. H., 131
Leavis, Q. D., 22, 46
"Legends of the Province-House," 10, 20, 64, 80, 101, 103, 104–17
Levin, David, 78
Lewis, R. W. B., 142
"Lily's Quest, The," 142–43
"Little Annie's Ramble," 23, 24, 47, 50, 64
Longfellow, Henry Wadsworth, 3, 21, 86, 157, 158, 161, 166, 169, 173, 182
Longinus, 118
Luedtke, Luther S., 74, 144, 182
Lundblad, Jane, 25

Male, Roy R., 7, 8, 18
Marble Faun, The, 3, 8, 20, 21, 74, 96–100, 141, 181–85, 186–91
Martin, Terence, 103
Martin, Wallace, 15, 37, 69, 150
Matthiessen, F. O., 10, 55, 76, 117, 187, 191
"May-Pole of Merry Mount, The," 20, 22, 26, 27, 47, 50, 102–04, 183
McWilliams, John P., Jr., 107
Melville, Herman, 3, 14, 55, 142–43, 152
Metadiegesis, 70–100 passim, 124–28, 178
Metalepsis, 36, 59, 66–67, 71, 77–78, 84, 93, 127, 190
Michael, John, 187
Miller, Edwin Haviland, 8, 9, 73–74, 161, 185
Miller, James E., Jr., 150
Millington, Richard H., 13, 127, 161

"Minister's Black Veil, The," 22, 26, 27–28, 39, 47, 181
Mizruchi, Susan, 10, 117, 118, 123, 197
*Mosses from an Old Manse,* 20, 35, 72–73, 74, 138
"Mr. Higginbotham's Catastrophe," 34–36
"My Kinsman, Major Molineux," 15, 23, 48, 83, 107, 162–64
"My Visit to Niagara," 105

Narratee, 51, 57–59, 61
Narrative authority, 5–6, 16, 20, 22–46, 54, 62, 70–100, 102–04, 105–17, 119–20, 124, 126–28
Narrative discourse, 16, 42, 56–59, 64–69, 128
Narratology, 15–18, 50–51, 55, 65–66, 68, 78, 85, 87, 104, 106, 117–18, 124, 128, 151, 156
"New Adam and Eve, The," 138–41
New Criticism, 8, 10, 17, 49
Newberry, Frederick, 10, 101, 103, 104, 106
Newman, Lea B., 39, 55, 75, 77, 165
"Night Sketches," 48, 60, 64–69, 164, 168

"Old Esther Dudley," 104, 113–16
Ong, Walter, 69
Orians, G. Harrison, 10, 103

"Passages from a Relinquished Work," 35, 144
Pauly, Thomas H., 50
Pearce, Roy Harvey, 117, 123
Poe, Edgar Allan, 11, 71, 78, 86, 176
Ponder, Melinda, 84
Prince, Gerald, 15, 23, 57, 83
Progress, belief in, 131, 132, 137–38, 141, 152, 153, 189
"Prophetic Pictures, The," 26, 109
Prufrock, J. Alfred (Eliot), 137, 175, 177–78

Quest, romantic, 41, 44, 131, 132, 141, 142–53, 155, 162–63, 165, 166, 178

Rahv, Philip, 182
"Rappaccini's Daughter," 7–8, 20, 59, 71–78, 86, 97
Reed, P. L., 104
Reilly, Cyril A., 152

Reynolds, David S., 14
Richards, Jeffrey H., 65
Ricoeur, Paul, 4
"Rill from the Town-Pump, A," 23, 24
"Roger Malvin's Burial," 48, 161–62
Romance tradition, 10, 12–15, 38, 86, 88, 89, 121, 128
Romanticism, 21, 129–54, 155, 163, 189

*Scarlet Letter, The,* 11, 74, 86–87, 88, 94, 133, 137, 138, 141, 159, 169–72, 184, 185, 188
Scholes, Robert, and Robert Kellogg, 23, 56
Schorer, Mark, 49
Shakespeare, William, 73–74, 132
"Sights from a Steeple," 23, 24, 47
Simpson, Claude M., 190
"Sister Years, The," 51–54, 55
Smith, Julian, 104, 108
Spengemann, William C., 155, 161
St. Armand, Barton Levi, 177
Stern, Milton R., 139, 157, 187–88, 191
Stock, Ely, 150
Stowe, Harriet Beecher, 156, 157, 167, 176
Structuralism, 15–17, 18, 20, 71
Stubbs, John Caldwell, 110
"Sunday at Home," 23, 24, 25, 47
Swann, C. S. B., 35, 45

*Tanglewood Tales,* 110
Thompson, G. R., 18–19, 46, 69, 78, 84, 140
Thoreau, Henry David, 132, 135, 137
Thorpe, Thomas Bangs, 71
"Threefold Destiny, The," 144–47, 148, 149, 150, 151, 153, 160
Todorov, Tzvetan, 11, 15, 16, 32–33, 42, 58, 69, 98, 112, 127
"Toll-Gatherer's Day, The," 48
Tompkins, Jane, 3–4, 14, 159, 160
Tuckerman, Frederick Goddard, 157, 158–59
Turner, Arlin, 68

Updike, John, 161

Van Tassel, Mary, 50, 64
"Village Uncle, The," 165–66
"Vision of the Fountain, The," 23, 25–26, 48, 99

Wagenknecht, Edward, 55
Waggoner, Hyatt H., 64, 65, 68, 117, 118
"Wakefield," 22, 43–45, 47, 50, 93, 144,
   147–49, 150, 151, 169
Walsh, Thomas F., 37, 38, 43
Warhol, Robin, 15, 23, 83
Warner, Susan, 21, 157, 159–61, 166, 173,
   176, 179, 180, 182, 185
Way, Brian, 153
Webster, Grant, 48–49
"Wedding-Knell, The," 39–40

Whipple, Edwin, 124
White, Hayden, 117
Winters, Yvor, 76, 82
"Wives of the Dead, The," 19
Wordsworth, William, 135

"Young Goodman Brown," 5–6, 48, 73, 78,
   104

Ziff, Larzer, 134